THE CHILD AND HIS IMAGE

THE
CHILD
AND HIS
IMAGE

SELF CONCEPT IN

THE EARLY YEARS

EDITED BY

KAORU YAMAMOTO

PENNSYLVANIA STATE UNIVERSITY

HOUGHTON MIFFLIN COMPANY   BOSTON

NEW YORK   ATLANTA   GENEVA, ILLINOIS   DALLAS   PALO ALTO

ORIGINAL CONTRIBUTIONS BY

Whitfield S. Bourisseau, Mayfield Board of Education, Mayfield Heights, Ohio
Helen M. Felsenthal, Purdue University
Evelyn L. Kirkhart, Meadow View Farm, Hudson, Ohio
Robert O. Kirkhart, North Haven Medical Center, Cuyahoga Falls, Ohio
Carolyn E. Massad, Educational Testing Service, Princeton, New Jersey
Marjorie S. Snyder, Northeast Louisiana University
Kaoru Yamamoto, Pennsylvania State University

WITH THE ASSISTANCE OF

Mildred L. Hathaway, Cleveland Heights–University Heights Board of Education, Ohio
Edward A. Karns, Parma Board of Education, Parma, Ohio
Beverly H. Lewis, Campus School, State University of New York at Geneseo
Louise Liske, Brady Lake School, Brady Lake, Ohio
Jennifer Loehr, Indiana State University, Terre Haute, Indiana
Hilda Stocker, Cuyahoga County Board of Education, Cleveland, Ohio
John Stockwell, Michigan City Schools, Michigan City, Indiana
Nicola Turner, Indiana State University, Terre Haute, Indiana
Marilyn J. Wenger, Parma Schools, Parma, Ohio

Printed in the U.S.A.

Library of Congress Catalog Card Number: 72-163283
ISBN: 0-395-12571-5

CONTENTS

PREFACE

This book is first and foremost for our young colleagues who are now preparing themselves for teaching in elementary and pre-elementary schools. It is additionally for classroom teachers and supervisors at these levels of education. As an end product of cooperative efforts among seven authors (two in curriculum and instruction, one in clinical psychology, one in school psychology, and three in educational psychology), it represents a broad range of experience and scholarship, though the overall humanistic concern must be apparent to readers. After individual chapters had been prepared, reviewed, and revised, the authors met to examine each other's contribution, as well as all chapters in toto. With the help of nine discussants (three college students, three classroom teachers, one school supervisor and two curriculum supervisors), they considered various relevant issues and then proceeded to revise their respective chapters again. A portion of the discussion at this meeting is presented in the final chapter as a unique form of summary. Besides, the authors benefited much from the careful reviews of the whole manuscript by Professor Robert H. Anderson of Harvard University, Professor Frank J. Estvan of Wayne State University, and Professor Philip Lambert of the University of Wisconsin. We hope that readers enjoy this volume as much as we did preparing it. If they find any merit in the book, the credit belongs to our own good teachers who, through their life, taught us to seek wisdom, humility, and compassion.

KAORU YAMAMOTO

INTRODUCTION

In view of the tremendous interest that today's teachers and parents are showing in early childhood, and especially the wider appreciation of the importance of healthy selfhood, a great need exists for informed and practical commentary. This book is a remarkable response to that need; it represents in fact a kind of milestone in the literature bearing on early childhood.

Self concept, self image, self esteem—these and similar terms have appeared with increasing frequency, and there is much that has already been learned even as more extensive research proceeds. One must struggle with the available writings, however, to find materials and proposals that can be understood and utilized by practicing educators. Few writers have troubled to prepare solid but easily-comprehensible treatises on the nature and nurture of self in the early childhood years, and most of the material that *is* available is not specifically concerned with the development of self concept in young children. Even more neglected is discussion of self and its nurturance in *educational* contexts, presented in ways that will be visibly useful to teachers, those who would become teachers, and others with child-service roles.

This book, then, is aimed at those who are or will be working with children, and it seeks to provide them not so much with theory (although it is suitably included), but with concrete, useful, and practical information. The focus of attention is generally upon children between the ages of three and ten, although children in the upper-elementary years are not overlooked. Experienced teachers and advanced students will find much that meets their needs, but the authors have particularly aimed to serve college students studying education, human development, social work, and nursing, along with paraprofessionals, volunteer teachers, Sunday-school teachers, and interested laymen.

Yamamoto, whose opening chapter establishes a high standard of both thought and presentation, was the guiding spirit of the project. In his final chapter, he brings into focus both the major concepts and the essential viewpoint on which the volume is based.

In the second chapter, Massad examines the world of communication as it is experienced by the child, and she draws on the important contributions of researchers such as Piaget and Vygotsky prior to an examination of the educational importance of communication. This leads nicely into Chapter Three, in which Snyder helps us to see how various attitudes, policies, procedures, and interactions within the school environment influence the developing self. Various teaching strategies are described, and their practical applications are discussed. Symbolically, the chapter concludes with a section on the humanization of schools.

Crucially important are Chapters 4 and 5, in which are examined techniques of appraisal and of amelioration. Bourisseau explains both formal and informal approaches to assessment and evaluation, and readers will especially appreciate the conclusion of her chapter, in which are presented fifteen suggestions that may be useful in both the home and the classroom for helping a child develop a positive identity. This provides an excellent bridge to the chapter by the Kirkharts, which suggests techniques and approaches for dealing with children's problems. Many readers will find of special interest the discussion of psychological pathogens, the conditions that predispose a child toward bruises of the self system. The case studies in this chapter, illustrating symptoms of psychological distress, are also of notable interest.

Chapter 6, by Felsenthal, adds breadth to the volume by examining the role played by parents. The parent, she rightfully argues, is the key person in the development of the child's self concept. In the chapter, which amply supports that assertion, is included information that not only parents but the professionals who function in helping roles can profitably employ.

An attractive feature of the book is that its several authors worked very hard at coordinating their material, including a wide range of materials related to the main theme, and providing for the reader a volume that is much more integrated than the usual collection of essays. One proof of this is the final chapter and the way that it came into being: during a conference of the authors, in the course of which each chapter was examined both as a separate entity and as a part of the whole, enabling them to unify their material and also yielding some interesting additional observations and source references. The reader will probably enjoy the opportunity that this final chapter provides for "eavesdropping" on the authors at work and for at least vicariously participating in the sort of dialogue that the volume should, and can, stimulate among teachers, college and university students, and others who seek to know more about the self and its nurturance.

ROBERT H. ANDERSON
HARVARD UNIVERSITY

THE CHILD AND HIS IMAGE

ONE · THE CONCEPT OF SELF:

INTRODUCTION

Kaoru Yamamoto

Man is an enigma. He is but a transient in the universe; yet he is aware of eternity. He is a feeble being; yet his faith moves a mountain. He is a whole; yet he can be both the subject (*I*) and object (*me*) of his life without splitting himself in two.[1]

Suppose I underwent some harrowing experience, say, a fire, an accident, or a death in the family. In the most fundamental sense, what I lived through cannot be communicated to anyone else. Much of the experience undoubtedly remains outside my consciousness and only a small portion will be accessible for me to recount. Moreover, the moment I begin describing how I felt or what I did, I must in fact treat myself as if I were some other being. I can perhaps produce a few descriptions understandable to others, but the more generalized portrayal I make of myself, the further away I actually get from my unique and intimate experience. In the end, I will have described *me* more or less as an object of my awareness in just about the same way I treat everyone or everything else I encounter. Where, meanwhile, is *I*, the subject itself which has done all this experiencing and describing? This *I*, the elusive actor, is unexplainable and unpredictable.[2] That is why man forever remains a mystery even to himself.

Be that as it may, the composite of all the descriptions, verbal, pictorial, or otherwise, of *me* is what I call my *self concept*. It naturally reveals a lot about myself, but it does not tell everything. Most importantly, as suggested above, it cannot depict the subjective *I* without turning it into an objective *me*, thus leaving out the essence of what it

[1] This fundamental capacity can nevertheless be misused in various neurotic forms. Cf. May, Rollo; Angel, Ernest; and Ellenberger, Henri F. (eds.). *Existence*. New York: Basic Books, 1958.

[2] Mead, George H. "Self." *George Herbert Mead on Social Psychology*, ed. Anselm Strauss. Chicago: University of Chicago Press, 1964. Pp. 199–246.

tried to describe. In other words, my *self* is more inclusive as a construct than my *self concept* since the *self* is both the knower and the known, both *I* and *me*. How such a feat is possible, or where such capabilities specifically originate (i.e., nature vs. nurture), is an academic question for our present purposes.[3]

What is to be remembered is that the *self concept* is a composite, but imperfect, representation of the *self*. The self concept contains all kinds of descriptions of the objective *me*, not only the portraits rendered by the individual but also his impressions of his portraits done by either himself or someone else. This feature (the self-reflexiveness of any symbolic process[4]) often leads to gross misinterpretation of the self, the whole being, even by the very person in question. For example, a child draws a picture of himself. He can then go on drawing a picture of this picture of himself, another picture of the second picture of the first picture of himself, and so on and on. He can do the same with any portraits other people draw of him. All these pieces are a part of the enormous collection the child amasses in the name of his self concept. Every one of the pictures has his likeness somewhere, but it is safe to guess that the child, as depicted in the ninth, fifth, or even second, picture, hardly resembles him in the first which, to begin with, is but a pale facsimile of this live human being in all his misery and splendor. If anyone, including the child himself, believes that the youngster is in fact nothing more than what these incomplete portrayals collectively delineate, he will be woefully mistaken. No composite description tells the whole story of the objective *me*, much less that of the subjective *I*. The *self concept*, therefore, is not the same as the *self* and, in general, "A map is *not* the territory it stands for; words are *not* things."[5]

---

[3] Interested readers should consult Mead's original articles (n. 2) as well as some critiques of his position, e.g., Kolb, William L., "A Critical Evaluation of Mead's 'I' and 'Me.'" *Social Forces*, 22:291–296; March 1944, and Kohlberg, Lawrence, "Stage and Sequence: The Cognitive-Developmental Approach to Socialization." *Handbook of Socialization Theory and Research*, ed. David A. Goslin. Chicago: Rand McNally, 1969. Pp. 347–480.

[4] Johnson, Wendell. *People in Quandaries.* New York: Harper and Row, 1946.

[5] Hayakawa, S. I. *Language in Thought and Action.* 2d ed. New York: Harcourt, Brace and World, 1964. P. 314.

LOOKING-GLASS SELF

In the formation of self concept, most theorists agree, social interactions are of crucial importance.[6] While the contribution of organic sensations and direct body awareness ought not to be ignored, a concept of self can scarcely be developed without adequate interpersonal relations. Man perceives and defines himself as he believes others perceive and define him, thus "the reflected or looking-glass self" (after Charles Cooley). Ralph Ellison was describing this feature of the reflected self when he made his character in *Invisible Man* explain, "I am invisible, understand, simply because people refuse to see me. . . . you often doubt if you really exist. You wonder whether you aren't simply a phantom in other people's minds."[7]

From the very first stage of his development, a child finds himself in a matrix of cultural values, and growth (through both maturation and learning) is buttressed by his awareness of increasing social stature. While the patterns of child-rearing are quite varied among different societies and at different times,[8] every culture provides a sense of security and continuity and also offers a full array of models and experiences. These are the common foundation of a group identity, but a child can selectively respond to them to develop his individual style. Learning the culturally meaningful ways of life seems to be facilitated

[6] Baldwin, James M. *Social and Ethical Interpretations in Mental Development.* New York: Macmillan, 1897.

Cooley, Charles H. *Human Nature and the Social Order.* New York: The Free Press, 1956.

James, William. *Psychology: The Briefer Course,* ed. Gordon W. Allport. New York: Harper and Row, 1961.

Royce, Joseph R. (ed.). *Psychology and the Symbol.* New York: Random House, 1965. See, especially, chapters by Bertalanffy and Hayakawa.

Sullivan, Harry S. *The Interpersonal Theory of Psychiatry.* New York: W. W. Norton, 1953.

[7] Ellison, Ralph. *Invisible Man.* New York: Random House, 1952. P. 3.

[8] Minturn, Leigh, and Lambert, William W. (eds.). *Mothers of Six Cultures.* New York: John Wiley and Sons, 1964.

Whiting, Beatrice B. (ed.). *Six Cultures.* New York: John Wiley and Sons, 1963.

Whiting, John W. M., and Child, Irvin L. *Child Training and Personality.* New Haven, Conn.: Yale University Press, 1953.

by children's play and games. In his earliest encounters with his body and with various artifacts, a child first explores for the pure delight of functioning. Later, increasingly deliberate manipulation follows for the pleasure of being the cause of events, thoughts, and actions. Thus, the child attains a certain rudimentary sense of mastery over his world.[9] The idea of order and predictability is established first, and, afterward, the concept of chance is introduced as a case of random interference with the underlying regularity.

The child's basic trust in other humans is also built upon the principle of steadiness or nonrandomness. On this foundation, he is to develop a reciprocal interpersonal perspective by playing alone, first directly imitating others and subsequently taking roles of both participants in the imagined interaction. The role-playing allows him to experience, or at least approximate, the type of response which his own action elicits in others. Without such a repertory of shared attitudes, feelings, and acts, it is obvious that communication with others is severely restricted.

Still, at this point of play the various roles lack any internal consistency and the child is bound to the specific temporal and situational contexts. It takes various games of strategy (as distinguished from those of chance) to make him assume the roles of all other players simultaneously prior to taking his own action. "A young child may *play* in the sense of taking the role of a series of significant others, but until he grasps the structure of the rules which make a game a game—that is until he can govern his ongoing conduct in the light of what we call the referee's perspective, or in Mead's terminology, the 'generalized other'—the child is only *playing* and not *gaming.*"[10] In this connection, it is interesting to note the prevalence of similar kinds of games in various human communities.

One thing appears certain: children's playing is not recreation in the sense adults use the word. They are actually busy learning the general

[9] Erikson, Erik H. *Childhood and Society.* 2d ed. New York: W. W. Norton, 1963. P. 235.
[10] Moore, Omar K., and Anderson, Alan R. "Some Principles for the Design of Clarifying Educational Environments." *Handbook of Socialization Theory and Research,* ed. David A. Goslin. Chicago: Rand McNally, 1969. Pp. 571–613. Quoted from p. 579.

pattern of social relations within a given society. A fundamental communality of attitudes is thus insured to a large extent without suppressing the possibility of uniqueness in individual configurations of self.[11] These longitudinal changes in the form and function of play correspond to the growth sequence of images, thoughts, and language,[12] and the formation of self concept is well under way. Social sanctions, demands, rationales, and models are gradually translated into personal values and incorporated in the self.[13]

DIFFERENT FACES, DIFFERENT DRAMAS

It is difficult to study the development of self without reducing the dynamic process to some kind of static records for observation and analysis. As in a biopsy, where the state of living tissues is determined by a microscopic examination of isolated and dyed specimens, the functioning of the self must be inferred from two sources, neither of which provides totally satisfactory data on the live being under study. The first source is those who come in contact with a particular person, and the specimen, or his objective public identity, consists of the whole gestalt of public impressions accruing to his acts. The second source is the individual himself, and the specimen from this source, his subjective public identity, is his own perceptions of the objective public identity. The subjective public identity represents a stable reservoir of information for the self concept, which is his private identity.[14]

It is now generally acknowledged that a person's objective public identity is largely situationally defined. Depending upon the where, when, what for, and with whom of social relations, the public perception of a person may vary considerably. He himself adds to this variation by managing, consciously or unconsciously, his acts in such a way

[11] Mead, op. cit. (n. 2), pp. 234–235.

[12] Piaget, Jean. Play, Dreams and Imitation in Childhood. New York: W. W. Norton, 1962.

[13] Smith, M. Brewster. "Personal Values in the Study of Lives." The Study of Lives, ed. Robert W. White. New York: Atherton Press, 1963. Pp. 324–347.

[14] French, John R. P., Jr. "The Conceptualization and Measurement of Mental Health in Terms of Self-Identity Theory." The Definition and Measurement of Mental Health, ed. S. B. Sells. Washington, D. C.: U. S. Department of Health, Education, and Welfare, Public Health Service, 1968. Pp. 136–159.

as to control the impressions to be created in others.[15] Thus, the same youngster can be concurrently a bully to smaller children, a sissy to peers, a genius to a teacher, an angel to a mother, and a tyrant to pets!

But why should any man go to the trouble of staging different dramas for different audiences? The answer appears to lie in the fact that different groups maintain different sets of expectations. In conformance with his self concept, the person accepts some of these expected roles, while rejecting others, thus giving seemingly disparate performances from one setting to another. Studies have shown that teachers and clinicians indeed hold different role expectations of a child and thus perceive the same action in different lights.[16] That behavior is to a considerable extent dependent upon a given situation has also been shown in and out of the classroom.[17] Finally, there are some indications that variations among individuals within the same setting are a function of their concepts of self.[18]

The danger of accepting and playing all expected roles to the hilt is too well known to be elaborated here. Sometimes, a child gives up his personal values and judgments in return for security and affection, real or imaginary, from parents, teachers, and others. He follows someone else's plans instead of his own and conflicting expectations play havoc with the poor child. In most cases, however, the young child manages

[15] Goffman, Erving. *The Presentation of Self in Everyday Life.* Garden City, N. Y.: Doubleday, 1959.

[16] Beilin, Harry. "Teachers' and Clinicians' Attitudes toward the Behavior Problems of Children: A Reappraisal." *Child Development,* 30:9–25; March 1959.

Tolor, Alexander; Scarpetti, William L.; and Lane, Paul A. "Teachers' Attitudes toward Children's Behavior Revisited." *Journal of Educational Psychology,* 58:175–180; June 1967.

Wickman, E. K. *Children's Behavior and Teachers' Attitudes.* New York: Commonwealth Fund, Division of Publications, 1928.

[17] Barker, Roger G. *Ecological Psychology.* Stanford, Calif.: Stanford University Press, 1968.

Gump, Paul V. "Environmental Guidance of the Classroom Behavioral System." *Contemporary Research on Teacher Effectiveness,* eds. Bruce J. Biddle and William J. Ellena. New York: Holt, Rinehart and Winston, 1964. Pp. 165–195.

[18] Rosenberg, Morris. *Society and the Adolescent Self-Image.* Princeton, N. J.: Princeton University Press, 1965.

Sears, Pauline S., and Sherman, Vivian S. *In Pursuit of Self-Esteem.* Belmont, Calif.: Wadsworth Publishing Co., 1964.

to develop into a social yet individual being, for his self concept serves as a guide for action and helps to keep the pattern of dynamic growth reasonably consistent, unified, and purposive.[19]

"The basic purpose of all human activity is the protection, the maintenance, and the enhancement not of the self, but of the self-concept, or symbolic self."[20] The distinction here between the *self* and the *self concept* is important. As mentioned earlier, what is perceived and stated as *me* cannot tell everything there is about the *self* and, further, the *self concept* may or may not correspond fairly to the *self*. Since, however, this symbolized version is the only immediately available portrayal of the self, "Most of the ways of behaving which are adopted by the organism are those which are consistent with the concept of self."[21]

Now, the trouble is this: "The self is constantly undergoing change, but the self-concept is slow to change."[22] As a result, there can develop a gap, at times quite large, between the *self concept* (map) and the *self* (territory), and emotional strain and social difficulties may ensue. If a person is preoccupied with the preservation of his present self concept, he follows the map and may plunge into a pond, still insisting that a road ought to be there as the map says. Under certain circumstances he feels much too threatened to take his eyes off the map and his need for certainty and security leads him to engage in self-defeating activities.

To benefit from all his experiences and to grow continually, therefore, man must allow for the unsettling possibility, nay, probability, of discrepancies between the self and the self concept. He must be prepared to "enhance" the concept in the sense of approximating it closer and closer to the self—this is the meaning of self-acceptance. Of course, an individual does not accept his self once and for all as an accomplished fact. Acceptance of the self is instead a process through which he comes to know and appreciate himself better and, as a corollary, to understand others better. It goes without saying that such efforts at self-acceptance presuppose some fundamental faith in a self which is

[19] Lecky, Prescott. *Self-Consistency*. Garden City, N. Y.: Doubleday, 1969.

[20] Hayakawa, S. I. *Symbol, Status, and Personality*. New York: Harcourt, Brace and World, 1963. P. 37.

[21] Rogers, Carl R. *Client-Centered Therapy*. Boston: Houghton Mifflin, 1951. P. 507.

[22] Hayakawa, *Symbol, Status, and Personality* (n. 20), p. 38.

much more than what the self concept currently depicts, basic respect for the wholeness and potential of human being, and a high regard for life. That, essentially, is the meaning of self-esteem.

COLORING THE CONCEPT OF SELF

We have indicated the interactional basis for the development of the concept of self. As every one of the millions of tiny droplets in a rainbow reflects the full spectrum of the sun's rays, so does each individual in a given society reveal in himself the range of experience available in that particular culture. Configurations of self may vary, but the basic components are the same; hence, the transmission of culture is insured at a molecular level. Realization of this fundamental communality has been expressed by different observers in such concepts as the collective or transpersonal unconscious (Carl Jung), interrelatedness of fate (Kurt Lewin), or, at a less generalized level, national character.[23] What coloring is the American culture likely to add to the self concepts of children? Let us take a look at a few examples.

THE RACE SET BEFORE US

First, consider the matter of competitive standards in judging a person's worth. In its two hundred years of history, American society has stressed "whatness" (achievement; making something out of oneself), possibly to compensate for its short balance on the classic "whoness" (origin). Status depends upon one's achievements rather than upon one's lineage. This encourages competitive performance, since someone must lose if another wins. "It seems fair to say that patterns of coping both with desired objects and with the interference which other people offer in pursuing these objects are learned at the same time and under the same conditions, so that the process of developing a way of pursuing goals involves the development of competitive

[23] McGiffert, Michael (ed.). *The Character of Americans.* Homewood, Ill.: The Dorsey Press, 1964.
Sellin, Thorsten (ed.). "National Character in the Perspective of the Social Sciences." *Annals of the American Academy of Political and Social Science,* 370:1–163; March 1967.

techniques. This means that maturity in goal definition and in goal-seeking techniques is usually paralleled by maturity in competitive techniques."[24]

Although equalitarianism and hereditary stratification offer some counterbalancing forces in our society,[25] there is no denying that American schools place an enormous emphasis upon competition and keep their pupils under pressure.[26] A child is to learn how to get along with his peers so long as this does not interfere with his efforts to get ahead of them. Most of our educational experiences are means to an end of social achievement and they are seldom savored for themselves. Competence motives are not well developed, while children are driven by the nightmare of failure.[27] The complementary functioning of the motivation to achieve success and that to avoid failure merits some additional comments.[28]

When faced with a task, some are driven strongly by a dream of success, while others are chased by a threat of failure. Nonattainment of specific goals or standards would not be threatening in itself, were it not for the fact that the sense of failure is aggravated by three possibilities.[29] The first is objective losses and damages; for example, no supper or dessert, exclusion from play activities, or physiological injuries. The second is social devaluation, namely, a lowering of one's stature in the perceptions of others; and the third is self-devaluation. Both the second and third types of experience can directly contradict one's self concept and may therefore lead to numerous tactics of counteraction. Three familiar modes of handling such experiences are attack, escape, and avoidance in mental, as well as physical, behavior.

All-out, often desperate, efforts may enable a person to accomplish

[24] Murphy, Gardner. *Personality.* New York: Basic Books, 1966. P. 526.

[25] Gardner, John W. *Excellence.* New York: Harper and Row, 1961.

[26] Yamamoto, Kaoru. "Children under Pressure." *Teaching: Essays and Readings,* ed. Kaoru Yamamoto. Boston: Houghton Mifflin, 1969. Pp. 113–128.

[27] Clausen, John A. (ed.). *Socialization and Society.* Boston: Little, Brown, 1968.
Henry, Jules. *Culture against Man.* New York: Random House, 1963.
Moore and Anderson, op. cit. (n. 10).

[28] Atkinson, John W., and Feather, Norman T. (eds.). *A Theory of Achievement Motivation.* New York: John Wiley and Sons, 1966.

[29] Birney, Robert C.; Burdick, Harvey; and Teevan, Richard C. *Fear of Failure.* New York: Van Nostrand-Reinhold, 1969.

the task and to protect his self concept. The cost tends to be high and he risks complete disorganization in the case of an ultimate failure. This tactic of full mobilization at all times has ominous implications for a child. Imagine that every bit of positive social valuation is made contingent upon high-level performance in academic, athletic, or any other activities, under the threat of severe physical and emotional penalties and social shaming. The child is treated as worthless unless he is Number One and his life is nothing but a continuous test of his performance. He has no time to be a child because he must always be on the alert for another critical challenge and another and still another. He knows of only one way to gain some semblance of love from others, but, alas, this is to compete against them and beat them, precisely the worst imaginable way of endearment. As hard as he may try to maintain himself at the top, a day will finally arrive when he finds it utterly impossible to remain there. Woe to him, for that is the day the world collapses inside and outside him: no alternative means of handling the situation are available, no reserve energy is left, and no friend or self-respect is to be found. Do not think, even for a moment, that such an example is merely hypothetical; many unfortunate children literally exert themselves to death, at least psychologically if not physiologically.

Where a frontal attack fails, some diversionary tactics may prove useful. For example, a child simply shows no interest at all in the task, complains about distractions, gets incapacitated with anxiety or becomes physically sick, works instead on his favorite tasks, does not recognize where he is failing, raises doubts about the fairness and importance of the task itself, forgets the assignment completely, comes up with excuses for not trying the task, or becomes totally dependent upon adults. In all these and other behaviors we see examples of such processes as rationalization, repression-suppression, displacement, detachment, regression, somatization, and the like. These may or may not make sense to outsiders but they certainly serve a purpose. They may or may not work, and sometimes these tactics become quite maladjustive so far as the whole child is concerned.

The nightmare of failure tends to be compensated by the creation of a rigid and idealized self concept, that is, a much distorted image of the self. We find the most extreme form of this in psychotics, but the self-blinding and self-estranging qualities of this process are no less apparent in neurotic individuals.[30] Let us remember that "neurotic conflict is quite literally a question of keeping a perennially beautiful self-picture before the eyes. It is because the *picture* rather than the person is besmirched or mutilated that neurotic breakdown occurs."[31] But a picture of what kind of person—an ordinary man who has made something of himself, proud yet uncertain, competitive yet gregarious, successful yet fearful? Is that how our culture colors him? Is the picture worth reproducing?

SUNDERING OF MEN

In the last section we mentioned three social philosophies, namely, equalitarianism, competitive performance, and hereditary stratification. Although we would like to deny it, there is a place in American society for the last. Indeed, privileges assigned on the basis of the accidents of birth are much too familiar for us to ignore. One of the most glaring examples of the functioning of this philosophy is the lower status accorded members of various ethnic minority groups.

The principle of the "looking-glass self" is nowhere more clearly demonstrated than in the concept of self of, say, black and white Americans. A child first develops the so-called race awareness at the surprisingly early age of two or three and then establishes his race preferences approximately between the ages of four and seven.[32] It is a sad observation that "Negro children from three through six tend to have an uncritical preference for white skin color,"[33] thus marking the

[30] Horney, Karen. *Our Inner Conflicts.* New York: W. W. Norton, 1945.

[31] Murphy, op. cit. (n. 24), p. 561.

[32] Allport, Gordon W. *The Nature of Prejudice.* Abridged ed. Garden City, N. Y.: Doubleday, 1958.

Goodman, Mary E. *Race Awareness in Young Children.* 2d ed. New York: Collier Books, 1964.

[33] Clark, Kenneth B. *Prejudice and Your Child.* 2d ed. Boston: Beacon Press, 1963. P. 48.

Interested readers are referred to a recent methodological discussion on the observation here: Greenwald, Herbert J., and Oppenheim, Don B. "Reported Magnitude of Self-Misidentification among Negro Children—Artifact?" *Journal of Personality and Social Psychology,* 8:49–52; January 1968.

initial phase of their budding self-rejection and self-hatred. Note here that their concept of self reflects their low valuation by generalized others, while their rejection is directed not toward the self concept per se but toward the self as a whole. The map in this case is a quite distorted representation of the territory, but, no matter, a black child is led to believe in its authenticity and, as a result, he rejects and hates himself as a human being. In the same vein, a white child also believes in a distorted map of his own and behaves as if he were superior to his black brother. Prejudice hurts both children.

Social phenomena of poverty, segregation, and family disorganization have perpetuated the vicious circle of rejection by others, of oneself, and of others.[34] When we learn of the sometimes surprising effects upon black children of a bit of confidence and pride, inspired by adults' faith in them and reflected in their academic and social performance,[35] we should perhaps rather lament the depth of the underlying hopelessness thus revealed than congratulate ourselves for rediscovering the principle of self-fulfilling prophecy.[36] Man lives by his dream, and when

[34] Coles, Robert. *Children of Crisis.* New York: Dell Publishing Co., 1968.

Rainwater, Lee, and Yancey, William L. *The Moynihan Report and the Politics of Controversy.* Cambridge, Mass.: The M.I.T. Press, 1967.

[35] Anderson, Margaret. *The Children of the South.* New York: Dell Publishing Co., 1967.

Clark, Kenneth B. *Dark Ghetto.* New York: Harper and Row, 1965. Especially Chapter 6.

[36] The much publicized, recent study of the possible effects of teacher expectations upon pupil achievement by Robert Rosenthal and Lenore Jacobson (*Pygmalion in the Classroom.* New York: Holt, Rinehart and Winston, 1968) would appear to merit a closer methodological scrutiny. For a series of discussions on this work, consult the following:

Claiborn, William L. "Expectancy Effects in the Classroom: A Failure to Replicate." *Journal of Educational Psychology,* 60:377–383; October 1969.

Gephart, William J. "Will the Real Pygmalion Please Stand Up." *American Educational Research Journal,* 7:473–475; May 1970.

Rosenthal, Robert. "Empirical vs. Decreed Validation of Clocks and Tests." *American Educational Research Journal,* 6:689–691; November 1969.

Snow, Richard E. "Unfinished Pygmalion." *Contemporary Psychology* 14:197–199; April 1969.

Thorndike, Robert L. "Book Review of *Pygmalion in the Classroom* by Robert Rosenthal and Lenore Jacobson." *American Educational Research Journal,* 5:708–711; November 1968; and "But You Have to Know How to Tell Time." *American Educational Research Journal,* 6:692; November 1969.

his dream is killed, he is dead. Man lives and dies by his symbols.[37]

Faces change and their crosses vary. Still, *all* suffer from the often explicit social declaration: You are not one of us—you are not wanted here.[38] When the precarious tolerance of Mexican-Americans as potential peers is based upon the alleged "fact" of their inferiority, which is sustained by rationalizing stereotypes, and upon their "complete" Americanization in the sense of Anglo-conformity rather than either cultural amalgamation or pluralism, one wonders about the climate in which our children grow.[39] Seventy thousand law-abiding American citizens and their forty thousand immigrant relatives can be categorically declared military threats solely because of their Japanese ancestry and can be forcefully "relocated" in internment centers with the blessings of the Government. Such an act, producing an unfathomable degree of human tragedy and an estimated economic loss to these people of 350 to 500 million dollars, again makes us wonder about the coloring of our children's concept of self.[40] Further, the subjection of some six hundred thousand authentic Americans to a nearly perfect regimen of segregation and control after at least a full century of dishonorable treatment at the hands of newcomers,[41] and their reduction to the status of "stranger[s] in [their] homeland—America's prisoner[s] of war,"[42] force us to examine the kind of human image children see reflected in us.

[37] Smith, Lillian. *Killers of the Dream*. Garden City, N. Y.: Doubleday, 1963.

Utley, Robert M. *The Last Days of the Sioux Nation*. New Haven, Conn.: Yale University Press, 1963.

[38] Yamamoto, Kaoru. "Children of Those Who Are Not Like Us." *Teaching: Essays and Readings,* ed. Kaoru Yamamoto. Boston: Houghton Mifflin, 1969. Pp. 129–163.

[39] Heller, Celia S. *Mexican American Youth*. New York: Random House, 1966.

Simmons, Ozzie B. "The Mutual Images and Expectations of Anglo-Americans and Mexican-Americans." *Daedalus,* 90:286–299; Spring 1961.

[40] Grodzins, Morton. *Americans Betrayed*. Chicago: University of Chicago Press, 1949.

TenBroek, Jacobus; Barnhardt, Edward N.; and Matson, Floyd W. *Prejudice, War and the Constitution*. Berkeley, Calif.: University of California Press, 1968.

[41] Jackson, Helen H. *A Century of Dishonor,* ed. Andrew F. Rolle. New York: Harper and Row, 1965.

Van Every, Dale. *Disinherited*. New York: Avon Books, 1967.

[42] Cahn, Edgar S. (ed.). *Our Brother's Keeper*. Washington, D. C.: New Community Press, 1969. P. vii. (Distributed by World Publishing Co.)

The power which keeps men asunder works subtly but surely from one generation to the next, harming all it touches. Distinguishing marks are in the eyes of the beholder, and no observable or inferred variations in human characteristics would, in and of themselves, prescribe the differential treatments given their possessors. This point becomes clearer if we examine minority groups other than ethnic ones, for example, the mentally retarded, mentally ill, handicapped, criminal, and the like, to see how they are stigmatized and kept at arm's length.

MANY DISEASES AND PLAGUES AND EVIL SPIRITS

It was suggested above that deviance is not inherent in any particular patterns of behavior or physical attributes. The social audience determines whether certain individuals should be regarded as different by attaching degrading labels and interpretations to some facets of their being. The group also defines the roles the deviants are expected to play. Hence, these individuals are classified by the group for the purposes of social management.

Three related aspects of the processes of categorization have been identified.[43] First, it seems customary for the society to decide, no matter how tenuous the basis for the decision, whether the individual involved is to be held personally responsible for the attributed deviance. This judgment of moral accountability determines whether the person will be punished (e.g., executed, as in the case of a murderer) or merely controlled by other means (e.g., trained if he is mentally retarded, rehabilitated if physically handicapped, or corrected if delinquent). Second, a decision is made on the basis of the prognosis of the imputed deviance on the degree of segregation to be imposed. For example, lepers and criminals are usually banished from the community rather completely for an extended period of time, while the unemployed and people suffering from venereal disease may be permitted to share many facets of normal social life with other citizens. Third, the extent of status degradation or discrediting is specified to justify the differences in affective treatment of the deviants. For example, tuberculosis and

[43] Freidson, Eliot. "Disability as Social Deviance." *Sociology and Rehabilitation*, ed. Marvin B. Sussman. Washington, D. C.: American Sociological Association, 1966. Pp. 71–99.

schizophrenic patients may be loathed, while those suffering from cancer or hearing loss may be regarded with less stigma. Epileptics, little people (dwarfs), and the disfigured may be "merely" feared and pitied, but homosexuals and drug addicts can elicit wrathful reactions in non-deviants.

Interestingly, most of the designated deviant acts or traits are not immediately harmful to the group. As in the case of carved demons and pictured gods, the individuals singled out personify the kinds of experience which fall outside the boundary of the accepted group norm. In this sense, the "different" ones serve to preserve stability in society by embodying otherwise formless dangers.[44]

The institutionalization of deviance is completed by various public ceremonies which initiate the chosen individuals into their distinctly deviant status. Penal verdicts, legal definitions of insanity or blindness, professional diagnoses of illness, and referrals to social agencies are some of the dramatic means of pronouncement. The process is essentially irreversible, as witnessed by the existence of few, if any, rituals to reinstate the deviant individuals in the larger society. The initiation ceremonies are generally conclusive because the group is trying to establish that these individuals are different in essence and not merely in their temporary life patterns.[45] The trick is to replace an old map with a new one and then claim that the territory itself is now in fact different.[46] It is thus argued that, beyond any shadow of doubt, "these deviants . . . belong to a fundamentally different class of human beings, or perhaps even a different species."[47]

[44] Erikson, Kai T. "Notes on the Sociology of Deviance." *Social Problems,* 9:307–314; Spring 1962.

[45] Garfinkel, Harold. "Conditions of Successful Degradation Ceremonies." *American Journal of Sociology,* 61:420–424; March 1956.

[46] Readers may be interested in a recent news item. It was reported that American and European analysts had discovered some puzzling changes in Soviet maps which seem to indicate a policy of distortion for the sake of national security. "According to the specialist, the Soviet Union's charts and atlases, once renowned for their standards of excellence, have been designed in the last few years to shift coastlines, towns, rivers and other map features at random by as much as 25 miles in a seeming attempt at deception." (*Minneapolis Tribune,* Sunday, January 18, 1970, p. 1B.)

[47] Scheff, Thomas J. *Being Mentally Ill.* Chicago: Aldine Publishing Co., 1966. P. 77.

But why, in this social process of differentiation, are certain charac- teristics (both attributes and actions) inclined to be singled out as the focus of attention? One reason seems to be that the unfamiliar disrupts the established basic rules of social interaction.[48] A disfigured baby, a man in a wheelchair, a blind young girl, an ex-convict, or a homosexual —all present a serious challenge to the accepted rules of conduct in face-to-face encounter, and society has few alternative modes of action to handle the many different combinations of man and situation.

Especially when visible impairment is involved, social relations tend to be strained by, among other factors, the aesthetic aversion shown by the normals and the functional limitations of the handicapped them- selves. Reactions to these two aspects of physical impairment are illus- trated by studies of children's preferences among a normal child, a child with crutches and a leg brace, a child in a wheelchair, a child with left forearm amputation, a child with a slight facial disfigurement, and an obese child. While the overall ranking among various age and ethnic groups appears to follow the order above with a remarkable uniformity, it was observed that the obese child (an aesthetic impairment) is the least liked by girls and the forearm amputee (a functional impairment) is the least liked by boys. The preference patterns did not change even when a factor of skin color was added to the stimulus figures. Unfor- tunately, children's negative attitudes seem to increase with age, and available evidence indicates the idea that physical impairment repre- sents only an initial barrier to social relationships does not receive strong support.[49]

In view of their generally negative public reception, it is no wonder that those classified as deviant are inclined to be frustrated, unhappy, and often hostile. For example, it has been reported that children who have an upper and/or lower extremity amputated are highly sensitive to social appraisal of themselves or of their injury, have a high propor- tion (ca. 40 percent) of inadequate adjustment, and receive low parental acceptance. Further, both emotionally disturbed children and deaf children have been found to show deprecating attitudes toward them-

[48] Goffman, Erving. *Interaction Ritual*. Garden City, N. Y.: Doubleday, 1967.
[49] Richardson, Stephen A. "The Effect of Physical Disability on the Socialization of a Child." *Handbook of Socialization Theory and Research*, ed. David A. Gos- lin. Chicago: Rand McNally, 1969. Pp. 1047–1064.

selves and toward others, especially those who are impaired in ways different from their own.[50]

This last observation is sadly quite significant: the spurned minority members not only hold themselves in low esteem but also actively reject those who are in a similarly unfortunate position. Lacking fundamental faith in themselves, they are too insecure to show any tolerance of others in need. Trust in and love for others do not grow in the hotbed of contempt of self. "The great commandment of religion, 'Thou shalt love thy neighbor as thyself,' might now be better interpreted to mean, 'Thou shalt love thyself properly, and then thou wilt love thy neighbor.' "[51] Affirmation of self precedes one's affirmation of others, and an *authentic* adult can do much to induce and bolster a child's affirmation of himself by displaying rich and open feelings toward him, by showing unyielding confidence in him, and by providing and sharing with him genuine human encounters.[52]

TO A DIFFERENT DRUMMER

We have been describing several selected aspects of the American social milieu to show some common denominators in the developmental process of self. In this connection, it is important to note that clear models are not readily available to guide children in becoming a healthy being. Warnings of potential pitfalls abound, but positive guidelines are hard to find. The typical definition of a healthy individual is more heavily dependent upon our knowledge of the sick than upon our understanding of the well-functioning. Hence, a person is by definition healthy unless he is sick, and the whole argument is sustained

[50] Blanton, Richard L., and Nunnally, Jum C., Jr. "Semantic Habits and Cognitive Style Processes in the Deaf." *Journal of Abnormal and Social Psychology*, 68:397–402; April 1964.

Rosengren, William R. "The Self in the Emotionally Disturbed." *American Journal of Sociology*, 66:454–462; March 1961.

Siller, Jerome. "Psychological Concomitants of Amputation in Children." *Child Development*, 31:109–120; March 1960.

[51] Liebman, Joshua L. *Peace of Mind.* New York: Simon and Schuster, 1946. P. 43.

[52] Moustakas, Clark. *The Authentic Teacher.* Cambridge, Mass.: Howard A. Doyle Publishing Co., 1966.

by "what is present when health is absent" rather than by "what is present when health is present."[53]

As indicated earlier, moral judgment of badness usually befalls those identified as deviant, and in the realm of mental illness these people are likely to be uniformly called "abnormal." Similarly, the non-deviant are categorically called "normal," thus implying a certain degree of homogeneity among them. When we look for what is present when health is present, however, it is pertinent to point out that there can be another subgroup whose members are also "abnormal" but in a different way. They are not modal in the sense that their style of life tends to be better integrated and more purposeful and vital than that of the average group. Beyond attaining the minimum level of acculturation required for ordinary coping and social functioning, these people seem to be more open, autonomous, and self-accepting than the "normal."[54] Studies have characterized these "healthy" ones as emotionally stable, tolerant of ambiguity, resilient and flexible, trusting of self and others, competent and imaginative, ethical and dependable, guided by a unifying philosophy of life, and enjoying life with all its joys and sorrows. It appears that consensual identification of these exceptional individuals is not particularly difficult.[55]

One cluster of characteristics in this overall configuration of the healthy life style is often called creativity. The word is now a popular

[53] Barron, Frank. *Creativity and Personal Freedom.* Princeton, N. J.: Van Nostrand, 1968. P. 2.

[54] Jourard, Sidney M. *Personal Adjustment.* 2d ed. New York: Macmillan, 1963. Maslow, Abraham H. *Toward a Psychology of Being.* 2d ed. Princeton, N. J.: Van Nostrand, 1968.

[55] Allport, Gordon W. "Personality: Normal and Abnormal." *Personality and Social Encounter.* Boston: Beacon Press, 1960. Pp. 155–168.

Jahoda, Marie. *Current Concepts of Positive Mental Health.* New York: Basic Books, 1958.

MacKinnon, Donald W. "The Highly Effective Individual." *Teachers College Record,* 51:367–378; April 1960.

Shoben, Edward J., Jr. "Toward a Concept of the Normal Personality." *American Psychologist,* 12:183–189; April 1957.

Smith, M. Brewster. "Competence and 'Mental Health': Problems in Conceptualizing Human Effectiveness." *The Definition and Measurement of Mental Health,* ed. S. B. Sells. Washington, D. C.: U. S. Department of Health, Education, and Welfare, Public Health Service, 1968. Pp. 100–114.

White, Robert W. (ed.). *The Study of Lives.* New York: Atherton Press, 1963.

one. "It is more than a word today; it is an incantation. People think of it as a kind of psychic wonder drug, powerful and presumably painless; and everyone wants a prescription."[56] Parents want it in their children, if not in themselves, and teachers want it in their pupils—so long, naturally, as the young do not go too far! After all, creative people are not necessarily well-rounded and creative processes and products can be rather disquieting.

Now, there is no lack of scathing criticism of schools in America for not freeing children's capacity to learn. Curriculum is frequently characterized as trivial, fractionized, and irrelevant; instruction as impersonal, routinized, and unimaginative; and the total schooling experience as custodial, brutalizing, and indeed uneducative.[57] Granted that many of the objections are to the point, it would be much too naive to accuse the school of not releasing children's potential when the whole society is in fact wary of such possibilities.[58] The school is an easy scapegoat but that does not change the character of our culture.

In addition to this underlying resistance against innovations as well as innovators, there are two factors which tend to slow us down in creating measures to "train" children for creativity. The first is that even if we could identify those social and educational conditions which are believed to have contributed to the development of creativity in the past, we would be less than certain whether the same relationship can be replicated in today's world.[59] It is difficult enough to sift out nuggets

[56] Gardner, John W. Self-Renewal. New York: Harper and Row, 1965. P. 32.
[57] Some samples include:
Friedenberg, Edgar Z. Coming of Age in America. New York: Random House, 1967.
Goodman, Paul. Compulsory Mis-education and The Community of Scholars. New York: Random House, 1966.
Holt, John. How Children Fail. New York: Pitman Publishing Corp., 1964.
Kozol, Jonathan. Death at an Early Age. Boston: Houghton Mifflin, 1967.
Postman, Neil, and Weingartner, Charles. Teaching as a Subversive Activity. New York: Delacorte Press, 1969.
Silberman, Charles E. Crisis in the Classroom. New York: Random House, 1970.
[58] Henry, op. cit. (n. 27).
Mayer, Martin. The Schools. Garden City, N. Y.: Doubleday, 1963.
Schrag, Peter. Voices in the Classroom. Boston: Beacon Press, 1965.
[59] MacKinnon, Donald W. "Instructional Media in the Nurturing of Creativity." Instructional Media and Creativity, eds. Calvin W. Taylor and Frank W. Williams. New York: John Wiley and Sons, 1966. Pp. 179–216.

without being bothered by the possibility that all the fruits of hard labor are nothing but fool's gold! The second factor is simply that we have little genuine understanding of the creative process, and we are accordingly not sure how to proceed in our conscious efforts to nurture creativity.[60]

"Perhaps some day we shall know how to heighten creativity. Until then, one of the best things we can do for creative men and women is to stand out of their light."[61] Perhaps some day we shall know how to facilitate the development of healthy individuals. Until then, one of the best things we can do is to have faith in our children and, within certain defined limits, to let them be. Because, in this effort, the young are on our side with ". . . one of the most splendid qualities of the child's soul—optimism. All children between the ages of two and five believe (or yearn to believe) that life is meant only for joy, for limitless happiness, and this belief is one of the most important conditions for their normal psychological growth."[62]

IMITATION OF LIFE

"How one hates to think," Anne Morrow Lindbergh once observed, "of oneself as alone. How one avoids it. . . . We seem so frightened today of being alone that we never let it happen."[63] The fear is dissipated by, among other means, some of man's most ingenious inventions, namely, the devices of mass communication. Printed matter, photographs, radio, movies, television, and other devices singly and jointly help us to avoid this frightening feeling. Present-day mass communication is extraordinarily pervasive, and highly specialized.

It has in fact been said that "mass communications now fill more than one half of an American adult's leisure time" and also that they "command more of a child's life than any other waking activity, including school."[64] Mass communications thus expose a large number

[60] Ausubel, David P. Educational Psychology. New York: Holt, Rinehart and Winston, 1968.

[61] Gardner, Self-Renewal (n. 56), p. 35.

[62] Chukovsky, Kornei. From Two to Five. Berkeley, Calif.: University of California Press, 1963. P. 42.

[63] Lindbergh, Anne M. Gift from the Sea. New York: Random House, 1955. P. 41.

[64] Schramm, Wilbur. "Mass Media and Educational Policy." Social Forces Influencing American Education, Sixtieth Yearbook of the National Society for the

of people to recent or current events in widely-scattered locales, even including the other side of the moon. Children raised in the world of ready accessibility to television are expected to be somewhat different in their *Weltanschauung* than those who have had only printed materials. They may have never been west of the Mississippi, but they are vaguely aware of people and things beyond. They may have never seen an ocean, but they are remotely conscious of worlds on the other shores. The messages may not be received and/or utilized but, all the same, they are there, available to anyone.

Ironically, a typical message in mass communication remains "munication" rather than "communication." That is to say, the flow of information is one-way and the action is basically unilateral. The built-in technical rigidity of many a mass communication system exerts powerful standardizing pressure on the contents and contexts of transmission, while the members of its large, heterogeneous, and anonymous audience are inclined to feel loss of individuality and initiative.[65] It has been observed, moreover, that people tend to see and hear only those messages agreeable to their predispositions. Because of this process of selective exposure consistent with one's concept of self, mass communications are more likely to reinforce and elaborate man's existing life style than to redirect or convert him to different positions or to create new tastes in him. Accordingly, it is usually the less secure and less mature among children who depend heavily upon such sources as television and comic books for escape, and it is the better-educated adults who seek culturally refined communications when, logically, the less-educated need these more.

On the receiving end, in addition, the effects of any communication tend to be mediated by opinion leaders, who, in their respective spheres of influence, personalize a message for wider and easier acceptance. This two-step flow of communications requires, as well as allows,

---

Study of Education, Part II, ed. Nelson B. Henry. Chicago: University of Chicago Press, 1961. Pp. 203–229. Quoted from p. 208.

[65] Foote, Nelson N. "The New Media and Our Total Society." *The New Media and Education,* eds. Peter H. Rossi and Bruce J. Biddle. Garden City, N. Y.: Doubleday, 1967. Pp. 382–415.

Janowitz, Morris, and Street, David. "The Social Organization of Education." *The New Media and Education,* eds. Peter H. Rossi and Bruce J. Biddle. Garden City, N. Y.: Doubleday, 1967. Pp. 227–265.

the significant others in a child's life to play a crucial role in determining the results of learning. Parents and teachers alike exert an important influence as mediators and models with definite views and values.[66] It is largely for them to turn the typical passive reception of second-hand experiences into an active intake and integration on the part of the young. It is for them to transform children's learning from one of safe, vicarious participation to that of concerned involvement.

Without the helping hand of adults, however, children will find it difficult to develop and exercise control over their actual environment and will tend to be resigned to "half lived, but never truly felt"[67] experiences. They may become familiar with an imitation of life but not with life itself. When a noted mountaineer and survival school instructor comments that many people, young and old alike, nowadays forget that meat, vegetables, and milk are not manufactured neatly and endlessly in the supermarket, he is telling us something of the seriousness of this alienating trend in modern life. Men are born and die daily on television. Even the astounding feat of man's ascent to the moon and return seems to be a matter accepted calmly as routine. We witness these wonders but take them for granted without any genuine involvement, comprehension, or appreciation.

In this climate of expanding knowledge and skills unaccompanied by wisdom and compassion, children are indeed hard-pressed to learn a disciplined way to transcend immediate relevance and convenience so as to foster a sense of historical significance. If they are to stop at what appears to count merely here and now, not much hope exists for four billion people in this world to develop the precious awareness of the interrelatedness of human fate. But where else other than the school can our young be systematically and deliberately initiated into a lifelong search for the sense of being one with themselves and with others?

[66] Berelson, Bernard, and Steiner, Gary A. *Human Behavior*. New York: Harcourt, Brace and World, 1964. "Mass Communication," pp. 527–555.

Maccoby, Eleanor E. "Effects of the Mass Media." *Review of Child Development Research*, Vol. I, eds. Martin L. Hoffman and Lois W. Hoffman. New York: Russell Sage Foundation, 1964. Pp. 323–348.

Wright, Charles R. *Mass Communication*. New York: Random House, 1959.

[67] Glynn, Eugene D., as cited in Schramm, op. cit. (n. 64), p. 213.

THE WAY AHEAD

This, then, is a cursory introduction to the mystery of self and the concept of self. No scholar worthy of the name would dare claim to understand the enigma of man, but, on the other hand, no practitioner can escape facing it every day. Teachers must know their children and that means they must know themselves. Knowing, in this context, is not the same as objective observation and description. Instead, it is the experiencing of the wholeness of man through reflection upon one's self in relation with another's. One cannot help being subjectively involved and being touched by the interaction, since the "essence of man which is special to him can be directly known only in a living relation. . . . *I* and *Thou* exist only in our world, because man exists, and the *I*, moreover, exists only through the relation to the *Thou*."[68]

In the ensuing chapters, six authors will be discussing different facets of self and the concept of self in young children. I defer to these colleagues for specific lists of references recommended for further examination. If nevertheless, I may be bold enough to suggest my own writings on related topics, I would name the following.

"For Each Tree is Known . . . ." *Teaching: Essays and Readings,* ed. Kaoru Yamamoto. Boston: Houghton Mifflin, 1969. Pp. 249–260.

"Planning and Teaching for Behavioral Change." *The Elementary School: Principles and Problems,* eds., Joe L. Frost and G. Thomas Rowland. Boston: Houghton Mifflin, 1969. Pp. 344–363.

To be quite honest, though, I myself would rather read the enjoyable and thoughtful titles listed below.

Axline, Virginia M. *Dibs: In Search of Self.* Boston: Houghton Mifflin, 1964. (Available in paperback as a Ballantine Book, U-6109.)

Baruch, Dorothy W. *One Little Boy.* New York: The Julian Press, 1952. (Available in paperback as a Delta Book.)

Rogers, Carl R. *On Becoming a Person.* Boston: Houghton Mifflin, 1961.

Closer to the classroom are the following accounts by three excellent teachers.

[68] Buber, Martin. *Between Man and Man.* New York: Macmillan, 1965. P. 205.

Ashton-Warner, Sylvia. *Teacher.* New York: Simon and Schuster, 1963. (Available in paperback form as both the original publisher's Essandess Paperback, 1966, and a Bantam Book, NM-1028.)

Marshall, Sybil. *An Experiment in Education.* New York: Cambridge University Press, 1966. (Available in both hardbound and paperback editions.)

Moustakas, Clark. *The Authentic Teacher.* Cambridge, Mass. Howard A. Doyle Publishing Co., 1966. (Paperbound.)

RECAPITULATION—THE MATTER OF SEMANTICS

As you will undoubtedly note, the seven contributors are essentially of a mind in their overall orientation to the subject of the self concept. However, it cannot be expected that they all agree in the precise usage of words in their respective chapters. To minimize possible confusion, therefore, let me briefly repeat the manner in which various expressions are used in relationship with each other more or less throughout the book.

First of all, the *self* refers to the whole of our being, the totality of who we are, including both the subjective (*I*) and objective (*me*) of our experience. We are at best only vaguely cognizant of the underlying processes and the enigma is probably never known to us in its entirety. Still, we must keep fundamental faith in our being, have a basic sense of *self-esteem* or *self-respect,* and speak of *self-actualization* in terms of the believed potential in the *self.* Without such underlying trust in ourselves, we may indeed reveal nothing but the depravity of man against himself and others.

Most of our thought and action are based, however, on the *self concept* which is the symbolic representation of *self.* Formulation, maintenance, and revision of this composite *image of self* (or *self image*) are much influenced by the reflexive nature of any such abstracting operation and, hence, the phrase, the *looking-glass self.* Distortion and coloring of the *self concept* are commonplace, and even within a reasonable range of accuracy, the image can be generally favorable (positive) or unfavorable (negative). Beyond certain limits, naturally, such misrepresentation will result in outright *self-deception.*

Our life styles inevitably reflect how we see ourselves, and clinicians have developed means to get a quick, though very approximate look at the images of self by asking people to describe their *me* in relation to the here and now (*actual self*), a desired model (*ideal self* or *self-ideal*), the presumed perceptions by others, or whatever additional referents. All these are components of the total configuration of *self concept* which we act to preserve and enhance. The efforts may unfortunately become *self-defeating*, unless we are conscious of the fact that there is a lot more to the territory (*self*) than to the map (*self concept*). If we have such *self-awareness* and if we have the basic *self-esteem*, we can then allow ourselves to develop the attitude of *self-acceptance* and enhance the *self concept* in the wholesome sense of its closer and closer approximation to the *self* regardless of the risks involved.

One of our crucial tasks is to see to it that a profound sense of respect for the *self* be fostered in the young and that the willingness to accept the *self* be nurtured. Humility for one's limited awareness, hope for potential growth, and trust in fellow humans all derive from the same root of affirmation of one's being. If so raised, our children will come a step closer to the goal of loving life and living it.

TWO · THE DEVELOPING SELF:

WORLD OF COMMUNICATION

Carolyn Emrick Massad

*It's the connection between language and experience
that offers children human wholeness.*[1]

The self concept develops as the individual matures and
learns about his environment and himself. Maturation plays an important
role, but of equal or possibly even greater importance is conscious and
subconscious learning. How might the self concept be learned? As
with the formation of any other concepts, there are three major possibilities: (1) the self concept may be learned from direct experience or
perception of the physical world without any social mediation; (2) the
self concept may be socially mediated without language; (3) the self
concept may be socially mediated and the mediation is through language.
All three kinds of learning probably occur. The age, physical condition,
and environment of the individual are the factors which are most likely
to determine, together or independently, the particular kind of learning
involved.

Learning about what is self and what is not self from direct experience or perception of the physical world without any social mediation is
a child's first major step in his orientation to the world. An infant will
watch his own hands and feet in motion, at times pull his own hair, and
put his fist and toys in his mouth. As the child grows he perceives

[1] Martin, Bill, Jr. *The Human Connection: Language and Literature.* Washington, D. C.: National Education Association Department of Elementary-Kindergarten-Nursery Education, 1967. P. 35.

more of his environment and learns about himself in relation to other objects in the world.

Very early in life, the child becomes aware of the other people in his environment. It is at this point that a child's perception of what is self and what is not self may be socially mediated, communication being a primary factor in the process.

But what is meant by the term communication? Is it the verbal exchange of information among people? Yes, but this is only one face of the coin. Communication is much more. It includes all behavior, both conscious and subconscious, by which people influence each other.

NONVERBAL COMMUNICATION

A child's perception of what is self and what is not self may be socially mediated without language. An infant does not sense his mother's love because she says the words "I love you" (although in time he may learn to associate the voice with his mother). The face that he sees when he wakes or when he cries, the hands that hold him firmly yet gently, and the dependable provision made for each of his many needs develop in him feelings of trust and security. Later father, brothers, sisters, and playmates gradually become a part of his experience and he learns to relate himself to them. Eventually, due to the processes of social interaction, the child acquires a system of communication that is common to his cultural group. Language is only one part of that system.

But once language is learned, what are the other ways in which an individual communicates? Remember the saying "actions often speak louder than words"? Well, at times they do, but often so subtly that even the people involved are not aware of the fact that communication is taking place.

In studying human behavior, culture, and communication, several psychiatrists, psychologists, anthropologists, and linguists have studied nonverbal communication. The effects that body language, concepts of time and space, play activities, laughter, and crying have on interpersonal relations are some of the major areas studied.[2]

[2] Hall, Edward T. The Silent Language. Greenwich, Conn.: Fawcett Publications, 1959; and The Hidden Dimension. Garden City, N. Y.: Doubleday, 1966.

Birdwhistell, Ray L. Kinesics and Context. Philadelphia: University of Pennsylvania Press, 1970.

(continued on next page)

BODY LANGUAGE

What is body language? Well, take a moment from your reading and consider the position you have taken to read this text. Are you lying down or sitting in a comfortable easy chair? If so, chances are that you are reading for pleasure or, at least, have voluntarily elected to read the book. However, if you are sitting at a desk or table it is likely that you are studying the text for an explicit purpose. A frown, a smile, a nod of the head, the way you fold your arms or hands may also tell an observer something about how you feel about what you are reading. This is body language.

A study of body language reveals that there are socio-cultural codes that include such things as gender signals. An example of just such a signal is the way in which American males generally cross their legs, one ankle on the other knee, as opposed to the knee-on-knee position typical of American females.[3] Also, certain gestures of the hands, arm positions, and ways of walking have come to be identified with females as opposed to males, and vice versa.

The fact that German university students indicate respect by rising as the professor enters the classroom is another example of a socio-cultural code. Still other examples of respect signals are a young American male's holding a door open for a woman or relinquishing his seat to an elderly gentleman.

Whether one realizes it or not, he is communicating with his body language. An awareness of this language can be of particular help to those who wish to understand and improve social interaction.

Ruesch, Jurgen, and Bateson, Gregory. *Communication: The Social Matrix of Psychiatry.* New York: W. W. Norton, 1968.

Fast, Julius. *Body Language.* New York: M. Evans, 1970.

Fromm, Erich. *The Forgotten Language.* New York: Grove Press, 1951.

Berlyne, D. E. "Laughter, Humor, and Play." *Handbook of Social Psychology,* ed. Gardner Lindzey. Cambridge, Mass.: Addison-Wesley Publishing Co., 1969. Pp. 795–852.

Tagiuri, Renato. "Person Perception." *Handbook of Social Psychology,* ed. Gardner Lindzey. Cambridge, Mass.: Addison-Wesley Publishing Co., 1969. Pp. 395–449.

[3] Davis, Flora. "The Way We Speak 'Body Language.' " *The New York Times Magazine,* May 31, 1970. Pp. 8–9.

CONCEPTS OF TIME AND SPACE

The time of day is very significant in certain contexts. For example, have you ever received a telephone call very early in the morning or around midnight? Remember your concern? Usually a call at such hours indicates an important or urgent matter. Or, do you ever remember being invited to a party the day it was to be given knowing that the party had been planned for at least a week earlier? You may have interpreted the situation to mean that you were an afterthought, or perhaps even a "fill-in" for someone who couldn't attend at the last minute. Yes, time affects interpersonal relationships.

Concepts of space also influence the way people feel about themselves and act toward each other. Remember when, as a child, you were given your "very own" drawer or closet space? Can you recall the feeling of resentment toward a sibling or friend who entered that area without your permission? Many young couples have similar feelings when their mothers and fathers enter their homes and try to tell them how to raise the baby, arrange the furniture, or cook the meal. One's concept of space, ownership of that space, if you will, is another important factor in social interaction.

PLAY ACTIVITIES, LAUGHTER, AND CRYING

Is there a difference between the woman who plays cards for fun and the pleasure of being with others and the woman who plays cards to win? The one playing for pleasure may laugh at one of her errors, but the one playing to win becomes quite cross at her own mistakes and generally intolerant of those who continually make errors. Even the very tactics taken to play a game tells something about the player. Is she shrewd and calculating in every move? Does she become visibly upset over the successful move of an opponent and give up trying to win? Or does she appear to enjoy the discomfort of a losing player by laughing and glancing at the loser with a look of arrogance? People at play are often communicating more than just verbally.

A hearty laugh generally tells us that someone has greatly enjoyed something funny. A suppressed giggle may indicate an attempt to cover up the humor of another's misfortune. Crying in adults may be for joy or for sorrow depending upon the situation; however, it usually indicates discomfort or unhappiness in infants and children. Often the nonverbal sounds that people make communicate as much or even more than any words.

LOOK AND SEE, TEACHER

Children communicate freely. They have not yet learned to be selective in sharing with others what they know or how they feel. Even as they learn the strategy of verbally concealing things from others, they may still communicate nonverbally with an interested observer.

Johnny who is always very slow in getting ready to join the reading group may be telling his teacher that he is insecure and feels that he does poorly. Mary who never volunteers an answer and moves restlessly in her seat when called upon may be saying that she feels inadequate also. Karen's sagging shoulders and frown as she works on her arithmetic problems could be saying that she doesn't understand them and may soon be giving up even though she doesn't want to. Bobby who likes to clown around in class and generally raises his hand even when he doesn't have the correct answer may be communicating to his teacher that he wants and needs attention. In working to understand children and guide their learning, it is up to the teacher to read the nonverbal signals of his pupils just as he would listen to their verbal statements.

However, when the teacher is from a socio-cultural group different from that of the children he teaches, he needs to learn something about the codes of the children's culture. Fuchs[4] tells of Jimmy, a bright boy who adheres to the male role characteristic of Hispanic culture, that is, *machismo* or the cult of maleness, the ideal role for males involving courage and strength as opposed to the female role characteristics of shame, resignation, and suffering. He would strut around the classroom like a young bantam rooster and frequently defy his female teacher, refusing to do any assignments that he associated with a feminine role. Fortunately, the teacher was sensitive to the situation and was able to resolve the problem with patience, understanding, and the help of others.

[4] Fuchs, Estelle. *Teachers Talk*. Garden City, N. Y.: Doubleday, 1969. Pp. 34–36.

Unfortunately, all such cases do not turn out as well as Jimmy's. Ignorance of a culture different from one's own often breeds distrust and misunderstanding. Being open and ready to learn about what is new and different promotes good will and leads to successful interpersonal relations with people from a different cultural orientation. Remember, too, the teacher communicates by his actions also.

A teacher who makes children wait great lengths of time for help or attention may be telling them that they are unimportant to him. A skillful teacher finds ways to reassure individual children that they are not forgotten even when they are not working directly with him.[5] Moving toward children rather than backing away indicates acceptance and willingness to help them. A gentle hand on a six-year-old's shoulder and a smile as he works on a drawing can indicate support for what he is attempting.

Nonverbal communication is important in the classroom.[6] It can help a teacher to understand his pupils and help them to understand him. To develop mentally healthy children, knowledge about nonverbal communication is essential.

VERBAL COMMUNICATION

Although learning about one's environment and self from direct experience with the physical world or through nonverbal communication is likely to occur more often for children from homes where language is not an important form of communication than for those children whose environment has a rich language orientation, it is generally agreed that as the typical child grows and learns the language of his socio-cultural group, his thought processes involve and may even be facilitated by his linguistic ability. Even the development of new concepts and the restructuring of old concepts occur more frequently through the mediation of language. To understand the process, it is important to know about the development of language facility.

[5] D'Evelyn, Katherine E. *Developing Mentally Healthy Children*. Washington, D. C.: American Association of Elementary-Kindergarten-Nursery Educators, 1970. Pp. 10–12.

[6] Galloway, Charles M. *Teaching Is Communicating: Nonverbal Language in the Classroom*. Washington, D. C.: National Education Association, The Association for Student Teaching, 1970.

As McNeill[7] indicates, normal children acquire language in an amazingly short period of time. Grammatical speech generally is not initiated before the age of eighteen months. Nevertheless, the foundation is complete by the time the child reaches three-and-one-half years of age. The basis for the language competency of an adult's grammar most likely emerges in the short span of two years—an astounding accomplishment when achievement in language is compared to growth in the other cognitive areas.

But specifically, what does occur in the speech development of the infant from birth to the age of two years? Researchers tend to agree that the vocalizations of the newborn infant are the basic components from which speech develops and are used even at the earliest stage in life to communicate needs or desires. In time, the normal child can comprehend other people, even before he is able to use words. By the age of one, the child can say a few words but the development of vocabulary is relatively slow until the last months of the second year when the speed of progress rapidly increases. At first, the child uses words in a generalized way, the use of words for specific meanings occurring later in the child's development. Words that name things are used first followed by verbs and adjectives; only the most advanced children may begin to use pronouns near the end of the second year. Also, children under two years of age will use single words for the same purpose that an adult would use a phrase or sentence because young children generally do not use combinations of words until much later.[8]

But what mental processes occur as the typical child's language develops? Is there a direct relationship between the two? If so, what is the relationship? And how does the child's language indicate what he thinks about himself and his world? In seeking answers to these questions, it is desirable to look at the work of Vygotsky and that of Piaget and his co-workers since they provide the most comprehensive

[7] McNeill, David. "Developmental Psycholinguistics." The Genesis of Language, eds. Frank Smith and George A. Miller. Cambridge, Mass.: The M.I.T. Press, 1966. P. 15.

[8] Carroll, John B. Language and Thought. Englewood Cliffs, N. J.: Prentice-Hall, 1964. Pp. 30–43.

Brown, Roger. Social Psychology. New York: The Free Press, 1965. Pp. 246–349.

treatment so far of the development of language and thought. Although their theories vary, they also bear striking similarities. Because Piaget's initial work preceded that of Vygotsky, a summary of his work is presented first.

PIAGET'S INTERPRETATIONS:
DEVELOPMENT OF LANGUAGE AND OF CONCEPT

In their recent writing, Piaget and Inhelder[9] state that "language does not constitute the source of logic but is, on the contrary, structured by it." This statement indicates the need to examine Piaget's theory of language development in the light of his theory of the cognitive development of children.

Although Piaget's earliest studies of children were concerned with the development of language and thought, he soon began to concentrate primarily on the thought processes. To Piaget, thought involves more than language. Mental operations (including internalized behavior and action) and representations (including language, auditory images, and visual images) are the elements of thought. For certain kinds of thought, such as logical thinking, operations are of primary importance and the verbalization of the thought may only help to consolidate and generalize it. In other instances, such as thinking verbal problems through, internal speech may control behavior.

Basic to Piaget's theories is the idea that as the child grows new conceptual schemata are continuously developing and are being integrated with existing schemata. Inhelder[10] defines schema as "the structure common to all those acts which—from the subject's point of view —are equivalent." That is to say, as the child develops he gradually yet continuously acquires an internal mental model of his environment, consolidating and integrating older conceptual structures with the newly developed ones.

In view of this idea, it is generally assumed that each individual looks at the world in his own way. Even when two individuals live in the

[9] Piaget, Jean, and Inhelder, Bärbel. The Psychology of the Child. New York: Basic Books, 1969. Pp. 89–90.
[10] Inhelder, Bärbel. "Some Aspects of Piaget's Genetic Approach to Cognition." Monographs of the Society for Research in Child Development, 27(2):19–40; 1962 (Serial No. 83). Quoted from p. 25.

same world they are not likely to have identical impressions of the common environment because the unique patterns of environmental interaction provide each person with his own unique impressions of what reality is. It is for this very reason that language is important. Language serves to group people who have achieved agreement as to the meaning of specific concepts.[11]

The language one speaks is part of one's social inheritance and is not necessarily indicative of personality; however, the common meaning that is conveyed through language permits other individuals to grasp some of what one thinks and feels. As Miller[12] presented it:

> Whether we like it or not, our listeners type us—stereotype us—according to the impression they gain from our verbal habits. Every word we speak is a shibboleth.

In other words, what one says is assessed by others. However, the evaluation is of the individual who is speaking; the language is but the medium through which the evaluation is made.

Although the child's development is seen as a continuous process, Piaget suggests that the child passes through the following universal stages in a fixed sequence.

Sensorimotor Intelligence (birth to 1½ or 2 years)
Preconceptual Thought (1½ or 2 to 4 years)
Intuitive Thought (4 to 7 or 8 years)
Concrete Operations (7 or 8 to 11 or 12 years)
Formal Operations (11 or 12 to 15 or 16 years)

These developmental periods are fixed only in that the child cannot omit any of them, even though overlapping between periods readily occurs. Also, the age ranges that Piaget indicates are broad and are by no means intended to be specific; they are instead flexible, dependent upon the individual child and the quality of the personal experiences to which he can relate.

For Piaget, these developmental stages provide the key to understanding the thought processes of children. Unless a child has reached

[11] Carroll, op. cit. (n. 8), p. 32.
[12] Miller, George A. *Language and Communication.* New York: McGraw-Hill, 1963. P. 119.

a certain level of maturation, he cannot perform certain mental operations. Therefore, it is important to look carefully at each of these periods.

Sensorimotor Intelligence. During the period of sensorimotor intelligence, the child is egocentric in the sense that the world is considered an extension of the self. The objects in the infant's immediate environment become the center of his attention as he is gradually learning to coordinate and control his perceptual-motor mechanisms. As the child recognizes that certain aspects of his environment are constants, he acquires internalized representational responses to these constants. That is, he has a mental picture of those objects or persons that are consistently a part of his environment and of those responses which are regularly associated with these objects or persons. Although not physically present, one such constant may be sufficient to elicit a customary overt response from the child. For example, the baby may begin to suck while no nipple is present, the assumption being that a thought of the nipple brought about such a response. Eventually, the child is able to separate the constant from his personal self.

The earliest substantives of the child's language occur during the sensorimotor period; they express commands or the child's desires to satisfy himself. As time goes on, the child's social environment exerts more and more influence upon the development of his mind—affecting the child's objectivity, speech, and logical ideas throughout his development. However, it is following the sensorimotor period that verbal behavior becomes more important in the thought processes of the child.

Piaget and Inhelder[13] indicate that the difference between verbal behavior and sensorimotor intelligence lies in the fact that verbal patterns can simultaneously portray all the components of a construct whereas sensorimotor processes move slowly from one factor to the next. A sentence such as "They built the bridge over the river" can quickly symbolize the series of events—covering an expanse of time and space —that are inherent in the meaning of the verbalization. Sensorimotor behavior is bound by the immediate time and space. The child can only consider the ball lying on the floor—as it is seen at a specific moment. He does not think of the ball as rolling until he sees it rolling nor does he think of the ball as having rolled in the past.

[13] Piaget and Inhelder, op. cit. (n. 9), p. 86.

Preconceptual Thought. In the second period of development, which is labeled preconceptual thought, the child learns symbolisms and "preconcepts." It is during this period that children ask, "What's that?" and thus acquire a repertory of names for things. A name becomes a symbol for the thing named—a major step in the development of the child's language. However, the child has not yet learned to form the concept of class as an adult sees it. The child recognizes a distinguishing characteristic that permits him to set groups of objects, persons, or events apart from other groups, but he may fail to realize that the objects within the group are different. The name for new similar objects may always be the same, but the child does not yet realize that each object is a separate entity with specific characteristics that differentiate it from the rest of the group. For example, a child looking out the window does not know whether he sees a succession of unfamiliar men go by or whether the same man keeps reappearing. For the child, the distinction does not exist. The men are all "man" to him. Or perhaps the child sees a dog and is told that it is "doggie." All dogs that he sees he then calls "doggie." However, when he sees a cat, another furry, four-legged animal, the child is likely to call it "doggie" also. The child is reasoning transductively from the particular to the particular; that is, he is unable to differentiate characteristics of several specific objects belonging to one class. The objects are all the same to him. He overgeneralizes. The term *preconcept* is used to define these ideas that lie somewhere between the child's concept of an object and his concept of a class.

But what if a two-year-old cries for his "cup" when his mother offers him milk in a new cup? Certainly, in light of the above discussion, "cup" would refer to all cups. Right? No, not necessarily so. The child's cup was a constant of his environment. He came to learn that "cup" meant *his* cup as "Mother" did not refer to all women but to someone who belonged to him. This is a good example of what occurs during the sensorimotor stage when the child recognizes and attaches himself to certain constants in his environment. The preconcepts represent those ideas that are new to the child; they have not been constants in his earlier life. As the child's language develops, it mirrors his more complex conceptual structures, and, during the period of preconceptual thought, his language indicates his overgeneralization beyond his sensorimotor constants.

Intuitive Thought. During the third period of development, intuitive thought, the child's reasoning is still greatly determined by his perceptions. The magician's tricks are a reality to the four- or five-year-old. Although he may count out a number of beads and place them in a glass, when the beads are poured into a taller and narrower glass the child believes either that there are more beads in the second glass because the level is higher or that there are fewer beads because the glass is narrower. The logical thought processes of an adult are absent.

The child's perceptual mechanisms play a major role throughout the first three stages of his development. What he has been able to see, feel, and hear has provided a basis for what the child believes and the structure of his thoughts. But how does he perceive himself in relation to the world? During the sensorimotor period, the child was clearly egocentric. How much of his egocentrism did he lose as he identified objects that were not immediately a part of himself? Perhaps the answer can be found by taking a look at the language of the child in the stage of intuitive thought.

In his studies of the verbal behavior of children from four to seven, Piaget[14] distinguishes two functions of language, the social and the egocentric. Egocentric speech indicates that the child has no concern for the listener; the child does not bother to know to whom he is speaking or whether he is being listened to. Socialized speech indicates that the child wishes to communicate with his listener; the child addresses himself to the listener, considers the listener's point of view, and tries to influence the listener or actually exchange ideas with him.

Piaget further defines egocentric and socialized speech by subdividing each into several categories. Egocentric speech includes the categories of repetition (the child reproduces sounds and words solely for the pleasure of talking), monologue (the child directs his speech to himself as if thinking aloud), and collective monologue (another person is related to the thought but is expected neither to listen nor to understand). Socialized speech includes: adapted information (an actual exchange of thoughts between the child and others occurs); criticism (the child remarks about the behavior of others); commands, requests,

---

[14] Piaget, Jean. *The Language and Thought of the Child.* Cleveland: World Publishing Co., 1955. Pp. 25–68.

and threats (in each of these a definite interaction takes place between the child and another person); questions (the child expects an answer); answers (the child responds to questions and commands).

But what portion of a child's speech is egocentric and what portion socialized? Piaget[15] found that for a child of six and one-half, 44 to 47 percent of the speech was egocentric. He further concluded:

> . . . we believe that the age at which the child begins to communicate his thoughts (the age when egocentric language is 25%) is probably somewhere between 7 and 8.

However, other investigators[16] question the proportion of egocentric speech reported by Piaget and claim that there are studies that show it to be much less. Piaget[17] more recently commented that the amount of egocentrism a child reveals depends upon the specific situation. Nevertheless, he maintains that the child does not speak from the point of view of the listener but speaks for himself until he reaches the period of concrete operations.

Today it is generally accepted that a child's speech serves primarily a social role. The child may talk about himself and his ideas between 30 and 40 percent of the time, but this may only reflect the desire to communicate his thoughts to others—to measure the *goodness of fit* between his ideas and his language.

Concrete Operations. The child of seven or eight begins to enter the period of concrete operations. It is at this point that the child starts to use certain logical thought processes. He begins to classify, conceptually order things according to relationships, and perform number operations.

Classifying is a mental process equivalent to the motor act of placing similar objects together. For example, the child is able to identify

[15] Ibid., p. 68.

[16] Isaacs, Susan. *Intellectual Growth in Young Children.* New York: Schocken Books, 1966.

McCarthy, Dorothea. "The Language Development of the Preschool Child." *Institute for Child Welfare Monograph Series,* No. 4. Minneapolis: University of Minnesota Press, 1930.

Vygotsky, Lev S. *Thought and Language.* Cambridge, Mass.: The M.I.T. Press, 1962.

[17] Piaget and Inhelder, op. cit. (n. 9), pp. 121–122.

separate groups of brown squirrels and gray squirrels and still realize that both groups are a part of a larger group; all are squirrels. Another example of the child's classifying ability is his realization that roses, lilies, and daffodils are all flowers.

In ordering things according to their perceived interrelationships, the child is able to visualize series of things. For example, he is able to put pegs of varying sizes into their respective holes in a peg board without using trial and error methods. Or, without a pause, he can build a pyramid from blocks of varying sizes.

The child's number operations constitute a blending of classifying and ordering operations. For example, he can group or identify nine objects as well as tell the order in which the number nine is placed in a sequence of whole numbers. That is, from a set of twenty triangles the child can select nine, when asked. Then, when the triangles are placed in a line, he is able to tell which is first, second, third, etc., through ninth.

Formal Operations. An eleven- or twelve-year-old child enters the period of formal operations. This is the period during which abstract thought develops and he begins to use reasoning powers similar to those of an adult. The child learns to manipulate ideas mentally without the assistance of concrete representations of those ideas; he can now perform mental operations upon other mental operations.

It is during these last two periods suggested by Piaget that the child's language ability facilitates his thinking to a greater extent than ever before. The child has learned the basics of his language system and proceeds to enrich it in the service of thought. From this point on a strong relationship between the language an individual employs and his mode of reasoning is observed.

VYGOTSKY'S VERSION: DEVELOPMENT OF LANGUAGE AND OF CONCEPT

On the one hand, Piaget suggests that language is structured by the thought processes and serves to facilitate thinking as the child develops. On the other hand, Vygotsky assumes that it is the language that structures—both consciously and subconsciously—the thought processes. To Vygotsky, language is the tool that gives power to the mental processes.

Basically, Vygotsky[18] describes thought and language as "two inter-secting circles" that might be illustrated as follows.

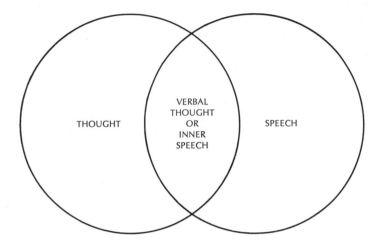

The intersection of thought and speech represents verbal thinking—the mental process involving logical and analytical thought. However, verbal thought is not possessed by the infant at birth but comes into existence as the child develops. Vygotsky proposes four stages of speech develop-ment[19] which help clarify our understanding of verbal thought.

Primitive Stage. The primitive or natural period is first. During this time thought and speech are completely independent of each other. A new-born infant would be at this stage of development—when thought is nonverbal and speech is nonintellectual.

Stage of Naïve Psychology. Second is the period of naïve psychology. The child becomes aware of his own body and his immediate environ-ment. In time, he takes the first step in exercising his practical intelli-gence when he begins to employ simple tools, such as a stick to pull something that is out of reach closer. At about the age of two, speech begins to serve the intellect as the child realizes that everything has a

[18] Vygotsky, op. cit. (n. 16), p. 47.
[19] Ibid., pp. 46–48.

name. Eventually the child starts to use correct grammatical forms even though he does not understand the logical thinking on which they are based. It is during this stage of speech development that the two developmental curves, one for thought and the other for speech, begin to unite.

Third Stage. In the third stage, which Vygotsky leaves untitled, the child begins to solve mental problems through the use of external processes, for example, counting on his fingers. Speech is egocentric, helping the child in his thinking: ". . . it serves mental orientation, conscious understanding."[20] However, Vygotsky differs greatly from Piaget as he suggests that egocentric speech develops along an upward rather than a downward curve, going though an evolution instead of an involution. Egocentric speech assists the child in the natural process of individualization, the pattern that each individual follows in his development. As the child moves from very socially-oriented thinking to the more individualized thought of the adult, egocentric speech becomes the speech for oneself, that is, inner speech or verbal thought.

Ingrowth Stage. Inner, soundless speech reaches full growth during the last period of speech development, the ingrowth stage. It is at this time that the child begins to use mental operations to solve problems, such as counting in his head. Logical thinking, the process of using "inherent relationships and inner signs,"[21] is now possible because the child can readily move back and forth between word and thought. In Vygotsky's[22] words: "Thought is not merely expressed in words; it comes into existence through them."

Because of his belief that language and thought are so closely related, it is important to understand Vygotsky's theory of concept development. The formation of concepts is initiated in earliest childhood but it is only at puberty that a child develops true concepts. Of course, he may understand a problem posed by an adult and determine ways of solving it, but this is possible only because the child employs the same means of understanding and communicating as an adult, namely language. How-

[20] Ibid., p. 133.
[21] Ibid., p. 47.
[22] Ibid., p. 125.

ever, the thinking activities of an adult vary considerably from those of a child because, while the adult's concepts are highly structured and thus permit intricate thought processes, the child uses only functional equivalents of concepts. That is to say, the child's "concepts" are very simple, based on the concrete or what he sees, feels, and hears, whereas an adult's concepts involve abstract thinking. To better understand Vygotsky's theory, let's look at the three stages of concept formation that he proposes.[23]

Phase One. The first step a young child takes toward concept development occurs when he creates unorganized groupings of inherently unrelated things, such as referring to all his toys as "ball" because ball was the first name learned to identify a plaything. This phase Vygotsky calls the period of unorganized congeries and it is roughly equivalent to Piaget's period of preconceptual thought. The child's immediate perceptions guide his thoughts about his world and himself.

Phase Two. The second phase on the road to concept development is thinking in complexes. Generally speaking, this phase corresponds to Piaget's periods of intuitive thought and concrete operations, although complexes in the earliest stages are comparable to Piaget's preconcepts. A complex consists of those things that a child mentally groups together because of the concrete—not abstract—relationships between objects as well as his subjective perceptions of them. For example, while an adult's concepts of higher mathematics—such as algebra—involve abstract thought, the child's complexes of mathematics involve those generalizations—such as geometric shapes or number—that are learned through concrete experiences by most elementary school children. However, it is important to note that Vygotsky[24] feels that "the lines along which a complex develops are predetermined by the meaning a given word already has in the language of adults." The child learns his complexes in terms of the speech of his socio-cultural group. For example, a child will say an object is "round" because that is the term the adults in his community have given to spherical, circular objects. Had the adults used a different label, such as *gub*, the child would use that label and say, "A ball is *gub*," rather than, "A ball is round." Thus,

[23] Ibid., pp. 59–81.
[24] Ibid., p. 67.

the child is able to communicate with the adult world even though his thought processes may differ from those of an adult.

Phase Three. Finally, the child reaches the point where he is able to synthesize as well as analyze on the abstract level. He has reached the third phase, the one in which true concepts are formed. This final phase would be comparable to Piaget's period of formal operations.

The fact that the adolescent and the adult may at times find it difficult to express a concept verbally does not necessarily mean that language has not aided in the formation of that concept. Vygotsky[25] points out that concept development is not always a deliberate, conscious process. Frequently an individual will subconsciously use concepts to analyze reality before analyzing the concepts themselves. Concepts of actuality formed without conscious effort are known as spontaneous concepts.

Other concepts, which Vygotsky calls scientific concepts, begin with a verbal meaning and are consciously formed, usually through instruction—although formal teaching, as in a classroom, need not take place. Such concepts provide the framework for the upward growth of spontaneous concepts which may eventually come into conscious and intentional use. Generally, once this has occurred, concepts are easily expressed verbally. For example, a child living in the United States learns to operate on the decimal system. Such learning is not consciously intentional but is, rather, obtained from interaction with the community and would be considered a spontaneous concept. Later, as he learns the broader concept of numerical systems and can deliberately use any system, such as base five or base four, the child would be using a scientific concept.[26]

However, scientific concepts may also grow down through the spontaneous concepts to function at an automatic, subconscious level. An example of the way in which spontaneous and scientific concepts move in reverse directions and often intersect may be illustrated in someone who is taking a course to learn a foreign language. Fluent, spontaneous speech in the new language is contingent upon conscious learning of vocabulary and grammatical forms pertinent to the language, whereas fluency in one's native language develops long before the conscious comprehension of syntax.

[25] Ibid., pp. 84–110.
[26] Ibid., p. 115.

Vygotsky assumes that concept development may be both conscious and subconscious. One's speech plays an important role in both, providing the structure along which development occurs.

WHAT OTHER RELEVANT RESEARCH TELLS US

The work of Vygotsky and Piaget provides some orientation to the problem of determining the relationship between thought and language. Although they differ as to which one—language or thought—exerts the greater influence, both Piaget and Vygotsky indicate that a strong relationship does exist between thought and language and that the child's speech may reflect his thoughts about the world and himself.

Others have also attempted to clarify the relationship between language and thought. Studies have indicated that a similarity exists between verbal learning and the logical form of concepts. The labels that one learns to attach to objects, persons, places, actions, and even feelings tend to be grouped in a hierarchical form in the individual's mind. The framework of these verbal groups is generally similar to the structure of the concepts formed by them.[27] For example, a child's "animal" embodies not only the entire verbal group that he has learned to call "animal" but also the logical organization of the concept which follows this verbal chain; that is, animal may define the subcategories dog, cat, monkey, etc., each of which has various other subcategories, and so on down the line.

Lantz (as cited by Brown[28]) indicates the importance of language to new learning, suggesting that an individual's ability to use language to code the objects of his environment corresponds to his ability to mentally store the referents. In other words, being able to encode into the language of one's socio-cultural group appears to be useful for information storage and retrieval.

However, the form that this memory speech takes may vary considerably from speech used to communicate with others. As Vygotsky[29]

---

[27] Underwood, Benton J. "Some Relationships Between Concept Learning and Verbal Learning." *Analysis of Concept Learning,* eds. Herbert J. Klausmeier and Chester W. Harris. New York: Academic Press, 1966. Pp. 51–63.

Staats, Arthur W., and Staats, Carolyn K. *Complex Human Behavior.* New York: Holt, Rinehart and Winston, 1963.

[28] Brown, op. cit. (n. 8), pp. 332–337.

[29] Vygotsky, op. cit. (n. 16), pp. 138–142.

points out, the speech used for oneself can be more abbreviated than the speech for others. A student's lecture notes often correspond in structure to inner speech and, therefore, are likely to be clear to him but totally incomprehensible to another who was not in attendance at the lecture. Inner speech carries with it an assessment of the situation and a projection of personal information into the thought. At times when the thoughts of communicating individuals coincide, external speech may indicate structures similar to those of inner speech—as when an individual gives abbreviated directions to a close friend knowing that they both have common knowledge of specific landmarks.

But what of those individuals who, for some reason, have been isolated from society and therefore prevented from learning language? Or what of those who were born deaf or mute? Are the thought processes of these people able to function without language? Several accounts available indicate that thinking can proceed without language.[30] At an early age the deaf and the mute learn by using the nonverbal systems of the intellectual structure. Later, with training, they may read and write; the deaf can also learn to speak. Clearly, the human capacity to think does not rely solely on the language-acquisition device of the intellect. An individual deprived of an environment in which to learn language certainly is not prevented from thinking; thought is possible without language.

Language, however, is one important means of communicating thoughts to others. The fact that human intellectual capacity and achievement is most often measured by verbal instruments reflects the importance of the language-thought relationship in typical people. Also, the role language plays in understanding human problems and behavior is well recognized by psychologists and psychiatrists today, a large portion of current knowledge stemming from the work of Korzybski, particularly his *Science and Sanity*.[31]

Studies of self concept frequently use verbal measures such as those

---

[30] Furth, Hans G. *Thinking Without Language*. New York: The Free Press, 1966.
  Itard, Jean-Marc-Gaspard. *The Wild Boy of Aveyron*. New York: Appleton-Century-Crofts, 1962.
  Brown, op. cit. (n. 8), p. 249.
  Chomsky, Noam. *Aspects of the Theory of Syntax*. Cambridge, Mass.: The M.I.T. Press, 1965. P. 56.
[31] Korzybski, Alfred. *Science and Sanity: An Introduction to Non-Aristotelian Systems and General Semantics*. Lancaster, Pa.: Science Press, 1941.

outlined in the work of Sears and Sherman.[32] Here language is used to analyze self concept. Also, Axline[33] gives some indication of how one's self concept may affect oral speech. She suggests that an individual's own personal world of meaning not only determines the kind of language he uses but also may determine the quantity of language used.

LISTEN AND READ, TEACHER

"Hear the children in the playground?" "Did you hear what Johnny said?" "Can you hear Mary tell her story?" All of these questions ask about hearing, the ability to perceive noise. Hearing becomes meaningful only when it involves listening, the ability to perceive what someone is saying. The latter ability is one that permits an individual to "tune in" others. "Tuning in" is what opens the door to understanding children and how they feel about themselves.

"See what terrible writing Billy has." "Look at Sue's written report." "See the children's letters." Seeing and looking at written words, like hearing noise, becomes meaningful only when it involves reading, the ability to comprehend what someone has written. Reading is another means of "tuning in" and finding out about a child's self concept.

Children are not always obvious in letting adults know about themselves and what they think. For this reason, it is important to listen attentively to what they say and read carefully what they write. By bits and pieces, over time, the child's natural speech and freely written language will provide the window to his mind, revealing his thoughts about himself and his world.

Being aware of the language development theories of people like Piaget and Vygotsky helps us understand what a child is communicating to us as well as helps us communicate with him. For example, knowing that a young child's speech is often directed to himself in what Piaget and Vygotsky call egocentric speech, we might observe young Jerry at play alone and frequently hear him say "Can't do that." Then, stop and think if he might have been consistently told that he can't do anything well because he is too young. Think of what his self concept might be! Later, as Jerry grows older and is asked by others to do things or

[32] Sears, Pauline S., and Sherman, Vivian S. *In Pursuit of Self-Esteem*. Belmont, Calif.: Wadsworth Publishing Co., 1965. Pp. 36–96.
[33] Axline, Virginia M. *Dibs: In Search of Self*. Boston: Houghton Mifflin, 1964.

respond to questions, does he usually say "It probably won't do . . ." or "I'm probably wrong . . ." even before attempting to respond to the request? Evidently, the "can't do it" has been reinforced in so many of his experiences that he believes himself incapable and, in order to protect himself from deeper humiliation, he makes it known to all within hearing that he doesn't have much faith in himself. Jerry is communicating. Is anyone listening?

What of Grace whose reading tests indicate that she is an above average reader for her grade level, but who always reads in low, almost inaudible tones and halting voice when called upon to read aloud in class? Also, in class discussions Grace usually sits quiet and passive or when she does offer her comments it is generally in a low, hesitant voice. Grace is most likely indicating that she has little confidence in herself. She's communicating. Who's listening?

Both Jerry and Grace need encouragement. Words of recognition that show they are valued as individuals and words of praise for what they do well can help both of these children develop healthy self concepts.

Careful reading of what children write in their essays can also tell a lot about how they feel about themselves and others. Do they write about the "I" in glowing, heroic terms? It could be that they think very highly of themselves, or it may also mean that they need to bolster themselves up because they feel that others lack confidence in them. Remember, more than just the verbal output or the correctness of expression needs to be evaluated in understanding children.[34] The context in which the words are placed as well as the children's actions give meaning to what is being communicated.

By listening to the children's comments and conversations or reading what they write, a perceptive teacher who is familiar with theories of language development can understand what the children say, can understand that their world of meaning may not be the same as his, and can work to give greater meaning to the children's lives.

Words in and of themselves have no meaning. The meaning lies within the people that use the words. The words an individual chooses and the way in which the words are used communicate the meaning. To learn what children mean when they communicate, we must "tune in" by being open, ready receivers of their words and actions.

[34] Mearns, Hughes. *Creative Power.* Rev. ed. New York: Dover Publications, 1958. Pp. 217–228.

EDUCATIONAL IMPORTANCE OF COMMUNICATION

The importance of communication has been recognized on the school scene. In a publication of the Association for Supervision and Curriculum Development, Ammons[35] proposes communication as a curriculum focus so that "areas of study may contribute to the child's ability to cope with his world in his own terms." The primary objective of the curriculum should be to help the child understand himself and his behavior in a social context and learn to make wise choices with which he can live. Traditional elements of the curriculum—such as reading, language arts, mathematics, social studies, science, art, and music—should be the means rather than the ends of the instructional program. Further, Ammons proposes that the curriculum be organized around types of behavioral objectives—cognitive, affective, and psychomotor—that would be realized through verbal and nonverbal activities. With such a program, the classroom would buzz from the children's involvement in such things as discussion groups, painting groups, drama groups, and listening groups.

Taking a close look at the communication system within the classroom, Gantt[36] suggests a way to classify pupil statements, thus providing the teacher with some cues about the pupil's developmental stage of thinking so that further instruction may guide the pupil to the next higher level of thinking. Questioning appears to be an important technique the teacher can use to guide the pupils' thinking. For example, if a pupil gives a "book definition" the teacher might ask, "Can you give me an example and tell me what that means to you?" or should a pupil make a confused statement the teacher might follow with, "Are you saying that . . .?"

Some schools, such as the one described by Strauss and Dufour,[37] have courses that focus on the development of a wholesome self concept through role-playing. Stress is placed on developing the ability to use language and actions for the express purpose of communicating thought

[35] Ammons, Margaret. "Communication: A Curriculum Focus." *A Curriculum for Children,* ed. Alexander Frazier. Washington, D. C.: National Education Association, Association for Supervision and Curriculum Development, 1969. P. 113.

[36] Gantt, Walter N. "Teacher Diagnosis of Pupil Verbal Cues to Thinking." *Educational Leadership,* 26:684–687; April 1969.

[37] Strauss, Jack, and Dufour, Richard. "Discovering Who I am: A Humanities Course for Sixth Grade Students." *Elementary English,* 47:85–120; January 1970.

and feeling because it is believed that the role one learns to play in relation to the social world not only determines his evaluation of and behavior toward others but also patterns the way in which he evaluates and behaves toward himself.

Educators have generally recognized that a pupil's level of achievement has a profound effect on his self concept and his subsequent attitude toward learning. In relation to the area of reading, it has long been recognized that failure prevents the child from satisfying his need for self-esteem because our culture emphasizes the importance of the skill.[38] Success in reading forms the foundation for achievement in many other areas of the curriculum which, in turn, promotes the development of a healthy self concept. For this reason, a great deal of time and effort has been devoted to developing effective reading programs so that all children may learn to read.[39]

Based on the belief that a child's creative expression not only permits others to appreciate him but also provides him with the means of raising his level of self-esteem, various language arts programs have been designed to help pupils learn to express their own ideas and feelings. Langdon[40] describes one such program in intensive writing. Encouraging children to recall an emotional experience and to write about it in a brief, simple, and honest way appears to be the key to a successful

[38] D'Evelyn, op. cit. (n. 5), pp. 17–18.

Smith, Henry P., and Dechant, Emerald. *Psychology in Teaching Reading.* Englewood Cliffs, N. J.: Prentice-Hall, 1961. Pp. 297–304.

Strickland, Ruth G. "Creating a Challenging Classroom Environment." *Reading Teacher,* 10:72–81; December 1956.

[39] Chall, Jeanne. *Learning to Read: The Great Debate.* New York: McGraw-Hill, 1967.

Gates, Arthur I. "The Tides of Time." *Reading and Realism,* ed. J. Allen Figurel. Newark, Del.: International Reading Association, 1969. Pp. 12–20; and "What We Know and Can Do About the Poor Reader." *Education,* 77:528–533; May 1957.

Grissom, Loren. "Characteristics of Successful Reading Improvement Programs." *English Journal,* 50: 461–464, 474; October 1961.

Moore, Robert H., and Carlton, Lessie. *Reading, Self-Directive Dramatization and Self-Concept.* Columbus, Ohio: Charles E. Merrill, 1968.

Strickland, Ruth G. "Building on What We Know." *Reading and Realism,* ed. J. Allen Figurel. Newark, Del.: International Reading Association, 1969. Pp. 55–62.

[40] Langdon, Margaret. *Let the Children Write.* London: Longmans, Green and Co., 1966.

intensive writing program. Langdon initiated the program by taking advantage of an unexpected visitor to her classroom, a large spider. She first asked the children to write a brief statement of how they felt about the spider; then a brief description was requested while she guided them with questions about how the legs looked and how the spider's appearance contrasted with the appearance of the web it had made. By the end of the school year the pupils' compositions reflected the enthusiasm they normally displayed when orally telling about one of their experiences.

Mearns[41] points out that every child has a gift and should be encouraged to use and develop his gift. He tells of a boy who was quiet and retiring in class but very able in bringing his baseball team to victory by means of his own colorful and abundant but nonstandard verbal expression. Encouraging him to write about baseball games, using his own language, opened the door for his progress in classroom communication.[42] Observing children at times when they are off guard—at recess or lunch, on school trips, at parties—generally provides the leads for discovering each child's special gift that can be used as a focal point to encourage him and guide his classroom efforts. Everyone has something to offer and be proud of.

A current trend in the schools appears to be that of encouraging the development of a healthy self concept in children through the various language arts. Projects in creative writing as well as presentations of sketches, plays, and debates are aimed not only at helping children learn language as such but also at developing all channels of communication in them. Having realized the importance of "tuning in" the pupils in order to plan appropriate instructional procedures, the schools are emphasizing the teaching of communication skills, the use of which also provides an individual with the means by which his self concept may become apparent to himself as well as to those with whom he interacts.

Both verbal and nonverbal systems of communication play a part in a child's development of the self concept. Also, both systems can help an interested individual discover a child's self concept. To understand children and help them along the difficult path to adulthood necessarily

[41] Mearns, op. cit. (n. 34).
[42] Ibid., pp. 268–269.

involves constant learning from them regarding how they perceive their world and themselves.

SUMMARY

As Smith[43] very interestingly portrays it, everyone goes through the lifelong process of accumulating his own particular information—concepts and self concept—that affects his thinking and behavior. Because the development of language and the development of concepts are generally believed to be related processes, an understanding of a child's self concept may be provided by studying his world of language. The way in which a child learns and uses his language tells a perceptive adult a great deal about him.

But language is not the total picture. Nonverbal communication is important also. Actions, concepts of time and space, laughter, and tears are some other keys to understanding children.

Reality as it exists in the mind of an individual is frequently symbolized in his speech and actions. Human communication generally reflects the conscious effort toward understanding among individuals. However, the fact that a communication system, once learned, most frequently operates at an automatic, spontaneous level permits an individual to release information that may be at a subconscious level also. It is in this manner that both the conscious self concept and the subconscious self of an individual may become apparent.

To promote the development of a healthy self concept in a child, adults first need to understand how the child feels about himself and his world; then, they need to communicate their support of and interest in him. Let him know that he is wanted and respected. A nod of approval, a smile, or an arm around the shoulder, a simple "Good work" or "Job well done" communicate a great deal.

SUGGESTED READINGS

Birdwhistell, Ray L. *Kinesics and Context*. Philadelphia: University of Pennsylvania, 1970. This study indicates how much a child must learn

[43] Smith, Robert P. *Got to Stop Draggin' That Little Red Wagon Around*. New York: Harper and Row, 1969.

in order to express himself and communicate within his culture, human body motion being as much a part of the communication process as is verbal language. Here, also, is a detailed presentation of how human gestures and motions can be identified, coded, and interpreted.

Chase, Stuart. *The Tyranny of Words.* New York: Harcourt, Brace and World, 1938. What is meant by "meaning" is interestingly analyzed. The language one uses reflects a personal bias as well as cultural bias. Stressed is the importance of *good* language to improve communication among people.

Johnson, Wendell. *People in Quandaries.* New York: Harper and Row, 1946. The focus of this book is upon personal and interpersonal problems and how these problems can be understood and dealt with through the employment of general semantics. In a most practical vein, an interesting set of semantic exercises is found at the end of the text.

Pei, Mario. *The Story of Language.* New York: The New American Library, 1965. This is an entertaining study of language, its history, social function, and elements. It is also a study of man since language has served to facilitate and record his social development throughout the centuries.

Phillips, John L. *The Origins of Intellect: Piaget's Theory.* San Francisco: W. H. Freeman and Co., 1969. Presented is a general summary of Piaget's theory, written at a relatively nontechnical level. The author employs a number of pedagogical devices to explain the complexities of the theory as well as discusses the educational implications of Piaget's work.

Postman, Neil, and Weingartner, Charles. *Teaching as a Subversive Activity.* New York: Delacorte Press, 1969. Bringing meaning into the classroom and helping students learn how to learn is what the authors propose, suggesting the "inquiry method" as the alternative to less vital educational methods. The processing of knowledge through the conscious use of language is stressed since language is one determinant of how one perceives reality.

Smith, Robert P. *Got to Stop Draggin' That Little Red Wagon Around.* New York: Harper and Row, 1969. The priceless knowledge obtained, as well as the attitudes formed, in childhood go into the "little red wagons" that people drag around all their lives, influencing their actions. The story of one boy's childhood and how he loaded his "wagon" suggests the need for people to examine their own experiential backgrounds in order to get rid of impediments to desired behavior.

THREE · THE DEVELOPING SELF:

NURTURANCE IN SCHOOL

Marjorie S. Snyder

A teacher can never truly teach unless he is still learning himself. A lamp can never light another lamp unless it continues to burn its own flame. The teacher who has come to the end of his subject, who has no living traffic with his students can only lead their minds, he cannot quicken them. Truth not only must inform, it must inspire; if the inspiration dies out and the information only accumulates, then truth loses its infinity. The greater part of our learning in the schools has been wasted because for most of our teachers their subjects are like dead specimens of once living things with which they have learned acquaintance but no communication of life and love.[1]

SIR RABINDRANATH TAGORE

The social and scientific changes of the last two decades have been so rapid and pervasive that their full impact upon schools is difficult to appreciate. Most of us would welcome an opportunity to declare a moratorium on all on-going activities for a few years in order to evaluate and assimilate what is really of value in our work with children. Since this is patently impossible, we are perennially forced to live and work simultaneously in the past, present, and future. Such, in a sense, is the life of a teacher.

[1] From an inscription on the administration building at Santiniketan, a famous school established by Tagore at Bolpur, India.

CULTURAL/ENVIRONMENTAL DIFFERENCES AND LEARNING ABILITY

Research in psychiatry and psychology would seem to indicate that much of the learner's ability to use his power to learn is determined by his concept of self, his perception of the way others view him and his perception of the world and of his own goals, purposes, and values.[2] In other words, the learner's awareness, what he thinks and feels, is what primarily guides, controls, and regulates his performance. There is substantial evidence that the child reared in a climate of affection and understanding will have the freedom to grow and experiment without the fear of failure and rejection. The child with his security needs accommodated learns to accept himself and considers failing a task a learning experience. Conversely, the child reared in a climate of rejection is constantly forced to mobilize his defense mechanisms. It is not easy for the rejected child to value himself and develop confidence in his own worth, and this makes the task of the teacher more difficult.

Unfortunately, parental rejection is not the only reason for unflattering self concepts and depressed performance in children. The simple fact of cultural differences may be sufficient to send a child to school ill-equipped and already defeated.[3] For example, a recent study of mother-child communication systems sharply brings out some of the differences between middle-class and lower-class homes.[4] In contrast to the socio-economically handicapped mothers of the lower class, middle-class mothers elaborate more on what they say, use more complex and explanatory sentences, and give their child more information. They use language to encourage their child to reflect, to anticipate conse-

[2] Arieti, Silvano (ed.). *The World Biennial of Psychiatry and Psychotherapy,* I. New York: Basic Books, 1970.

LaBenne, Wallace D., and Greene, Bert I. *Educational Implications of Self-Concept Theory.* Pacific Palisades, Calif.: Goodyear Publishing Co., 1969.

Wepman, Joseph M., and Heine, Ralph W. (eds.). *Concepts of Personality.* Chicago: Aldine Publishing Co., 1963.

[3] Hess, Robert D. "Social Class and Ethnic Influences upon Socialization." *Carmichael's Manual of Child Psychology,* II, ed. Paul H. Mussen. 3d ed. New York: John Wiley and Sons, 1970. Pp. 457–557 (Chap. 24).

[4] Hess, Robert D., and Shipman, Virginia C. "Early Experience and the Socialization of Cognitive Modes in Children." *Child Development,* 36:869–886; December 1965.

quences of his actions, to avoid error, to weigh decisions, and to choose among alternatives. Regardless of the race of the culturally different child, his environmental relationships tend to leave him with a negative self concept. This, coupled with a mother-child communication system lacking in range or alternatives of thought, action, and cognitive meaning, cripples the child's ability to function in school. The culturally different child seems to enter school with a rather restricted language background characterized by a limited vocabulary, stereotyped expressions, short sentences, simple grammatical structure, lack of linguistic precision, substitutions of gestures for words, and with negative expectations for school experiences.

Family relationship structures as well as broader communication structures shape the individual's language and cognitive styles of problem solving. The lower-class mother tends to encourage compliance, passivity, and dependence upon authority, while the middle-class mother is inclined to anticipate an altogether different role for her child as a participating, active person with problem-solving abilities. These contrasting expectations are reflected in the children's behavioral repertoires in school.

It is axiomatic that we understand that needs are not the same for all people and the degree to which any needs are felt and met is dependent upon the individual. According to Maslow, we can think of two types of needs, namely, the D-needs (Deficiency or Basic), which are intrinsic and governed by a person's inner nature, and the B-needs (Being or Becoming), which determine what a person can be because they are extrinsic and governed by the environment. The Deficiency needs include (1) physiological needs, (2) safety and security, (3) love and belonging—being accepted and accepting others, and (4) esteem—respect for self and others. A person builds his fundamental sense of security and worthiness through the D-needs.[5] These low order needs must be met before the high order, B-needs can be fulfilled.

The B-needs are (1) information—a reaction to one's environment,

[5] Maslow, Abraham H. "Some Basic Propositions of a Growth and Self-Actualization Psychology." *Perceiving, Behaving, Becoming*, ed., Arthur W. Combs. Washington: Association for Supervision and Curriculum Development, 1962. Pp. 34–39; and *Toward a Psychology of Being*. 2d ed. Princeton, N. J.: D. Van Nostrand, 1968.

curiosity, and spontaneity, (2) understanding—discovery, a religious system and a faith, (3) beauty—esthetic appreciation and the development of one's innate talent, and (4) self-actualization—creativity, the ability to handle problems (i.e., conflict, anxiety, frustration, sadness, hurt, and guilt), and a conscience (the person wants and enjoys what is good for him). Transcendence of self is possible through self-actualization, and a fully-functioning person results, characterized by autonomy, openness, sensitivity, and integrity.

Getting back to the classroom, academic subjects, particularly reading, can help fulfill high order needs (information, understanding, beauty, and perhaps even self-actualization) but not the low order needs. Familial and environmental conditions must be ameliorated first so that the low order needs of disadvantaged learners will be met. If the low order or deficiency needs are not met, an individual will probably be unprepared to read and cannot benefit from instruction. Premature efforts at teaching are largely wasted. A teachable moment may come but the task cannot be accomplished, and this failure affects future achievement. The learner's response to the results of the learning experience determines whether the new behavior will be used or avoided, depending upon the satisfaction or the frustration of the experience.

THE SCHOOL AND THE INDIVIDUAL

The school as a social institution expresses and attempts to enforce prevalent social norms which represent society's idealized concept of its past, present, and future, although since American society is pluralistic with some common but many conflicting values, these social ideals are difficult to delineate. Less stable homes, more working mothers, and greater population mobility have made it necessary for social agencies, particularly the school, to assume a larger share of responsibility for the development of the young. One thing seems clear: the child for whom the school does not serve as a means of effective induction will find it difficult to become an accepted member of the larger society.[6]

Induction into the complex societal life is initiated by the child's

[6] Kimball, Solon T., and McClellan, James E., Jr. *Education and the New America.* New York: Random House, 1962.

assignment to school groups.[7] While efficient utilization of staff, materials, and facilities may be presented as an overriding basis for grouping for instruction, the real educational goal should be the most effective orchestration of the diversity in an individual classroom in order to provide meaningful learning for all. Groupings often give rise to labels which affect the behavior of both students and teachers. Labels may enhance learning or retard it, and the problem is to maintain the positive effects and to eliminate as many of the negative ones as possible. Any grouping should be provisional in nature and exist merely so long as it serves the needs of the pupils. Groupings should be flexible, and teachers and pupils should be free to move as their growth indicates.[8]

> What, then does grouping for teachability involve? First, the local school must decide the most effective criteria for grouping its students with the understanding that these are only starting points. Second, the individual progress of the students must be evaluated continuously, and wherever changes in pupil assignments are indicated, they should be made within the imaginative limits of the school. Third, flexible change based on realistic assessments of student needs and student growth should be characteristic of the entire school. Fourth, the professional staff should be in the process of growing personally and professionally.[9]

The two most influential rewards of learning seem to be the learner's satisfaction in his product and the group's approval. Unfortunately, most of the investigations of group interaction and influences have been conducted with adults. Recent research indicates that a child's classmates have far greater consequences for the child's intellectual, emotional, and social development than heretofore recognized.[10] The Coleman Report

[7] Dreeben, Robert. On What Is Learned in School. Reading, Mass.: Addison-Wesley Publishing Co., 1968.

[8] Goodlad, John I., and Anderson, Robert H. The Nongraded School. Rev. ed. New York: Harcourt, Brace and World, 1963.

Goldberg, Miriam L.; Passow, A. Harry; and Justman, Joseph. The Effects of Ability Grouping. New York: Teachers College Press, 1966.

Stoddard, George D. The Dual Progress Plan. New York: Harper and Row, 1961.

[9] Aspy, David N. "Groping or Grouping for Teachability." Contemporary Education, 41:306–310; May 1970. Quoted from p. 310.

[10] Butler, Annie L. Current Research in Early Childhood Education: A Compila-

showed that school performance depended less on facilities and teacher qualifications than on the characteristics of the child's schoolmates. Disadvantaged children who attended school with middle-class children tended to acquire the characteristics of the children in the class. Conversely, children from middle-class backgrounds who attended school with the majority of the class disadvantaged tended to acquire the speech patterns and lackadaisical attitudes toward school that the lower-class children display.[11] Other studies have shown that nonadaptive or antisocial behavior is as readily communicated as competence or constructive action. The influence of peer interaction on school achievement increases with age.[12]

THE TEACHER'S ROLE

Education as a profession has heretofore had its critics, but never has criticism been so prevalent. The daily paper reports the failure of the schools to teach the basic subjects because the teachers do not know them; professional journals question the utilization of research funds for more educational projects; television programs lament what children encounter in school; scholarly books document some glaring inequities and inadequacies in teacher education;[13] and some critics even suggest that colleges of education be abolished.[14] It is no wonder that teachers

---

tion and Analysis for Program Planners. Washington, D. C.: American Association of Elementary-Kindergarten-Nursery Educators, 1970.

[11] Coleman, James S., and others. Equality of Educational Opportunity. Washington, D. C.: U. S. Department of Health, Education and Welfare, Office of Education, 1966.

[12] Hartup, Willard W. "Peer Interaction and Social Organization." Carmichael's Manual of Child Psychology, II, ed. Paul H. Mussen. 3d ed. New York: John Wiley and Sons, 1970. Pp. 361–456.

[13] Boffey, Phillip M. "R & D Finding: Top Treasury Aide Decries Blind Faith Approach." Science, 170:512–516; October 30, 1970.

Jones, Richard M. Fantasy and Feeling in Education. New York: New York University Press, 1968.

Silberman, Charles E. Crisis in the Classroom: The Remaking of American Education. New York: Random House, 1970.

[14] Hall, Elizabeth. "Bad Education—A Conversation with Jerome Bruner and Elizabeth Hall." Psychology Today, 4:50–57; December 1970.

in general and professors of education in particular suffer somewhat paranoid feelings. But has anyone countered the foregoing criticisms with data that prove schools throughout the United States to be better than they have ever been? Alas, it is impossible to counteract the barrage, because no such evidence exists.

Since the 1930s, a goodly proportion of the efforts of educational researchers has been devoted to trying to identify the crucial factors in the classroom teaching-learning situation so that those factors may be more precisely controlled. At first, effort was directed to what a teacher *did*, and numerous comparative studies of teaching methods, curriculum content, and organizational practices were conducted. These studies allegedly yielded lists of effective and ineffective teaching methods, but by 1960 the conclusion was reached generally that more than half a century of research had not yielded meaningful, measurable criteria against which the majority of the nation's educators could evaluate themselves.[15]

During the 1960s, as a result of the growing national concern with mental health problems, investigations were made of the teacher's personality in terms of its contribution to teaching effectiveness. Undoubtedly, the personality of a teacher and his attitude toward and understanding of children are of paramount importance for the total social and emotional growth and adjustment of his pupils. A teacher's success in working with children depends to a great extent on his ability to gain insight into and to accept his own emotions and behavior.[16] For instance, in a longitudinal study involving female subjects, Lucio and his associates investigated the relationships of their emotional stability, general health, and classroom behaviors during student teaching with the first-, sixth-, and seventh-year in-service performance.[17] The less successful teachers were found to be less emotionally stable, more introverted, and more tense.

[15] Turner, Robert L., and Fattu, Nicholas A. *Skills in Teaching: A Reappraisal of the Concepts and Strategies in Teaching Effectiveness Research.* Bulletin No. 36. Bloomington, Ind.: Indiana University School of Education, 1960.

[16] Del Popolo, Joseph A. "Teacher Personality: A Concern of Teacher Education." *Peabody Journal of Education,* 43:50–55; July 1965.

[17] Lucio, William H.; Wenger, Marion A.; and Cullen, Thomas D. *Psychophysiological Correlates of Female Teacher Behavior and Emotional Stability: A Seven Year Longitudinal Investigation.* Washington, D.C.: U. S. Office of Education, 1967. (ERIC Microfiche No. ED-021-786, November 1967.)

STRESS AND TEACHING

Teaching tends to produce high-anxiety emotional states for various reasons. The number and variety of people to whom a teacher is accountable constantly expose him to conflicting and divergent expectations. The students, principal, supervisors, consultants, superintendent, parents, and the teacher himself all have thoughts and feelings about what kind of person he should be. His authority and responsibility are seldom clearly defined, and his daily interpersonal contacts often result in psychological and physical fatigue. Moreover, the demands of the job are very likely to be carried over into his personal life, and heavy pressure is placed on him for consistent behavior in and out of school.[18]

Anxiety is induced by the increasing number of children with little motivation to learn and with behavior problems; the need to counsel with troubled parents whose hopeless and helpless feelings are often manifested in hostile, defiant, indifferent, or demanding attitudes; and the fish-bowl exposure of teaching activities. Stresses which interfere with teacher competence arise frequently from the organizational climate in colleges of education and in the school systems, which make the teacher feel he risks being labeled a poor teacher if he expresses emotion; from the necessity of working with groups rather than with individuals as is the case in most of the other helping professions; from the teacher's role "in loco parentis" ("in the place of a parent"); from the conflicts between democratic ideals and training for skills in autocratic methods; and from the desire to keep discipline but also to be liked by the pupils.[19] These sources of stress which are more or less endemic to the school situation are augmented by the externally generated pressures of rapid changes taking place under the impetus of federal funding, legislation for ethnic integration, and demands for help for the culturally disadvantaged child. Many changes are demanded and instituted without adequate teacher participation in decision-making and planning or without careful teacher preparation. A good example is school desegregation. Legislation does not, in itself, circumvent human emotions or human ignorance.

[18] Waller, Willard. *The Sociology of Teaching.* New York: John Wiley and Sons, 1965.
[19] Solomon, James C. (ed.). "Neuroses of School Teachers: A Colloquy." *Mental Hygiene,* 44:79–90; January 1960.

One of the most important causes of anxiety for teachers is the ambiguity inherent in much of what he tries to accomplish. Even after the teacher has decided on goals for his work with students, he is plagued by lack of knowledge about specific actions to take to reach his goals and about the consequences of the actions when taken. Should he use discovery techniques, individualized instruction, ability grouping, audio-visual aids, programmed instruction, language experience curriculum, social activities, or the lecture? Should he use laissez-faire, democratic, permissive, or autocratic methods of control? Should he deal with feelings, facts, concepts, or the structure of knowledge? Nowhere in professional literature can he find a consensus on any one of these considerations. For that matter, he will find little consistent help in putting into operation the methods he finally chooses. Hence, ambiguity is implicit in almost every aspect of the teacher's professional life, and anyone who aspires to be a teacher must learn to tolerate it. He should, in fact, learn to take advantage of it to bring about constructive changes in himself and in his charges. "A lamp can never light another lamp unless it continues to burn its own flame" (Tagore); a teacher can never touch another mind unless he continues to grow himself.[20]

Both the individual and the institution which trains him should prepare him for some of the unavoidable stresses and strains of teaching. Vicarious experiences can be had through reading,[21] and practice teaching ought to provide a good specimen of the pressure under which the teacher is expected to operate.[22] An in-service training scheme recently proposed by Aspy and Roebuck tries to utilize a preventive approach to give the teacher enough control over the emotional environment in his classroom so that he can function effectively. The first step is understanding classroom interaction processes by means of a com-

[20] Combs, Arthur W. *The Professional Education of Teachers*. Boston: Allyn and Bacon, 1965.

[21] Fuchs, Estelle. *Teachers Talk*. Garden City, N. Y.: Doubleday, 1969.

James, Deborah. *The Taming: A Teacher Speaks*. New York: McGraw-Hill, 1969.

Wisniewski, Richard. *New Teachers in Urban Schools: An Inside View*. New York: Random House, 1968.

[22] Burkhart, Robert C., and Neil, Hugh M. *Identity and Teacher Learning*. Scranton, Pa.: International Textbook Co., 1968.

Shumsky, Abraham. *In Search of Teaching Style*. New York: Appleton-Century-Crofts, 1968.

prehensive model. Each teacher then applies various schemes of inter-action analysis to assess his classroom functioning in both affective and cognitive areas. After analyzing the data from his own class, the teacher decides what teacher and pupil behaviors seem feasible to change during the period of time he is responsible for that group of children. By repeating the analyzing process with the specific group of pupils, he will come to understand better what is effective for himself in inter-action with that group, and this is expected to help reduce ambiguity and the teacher's resulting anxiety.[23]

Poor mental health in a teacher has ominous implications indeed. In 1959 one report estimated that about three million pupils are daily ex-posed to teachers so emotionally disturbed that they should not be around children.[24] In 1968 a publication of the National Institutes for Mental Health stated: "It is estimated that as many as 500,000 children in this country suffer from psychoses and borderline psychotic conditions and that another million are afflicted with personality and character dis-orders. Of the 50 million school age youngsters, evidence suggests that between 10 and 12 per cent have moderate to severe emotional prob-lems requiring some kind of mental health service. . . . Among the 15 million youngsters in the United States who are being reared in poverty, *one out of three* has serious emotional problems that need attention."[25] It is true that "the teacher cannot be all things to all men, and there is grave doubt whether he can pursue the exacting career of educator while at the same time carrying on the exhausting job of meeting and grappling with the emotional needs and problems of his pupils."[26] Perhaps no one can blame him if he breaks down under all the pressure.

[23] Aspy, David N., and Roebuck, Flora N. "A National Consortium for Hu-manizing Education." Unpublished grant application to the National Institutes for Mental Health, Applied Research Division, October 1, 1970.

Roebuck, Flora N., and Aspy, David N. "The Anxious Teacher—A Necessary Ill?" Unpublished manuscript, Northeast Louisiana University, 1970.

[24] Kaplan, Louis. *Mental Health and Human Relations in Education.* New York: Harper and Row, 1959.

[25] National Institutes for Mental Health. *Mental Health Services for Children.* Public Health Service Publication No. 1844. Washington, D. C.: U. S. Govern-ment Printing Office, 1968. Quoted from p. 3.

See also National Institutes for Mental Health. *The Protection and Promotion of Mental Health in the Schools.* Public Health Service Publication No. 1226. Washington, D.C.: U. S. Government Printing Office, 1964.

[26] Joint Commission on Mental Illness and Health. *Action for Mental Health.* New York: John Wiley and Sons, 1961. Pp. 131–132.

Nevertheless, he owes it to his children to acquire sufficient knowledge and understanding of himself (that is, his self) so as not to hurt them in the name of teaching. Being a professional is not an easy task. "Only the strong need apply."[27]

TEACHER-LEARNER INTERACTION

At a convention in Houston, Texas, I witnessed an unexpected reunion of a teacher and a former student of hers. The keynote speaker, an eminent humanistic psychologist, entered the elevator with several people, one of whom was a retired teacher. Upon her inquiry whether he could possibly be the same boy who joined her third-grade class when he moved to this country from Russia, her name came to him and so did fond memories of her many kindnesses, particularly teaching him to speak and read English. Her humble response was gratifying to all on the elevator as she expressed her appreciation for his many contributions to childhood education. Was she proud!—and rightly so; yet she had willingly given her time and energy to a little, frightened immigrant boy without any thought of future returns. Teachers can be influential without realizing it.

Unfortunately, not much is known about the dynamics of teacher-pupil interactions in the classroom and how they affect the development of self concepts,[28] although some clues are available. For example, teachers who are high on self-esteem tend to be associated with groups of students who also have high self-esteem.[29] Superior students have better self concepts when the teachers provide "calm, acceptant teacher-pupil transactions with private individualized instruction and a concern for divergency, attention to the task, and the use of task-appropriate

[27] Wrenn, C. Gilbert. "The Culturally Encapsulated Counselor." *Harvard Educational Review*, 32:444–449; Fall 1962. Quoted from p. 449.

[28] See, however, the following:
National Society for the Study of Education. *The Dynamics of Instructional Groups*, ed. Nelson B. Henry. Fifty-ninth Yearbook, Part II. Chicago: University of Chicago Press, 1960.
Sears, Pauline S., and Sherman, Vivian S. *In Pursuit of Self-Esteem.* Belmont, Calif.: Wadsworth Publishing Co., 1964.

[29] Blume, Robert A. "How the Child Sees Himself May Relate to How the Teacher Sees Himself." *Michigan Education Journal*, 46:9–11; November 1968.

procedures and resources."[30] Teacher judgments about students' behavior are indicative of the basic values held by the teachers,[31] while favorable expectations by teachers may result in an increase in intellectual competence in students.[32] Apparently, academic achievement, emotional adjustment, and status within the peer group all contribute to the students' self concept in the educative process.

In lower grades, children are more often than not taught by female teachers. What about the possible effects of the sex of the teacher upon the pupil's concept of self? One admittedly inconclusive study revealed some trends suggesting that boys who have male teachers have better self concepts than boys who have female teachers, and that girls with female teachers in turn have better self concepts than girls with male teachers. Nevertheless, girls consistently had better self concepts than boys. Both sexes were very aware of their teachers' perceptions of them, but the teachers almost always underestimated the favorableness of students' self concepts.[33] An earlier investigation indicated a positive relationship between children's perceptions of themselves and their perceptions of teachers' feelings toward them, and between the latter and children's school performance.[34]

Do teachers act differently toward children in school depending upon pupil sex? Observations of teacher classroom behaviors tend to give an affirmative answer to this question.[35] Generally speaking, girls rarely

[30] Spaulding, Robert L. Achievement, Creativity and Self-Concept Correlates of Teacher-Pupil Transactions in Elementary School Classrooms. Final Report, U. S. Office of Education, Cooperative Research Project No. 1352. Hempstead, N. Y.: Hofstra University, 1965. P. 117.

[31] Combs, Arthur W., and Soper, Daniel W. The Relationship of Child Perceptions to Achievement and Behavior in the Early School Years. Final Report, U. S. Office of Education, Cooperative Research Project No. 814. Gainesville, Fla.: University of Florida, 1963. Pp. 140–149.

[32] Rosenthal, Robert, and Jacobson, Lenore. Pygmalion in the Classroom: Teacher Expectation and Pupils' Intellectual Development. New York: Holt, Rinehart and Winston, 1968.

[33] Williams, Rose Ann. "Self-Concept Relationships: A Study of Teacher and Student Perceptions." Unpublished doctoral dissertation, Indiana State University, 1970.

[34] Davidson, Helen H., and Lang, Gerhard. "Children's Perceptions of Their Teachers' Feelings toward Them Related to Self-Perception, School Achievement, and Behavior." Journal of Experimental Education, 29:107–118; December 1960.

[35] Davis, O. L., Jr., and Slobodian, June J. "Teacher Behavior toward Boys and

receive as harsh discipline in school as boys and are more likely to exhibit the behaviors valued by the teachers—neatness, cleanliness, conformity, mental passivity, and gentle obedience. Conversely, boys are more likely to receive harsher or angrier scoldings and are more likely to exhibit behaviors which annoy the classroom teacher—aggression, originality, manipulative curiosity, restlessness, and immaturity. In grading, girls are more likely to be given higher marks than boys who achieve at the same level.

The literature being amassed about sex differences in early childhood shows that while levels of intelligence are no different, girls excel in verbal abilities, talking, spelling, and writing. Boys excel in mathematics, science, and creative thinking. Some suggestions for improving the educational experiences of boys, at least until they mature enough to participate successfully in all areas of the curriculum, are: hiring more male teachers; adding more male school staff as co-principals, psychologists, counselors, supervisors, researchers, and others; employing young male teacher-aides for playground, lunchroom, and school bus duty; letting older boys work as tutors in kindergarten and first and second grades; delaying school entrance for half a year beyond the minimum legal age (in many states, five years by January 1 of the year of entrance); and separating classes by sex for academic subjects, while combining them for assemblies, lunch periods, recess, and some physical education. Opportunities for children to interact with a larger number and variety of male adults in school may be the first step in the right direction, although the nurturing warmth of a woman in a boy's early life should not be completely taken away in view of some evidence that it can aid him immeasurably in later life.[36] In any case, it is likely that teachers and

---

Girls during First Grade Reading Instruction." *American Educational Research Journal*, 4:261–269; May 1967.

Felsenthal, Helen M. "Sex Differences in Teacher-Pupil Interaction and Their Relationships with Teacher Attitudes and Pupil Reading Achievement." Unpublished doctoral dissertation, University of Iowa, 1969.

McNeil, John D. "Programed Instruction versus Usual Classroom Procedures in Teaching Boys to Read." *American Educational Research Journal*, 1:113–119; March 1964.

[36] Feather, Bryant, and Olson, Walter S. *Children, Psychology and the Schools.* Glenview, Ill.: Scott, Foresman, 1969.

McCandless, Boyd R. *Children: Behavior and Development.* 2d ed. New York: Holt, Rinehart and Winston, 1967.

(continued on next page)

parents can benefit their children by forgoing premature sex stereo-typing and providing diversified experiences for children of both sexes.

THEORETICAL BASES FOR TEACHING STRATEGIES

Professional study and interdisciplinary seminars help teachers who appreciate a diversity of viewpoints to determine which teaching strate-gies will be appropriate for the group with whom they are working and learning. But no formula exists for creating an educational environment which provides each child with the freedom to learn. One certainty is, however, that "the psychologically important dimension is what happens to the child: how he is handled, what knowledge he gains, what atti-tudes towards people he acquires."[37]

Human development can be characterized as the process of emer-gence of various control mechanisms involving both inhibition and facilitation. The child's first learnings are motor learnings, which play an important role, as the basis for elaborations and expansions, in estab-lishing later intellectual development. There is a pattern of development through which all children must pass, but individuals vary in the style and rate of progress. Anyone involved in education is very soon and very lastingly impressed with the extreme range of differences among normal children with respect to almost every major cognitive function. Unfortunately, school children are typically classified, and demands are made upon them, according to chronological age (which is only a physical definition of time); thus, the enormous individual differences among them are ignored.[38]

Pollack, Jack H. "Are Teachers Fair to Boys?" *Today's Health,* 46:21–26; April 1968.

Smart, Mollie S., and Smart, Russell C. *Children: Development and Relation-ships.* New York: Macmillan, 1967.

[37] Kagan, Jerome, and Whitten, Phillip. "Day Care Can Be Dangerous." *Psy-chology Today,* 4:36–39; December 1970. Quoted from p. 37.

[38] Peter, Lawrence J. *Prescriptive Teaching.* New York: McGraw-Hill, 1965. Pp. 16–41.

Readers who wish to investigate further are referred to the following discus-sions of individual differences:

Anastasi, Anne. *Differential Psychology.* 3d ed. New York: Macmillan, 1958.

Tyler, Leona E. *The Psychology of Human Differences.* 3d ed. New York: Appleton-Century-Crofts, 1965.

During the early years, it seems necessary and appropriate to emphasize training through sensory-motor modalities for subsequent intellectual and personality development. Concerning early training, three scholars from different countries, periods, and disciplines have made observations amazingly similar in their implications for education. The scholars are Maria Montessori, an Italian physician (1870–1952), Jean Piaget, a Swiss biologist and psychologist (1896–   ), and Jerome Bruner, an American psychologist (1915–   ).

MONTESSORI

Montessori has written extensively on intellectual training through sensory-motor modalities at ages three to six.[39] Because mental development in these early years proceeds at a rapid rate, this is a period, she felt, that must not be wasted. According to Montessori, a child undergoes "sensitive periods," during each of which he is particularly sensitive to certain stimulus modes and, hence, receptive to educational efforts made through the corresponding sense modalities. The nine overlapping sensitive periods and their respective areas of interest are as follows:

birth–3 years . . . . . . Absorbent mind
Sensory experiences
1½–3 years . . . . Language development
1½–4 years . . . . Coordination and muscle development
Interest in small objects
2–4 years . . . . Refinement of movement
Concern with truth and reality
Awareness of order sequence in time and space
2½–6 years . . . . Sensory refinement
3–6 years . . . . Susceptibility to adult influence
3½–4½ years . . . . . Writing
4–4½ years . . . . Tactile Sense
4½–5½ years . . . . . Reading

The environment in the Montessori classroom is designed to exclude distractions and to offer opportunities for constructive work. The

[39] Montessori, Maria. Dr. Montessori's Own Handbook. New York: Schocken Books, 1965; The Montessori Method. Cambridge, Mass.: Robert Bentley, 1965; and The Absorbent Mind. New York: Dell Publishing Co., 1969.

Montessori teaching method is divided into three parts: motor education, sensory education, and language. Great emphasis is placed on a thorough development of the five senses, and continuity between the three areas of training is established by special equipment adapted to preparing the child for each part. The materials used in Montessori classrooms are said to awaken the children's interest in learning and to teach them a love of learning for learning's sake. It should be noted that Montessori's innovations in education were based largely on her clinical observations of both mentally retarded and culturally deprived children. American Montessori schools are carefully organized according to the principles of Montessori and require their own graduate training for their personnel.[40]

PIAGET

Piaget's elaborate explanation of the sensory-motor nature of the very young child's intelligence is highly relevant to the Montessori method. He speaks of sensory-motor intelligence as the original stage or period of intellectual development, this limited form of intelligence predominating during approximately the first two years of life. It is only in Piaget's theory that one finds full recognition of the sensory-motor period as the base upon which the subsequent stages of intellectual development are built; other theorists have emphasized verbal development, the development of visual images and ideas, etc. According to Piaget, sensory-motor intelligence rests mainly on actions, on movements and perceptions without language, but these actions are co-

[40] Beck, Joan. *How to Raise a Brighter Child.* New York: Trident Press, 1967.
Fisher, Dorothy. *Montessori for Parents.* Rev. ed. Cambridge, Mass.: Robert Bentley, 1965; and *The Montessori Manual for Teachers and Parents.* Rev. ed. Cambridge, Mass.: Robert Bentley, 1964.
Hainstock, Elizabeth G. *Teaching Montessori in the Home.* New York: Random House, 1968.
Hertzberger, Herman. "Montessori Primary School in Delft, Holland." *Harvard Educational Review,* 39:58–67; November 1969.
Orem, Robert C. *A Montessori Handbook.* New York: G. P. Putnam's Sons, 1965.
Rambusch, Nancy. *Learning How to Learn.* Baltimore, Md.: Pelican Press, 1962.
Standing, E. M. *The Montessori Revolution in Education.* New York: Schocken Books, 1966.

ordinated in a relatively stable way under what may be called schemata (or structure). These schemata can be generalized in the child's actions and are applicable to new situations. For example, pulling on an object within reach constitutes a schema which can be generalized to other situations when another object rests on a support. In other words, a schema presupposes an incorporation of new situations into the previous schemata, a sort of continuous assimilation of new objects or new situations to the actions already schematized. *Assimilation* of new experiences to previously formed schemata and *accommodation* of behavior to external conditions are, in Piaget's view, the two major overall modes of interaction with the environment.[41]

Piaget terms the period at which Montessori training usually begins the "preoperational" period. Up to this point, intelligence refers largely to egocentrically organized actions and perceptions locked to the immediate space which surrounds the child. Passage to the preoperational period signifies that the child is ready to begin the long series of steps toward the ultimate mastery of interrelationships among symbols required for formal operations. Piaget has emphasized that the formation of later schemata and their effective maintenance is in part dependent upon external stimulation.[42] He also emphasizes the importance of variety in early experience. The variety is necessary for new experiences to be effectively assimilated. The original Montessori method, on the other hand, is not primarily designed to increase the variety of objects the child comes in contact with, nor is it intended to broaden the range of his sensory-motor interactions with the environment or of affective and motivational factors. However, no one would expect a set of educational devices, no matter how cleverly constructed, to provide all the requirements of optimal cognitive growth, namely, an effective overall equilibrium of the forces and structures within the child. For this reason, both Montessori and Piaget emphasize interactions with peers as the principal means of overcoming the child's egocentrism in learning.

Three parallels between Montessori and Piaget have been pointed out

[41] Maier, Henry W. *Three Theories of Child Development*. New York: Harper and Row, 1962. Pp. 75–143.

[42] Inhelder, Bärbel, and Piaget, Jean. *The Growth of Logical Thinking From Childhood to Adolescence*. New York: Basic Books, 1958.
Piaget, Jean. *Six Psychological Studies*. New York: Random House, 1967.

by Elkind.[43] First, they both have a predominantly biological orientation towards the thought and behavior of the child. They see mental growth as an extension of biological growth and governed by the same principles and laws. Secondly, both emphasize the normative (common) aspects of child behavior and development as opposed to the unique aspects of individual differences. They see an understanding of normal development as a necessary starting point for a full understanding of differences between individuals. Thirdly, both Montessori and Piaget manifest a genius for empathy with the child. Their insights into the child's mind were achieved by supposedly unbiased, astute, direct *observations* of the child, and these observations and insights, even without the buttressing of large-scale research, were later widely accepted. In fact, they have affected greatly the newer programs, particularly the preschool programs, offered the young child.[44] In addition, Montessori and Piaget look upon socialization of the child as the desired goal. The major difference between the two is that Piaget's contributions are primarily in the theoretical areas of logic and epistemology, while Montessori has contributed to child psychology and education.

Elkind also identifies three ideas more or less original with Piaget and Montessori:

> The first idea is that nature and nurture interact in a dual way. With respect to the growth of abilities, nature provides the pattern and the time schedule of its unfolding while nurture provides the nourishment for the realization of this pattern. When we turn to the content of thought, however, just the reverse is true; nurture determines what will be learned while nature provides the prerequisite capacities. A second idea has to do with capacity and learning. For both Piaget and Montessori, capacity sets the limits for learning and capacity changes at its own rate and according

[43] Elkind, David. "Piaget and Montessori." *Harvard Educational Review*, 37:535–545; Fall 1967.

[44] Elkind, "Piaget and Montessori," op. cit. (n. 43); and "Piaget's Theory of Perceptual Development: Its Application to Reading and Special Education." *Journal of Special Education*, 1:357–361; Fall 1967.

Also see the following:

Athey, Irene J., and Rubadean, Duane O. (eds.). *Educational Implications of Piaget's Theory*. Waltham, Mass.: Ginn-Blaisdell, 1970.

Elkind, David, and Flavell, John H. (eds.). *Studies in Cognitive Development: Essays in Honor of Jean Piaget*. New York: Oxford University Press, 1969.

to its own time schedule. Finally, the third idea is that repetitive behavior is the external manifestation of cognitive growth and expresses the need of emerging cognitive abilities to realize themselves through action.[45]

BRUNER

In his studies of children's thinking aimed at the improvement of educational practices, Bruner describes three systems (enactive, iconic, and symbolic) a child utilizes in the accommodation and assimilation of his environments. The enactive mode translates experience into an inner model through action; e.g., no words or diagrams are sufficient for transmitting the skills of bicycle-riding or ice-skating, and one must go through the motions.[46] Enactive representation, in other words, is based upon a learning of muscular responses and forms of habituation, and is apparently related to Piaget's sensorimotor stage of intelligence. It obviously lasts in human development much beyond the age of two and is involved in learning most of our physical skills. The enactive mode would also include visceral sensations and feelings and thus contribute the vital dimensions to social role-playing activities.

Bruner's second system of representation (iconic) depends on visual, aural, or other sensory organizations and upon the use of summarizing images. It is governed by perceptual organizations and transformations and is apparently related to Piaget's stage of concrete operations. The third system, consisting of words or mathematical language, is symbolic in nature. This system is highly productive, or generative, for ideas can be manipulated and transformed in ways that concrete objects cannot. This aspect of Bruner's theory appears to correspond to Piaget's stage of formal operations and also to relate to verbal utilization and performance.

Montessori, Piaget, and Bruner all describe, in different terminology, the process of the development of intelligence in the child's interweaving of cognitive and affective skills. They emphasize the value of

[45] Elkind, "Piaget and Montessori," op. cit. (n. 43), pp. 543–544.
[46] Bruner, Jerome S. On Knowing. Cambridge, Mass.: Harvard University Press, 1963; and Toward a Theory of Instruction. Cambridge, Mass.: Harvard University Press, 1966.
Bruner, Jerome S.; Goodnow, Jacqueline J.; and Austin, George A. "Selection Strategies in Concept Attainment." The Psychology of Language, Thought, and Instruction, ed. John P. DeCecco. New York: Holt, Rinehart and Winston, 1967. Pp. 238–245.

acquired experiences, from the concrete to the abstract. In each stage of development, the child has a characteristic way of perceiving and viewing his environment. At first, his perception is preverbal and not mediated by language, but later, it is mediated by some words and images. The child eventually becomes capable of some reasoning, and he is finally able to handle logical, even hypothetical problems quite rationally. In simple terms, the mind has predispositions, structure, and sequence, which through experience and maturation develop to greater complexity and greater capacity. But without the proper sub-stages the child cannot move from rote or relatively superficial learning to involved and meaningful understandings. The three theories differ in their interpretation of learning structure and discovery. Montessori and Bruner pre-package the arrangement of curricular experiences for children; while Piaget, admittedly no pedagogue, believes that mental activity, which when confronted with cognitive conflict operates to compensate, develops logical structures. Further implications for education can be made as research replications and evidence based on their theories are accumulated.

PRACTICAL APPLICATIONS OF TEACHING STRATEGIES

The nursery school, whether "traditional" or "development-oriented," has generally placed more emphasis upon the child's social and emotional development than on intellectual development, because the clientele is largely children who come from middle-class homes where parents have stressed intellectual development on their own. Most of the teachers have been trained to search for unconscious motivations and to provide activities which shape socially constructive behavior. The curriculum has, at least superficially, emphasized development of creativity, language, and interpersonal skills. However, some of the schools have flagrantly violated the intended freedom with outdated structure, activities, and materials, and because of this the whole nursery school system has been criticized by mental hygienists. Lately, on the other hand, the mental hygiene point of view has been attacked by critics as anti-intellectual for not stimulating formal learning.[47]

[47] Lavatelli, Celia S. "Contrasting Views of Early Childhood Education." *Childhood Education*, 46:239–246; February 1970.

Most of those who have devised programs to demonstrate that the early childhood years, rather than the primary grades, should be used to teach academic skills are educational psychologists. These preschool programs emphasize cognitive development and methods to speed up the acquisition of academic skills. Bereiter and Englemann, for instance, experimented in a school for disadvantaged four-year-olds with the children moving from class to class for formal lessons in arithmetic, pre-reading skills, and language.[48] Moore worked successfully with a "talking typewriter" to teach pre-reading skills to infants of two, and this equipment is now used in a few selected elementary schools and preschools.[49] Other experimenters have devised methods of teaching the alphabet and the sounds of letters to infants in an effort to accelerate reading acquisition. Overall, however, the trend appears to be toward an eclectic combination of structured, directed activities and nonstructured, relatively free activities.

After the child enters school, the programs available to him range from the traditional to some of the newer approaches utilizing a variety of organizational procedures. The British infant schools, for example, which enroll children from five to seven or eight years of age in classes of about 40, are characterized by informal methods. Some of the ways children learn in these schools are through small groups, older children teaching the younger, individualized instruction, freedom of choice, and the availability of many materials and activity centers. The structure and the choice of activities and materials in the British system provide better opportunities for acquiring concepts in academic subjects, and play is more explicitly used for cognitive growth. The theoretical basis is derived largely from Piaget and is coupled with a strong belief that telling is not teaching. In contrast, American preschools largely lack the informal age grouping and the training facilities for teachers to learn to appreciate the cognitive content of play.[50] Several organizational plans, e.g., nongrading, team teaching, and dual progress, which encourage

[48] Bereiter, Carl, and Englemann, Siegfried. *Teaching Disadvantaged Children in the Pre-School*. Englewood Cliffs, N. J.: Prentice-Hall, 1966.

[49] Moore, Omar K., and Anderson, Alan R. "Some Principles for the Design of Clarifying Educational Environments." *Handbook of Socialization Theory and Research*, ed. David A. Goslin. Chicago: Rand McNally, 1969. Pp. 571–613.

[50] Silberman, op. cit. (n. 13), pp. 207–264.

individualized instruction for continuous progress of each pupil, should be more seriously studied and implemented.[51]

Some innovative approaches to providing variation in mastery techniques have been introduced in American schools. Teaching machines and programed instruction based upon operant conditioning principles have been used in a number of schools to teach every age and ability level. Several sources of information about the various programs and methods are available.[52] While research evidence would indicate that, for certain purposes and with certain pupils, programed instruction or auto-instructional materials can be superior to classroom instruction accompanied by peer interaction, it seems reasonable to assume that their use with younger children would be limited largely to the mastery of basic skills. The principle of selective reinforcement also underlies the programs of behavior modification. The idea is a simple one but, as shown in a later chapter on remediation (Chapter Five), it is effective and may be particularly useful with "unsuccessful" pupils in school.[53] A related concept is that of behavioral instructional objectives, the specification of which often helps teachers to clarify for themselves what learning styles and teaching strategies are most efficient for what they want to accomplish in both the cognitive and affective domains.[54]

[51] National Society for the Study of Education. *The Changing American School,* ed. John I. Goodlad. Sixty-fifth Yearbook, Part II. Chicago: University of Chicago Press, 1966.

Hillson, Maurie. *Change and Innovation in Elementary School Organization.* New York: Holt, Rinehart and Winston, 1964.

[52] National Society for the Study of Education. *Programed Instruction,* ed. Phil C. Lange. Sixty-sixth Yearbook, Part II. Chicago: University of Chicago Press, 1967.

Lumsdaine, A. A., and Glaser, Robert (eds.). *Teaching Machines and Programed Learning.* Washington, D. C.: National Education Association, Department of Audio-Visual Instruction, 1960; and *Teaching Machines and Programed Learning, II: Data and Directions.* Washington, D. C.: National Education Association, Department of Audio-Visual Instruction, 1965.

[53] Bijou, Sidney. "Conversation with *Behavior Today.*" *Behavior Today,* 8:4; June 8, 1970.

McIntire, Roger W. "Spare the Rod, Use Behavior Mod." *Psychology Today,* 4:42–44, 67; December 1970.

Macmillan, Donald L., and Forness, Steven R. "Behavior Modification: Limitations and Liabilities." *Exceptional Children,* 37:291–298; December 1970.

[54] Gay, William O., and Stephenson, Bobby L. "A Systems Approach as a

Throughout the ages, teachers have used varied classroom teaching techniques, yet there is no technique of teaching which can be rated consistently good or bad. Some schools where there has been continuing lack of achievement among the youngsters have contracted with industrial concerns to upgrade their pupils' performance, measured by standardized achievement tests at prescribed testing periods. This so-called "performance contracting," for example at Texarkana, Texas-Arkansas, and Gary, Indiana, is obviously too new to allow any impartial assessment of all its technical and philosophical ramifications. It is clear that teachers are pressed hard to identify for themselves and for their pupils what education is all about, and how they can help in the process.[55]

Needless to say, the younger the child when he is exposed to appropriate teaching strategies for his particular learning style, the greater the possibility he will conceive of himself as a successful learner. Prevention is always more desirable than remediation, and any potential means for a better match between learning styles and teaching strategies merits careful exploration. Still, it must be remembered that efficiency is no substitute for human dignity and that education, and schooling also, is meaningless unless it is humane. A recent attempt at "emotional education" may shed some light on the feasibility of raising a generation of competent *and* compassionate human beings.[56] The "Living School" in New York City offers the usual academic subjects plus rational-emotive

"Method of Training Teachers of Mentally Retarded Students." *Education and Training of the Mentally Retarded,* 6:56–66; April 1971.

Mager, Robert F. *Preparing Instructional Objectives.* Palo Alto, Calif.: Fearon Publishers, 1962.

Stephenson, Bobby L. *An Investigation of the Psycholinguistic Abilities of Negro and White Children from Four Socioeconomic Status Levels.* Final Report, U. S. Office of Education, Bureau of Research Project No. 9-G-058. Monroe, La.: Northeast Louisiana University, 1970.

[55] Elam, Stanley. "The Age of Accountability Dawns in Texarkana." *Phi Delta Kappan,* 51:509–514; June 1970.

[56] Institute for Advanced Study in Rational Psychotherapy. "Emotional Education in the Classroom: The Living School." *Newsletter of the Institute for Advanced Study in Rational Psychotherapy,* 1:1–4; Spring 1970. (45 East 65th Street, New York.)

See also: Hymes, James L., Jr. "Making Tomorrow Now: The People Environment." *Childhood Education,* 47:122–125; December 1970.

guidance. The skill and communication subjects are taught individually, and the esthetic and recreational subjects are engaged in by the entire group and are conducted in a manner that fosters a wide range of opinion and expression. While skills and arts are being taught, the teachers are alert for unusual behaviors and guide the child to personal insight and changed attitudes and actions. Each child is taught how to acknowledge and identify his emotional states. If these efforts are successful, he will know himself as a worthy individual in the human race.

THE HUMANIZATION OF SCHOOLS

The complexities of a teacher's task are indeed overwhelming. The advance of technology, the interdependence of societies, the conflict of ideologies, and the inexorable crowding of the planet combine to stimulate a new awareness that the systematic development of human capability and understanding is indispensable to prosperity and peace. Schools are the agency most obviously responsible for such cultivation and conservation of human talents. Given all the perplexing and discouraging signs in our midst, is there any hope for humanized formal education?

Yes, there is, so long as we have enlightened and dedicated teachers. For instance, Robert Coles visited elementary schools in thirteen cities of varying size across the nation which offered special programs for low-achieving children from economically deprived minority groups. In each city, he interviewed school superintendents, principals, teachers, and individual pupils and found no lack of communication between teachers and pupils. Too often, however, the communication was on the level of despair, with low expectations on each side. Too often a child believed that his destiny had little to do with schooling or achievement as a student.[57] Fortunately, that is not all of Coles's story. He also found a number of unusual teachers, firm and tough, yet who in dozens of ways and on every possible occasion signaled their care and respect to the class sitting before them. These teachers were characterized by flexibility, or a willingness to forgo established and comfortable routines in the interest of reaching pupils who were quite often determined not to be reached. These seemingly impossible children then responded

[57] Coles, Robert. *Teachers and the Children of Poverty.* Washington, D. C.: The Potomac Institute, 1970.

with improved performance and newly awakened hope. The teachers created a reason for learning for the individual child and established an atmosphere of fairness and affection.

How can the teacher assist the child in the development of a feeling of adequacy and a desire to function well in the learning process? Each learner must perceive of himself as a person who is capable of performing adequately and who can learn to participate in the learning process. If we are to survive, the goal of education must be the facilitation of change and learning. When the teacher guides and facilitates learning, the child perceives of himself as a person who is free, self-initiated, and spontaneous.[58] As one of my own professors used to say, "The teacher of young children should have as his goal teaching so well that the day the children spend with him will be a better day in their life, because they have associated with him that day." If a teacher accepts this challenge, the children will meet a mature human being who never loses sight of the obligation involved in nurturing the young with whom he works. By these caring relationships, the self concepts of both teacher and children are enhanced. Out of such interactions will come young people who accept themselves, who have a genuine concern for others, and who can feel and think.

SUGGESTED READINGS

Athey, Irene J., and Rubadean, Duane O. (eds.). *Educational Implications of Piaget's Theory.* Waltham, Mass.: Ginn-Blaisdell, 1970. An anthology of articles discussing the application of Piaget's theory in the classroom and within various curricular areas.

Bronfenbrenner, Urie. *Two Worlds of Childhood: U.S. and U.S.S.R.* New York: Russell Sage Foundation, 1970. A leading psychologist compares the two cultures and examines provocative implications for the future for both societies.

[58] Rogers, Carl R. "The Interpersonal Relationship in the Facilitation of Learning." *Humanizing Education: The Person in the Process,* ed. Robert R. Leeper. Washington, D. C.: Association for Supervision and Curriculum Development, 1967. Pp. 1–17.

Coles, Robert. *Teachers and the Children of Poverty.* Washington, D.C.: The Potomac Institute, 1970. A psychiatrist's account of interviews with superintendents, principals, teachers, and individual pupils in thirteen cities of varying size which offer special programs for low-achieving minority children from economically deprived backgrounds.

Gordon, Edmund W. (ed.). "Education for Socially Disadvantaged Children." *Review of Educational Research,* 40:1–179; February 1970. A summary of the available information on the education of disadvantaged children with recommendations for improving current models, as well as suggestions for needed research.

Jones, Richard M. *Fantasy and Feeling in Education.* New York: New York University Press, 1968. A psychologist presents a theoretical and empirical account of curricular innovations which provide children and teachers with humanistic goals.

Maslow, Abraham H. *Toward a Psychology of Being.* 2d ed. Princeton, N.J.: D. Van Nostrand, 1968. This revision of a classic in humanistic psychology shows how recent research and thought have opened up a future built on the intrinsic values of humanity. The last chapter discusses basic propositions for creating a normative social psychology.

Myers, Patricia, I., and Hammill, Donald D. *Methods for Learning Disorders.* New York: John Wiley and Sons, 1969. Models of education based upon the strengths and weaknesses of children are studied in this textbook. It examines curricular systems which provide the matching of teaching strategies with learning styles.

Silberman, Charles E. *Crisis in the Classroom.* New York: Random House, 1970. A highly readable, scholarly analysis of current school practices with numerous examples of the beneficial and detrimental experiences children encounter in the name of education.

FOUR · TO FATHOM THE SELF:

APPRAISAL IN SCHOOL

Whitfield Bourisseau

Seek truth
No longer shadow reflections
Lantern flicker enlightenment
Misguided
Ignorant of symbol forces.
Seek rather
A growing comprehensive insight
Fusion of shadowless
Movements
Evolving in process.[1]

In recognizing the inevitability of rapid change in today's society, educators are challenged as never before to find the means of developing in youth a stable personality. The only predictions about the future that can be made with certainty are that it will be different and change will be a constant way of life. Supposedly, the well-adjusting personality, the stable and flexible person, can adapt to change, whereas the maladjusting personality feels threatened and becomes defensive, resistive, and often violent. The cure for these self-defeating coping strategies, so far as educators are concerned, lies not in emergency measures but rather in "the steady, consistent effort to make education

[1] Poem by Julius Stulman in *Fields Within Fields . . . Within Fields,* 2 (1); 1969. (New York: World Institute Council, 777 United Nations Plaza.) Quoted from p. 28. Reprinted by permission of the author.

more responsive to the real needs and essential quality of all human beings."[2]

Relevance in education is contingent first upon understanding the student, and secondly, upon individualizing the educational process. As a philosophical concept, individualized instruction meets little argument today. At the operational level, however, it provokes controversy —frequently quite heated—at the drop of a mortarboard.

Among several aspects of personality calling for better understanding, motivation possibly ranks first. Relative to achievement, motivation is perhaps even more complex and more significant than intelligence itself. Without adequate motivation the intelligent child is hardly a match for his less intelligent but highly motivated peer. A significant factor in motivation is anticipated success—the feeling that the task at hand can be completed. In fact, the realization has recently emerged that the child's *concept* of ability may be as crucial to his success as his ability per se. If a person feels he cannot produce, then the actual ability to produce is reduced or negated. By the same token, a success-oriented individual will often plunge into a project with little past experience and more often than not be successful. This feeling about ability is based on past experiences, physical, emotional, and psychological.

Although the importance of the self concept is an established fact and the literature is becoming increasingly productive, the concept continues to be elusive. The research is relatively limited, standardized measures are largely nonexistent, and terminology is obscure. Albeit limited, the research is consistent in reporting the relation between self concept and achievement, whether it be academic or social. Brownfain[3] found that college students with a stable self concept were better adjusted and freer of inferiority feelings and nervousness, were more popular, knew more people and were better known, and showed less evidence of compensatory behavior of a defensive kind than those students who had an unstable self concept. Wattenberg and Clifford[4] report that at the kindergarten level a self concept evaluation is a more

[2] Kunz, F. L., and Sellon, Emily B. "News and Views." *Main Currents in Modern Thought*, 25:145; May-June 1969.

[3] Brownfain, John J. "Stability of the Self-Concept as a Dimension of Personality." *Journal of Abnormal and Social Psychology*, 47:597–606; July 1952.

[4] Wattenberg, William W., and Clifford, Clare. "Relations of Self Concept to Beginning Achievement in Reading." *Child Development*, 35:461–467; June 1964.

accurate predictor of second-grade reading achievement than is a mental age evaluation.

Glasser[5] makes perhaps the strongest argument of all for the importance of the relation between self concept and achievement. He says that the whole of our society today is dichotomized between those who identify with success and those who identify with failure; not between blacks and whites or rich and poor. Glasser believes a child creates some feeling of who he is, that is, an identity, which will be either positive or negative. Ages five to ten are the critical years for this development, with the home and school as the major agents. In his book, *Schools Without Failure*, Glasser is highly critical of schools and the role they play in blocking the achievement of a success identity. School policies tend to reward those children who perform well and expose those who are unable to compete, and then emphasize academic material giving little encouragement to learning about oneself.

The role of the responsible elementary teacher today is expanding far beyond the teaching of academics. It is essential that the teacher know more about the children in his classroom; specifically, it is important to know how they feel about themselves. There is no one method by which this information is gleaned. The conscientious teacher will seek a broad exposure to the child's behavior in different ways and at different times. This chapter deals with some of the ways and means of reaching this goal.

SELF CONCEPT IN THE CHILD'S LIFE

The child's view of his environment and of his place in this environment determines his reactions and his behavior. One child may be challenged by the stimulation of environmental factors. Another child may see these same factors as overwhelming and thus will openly rebel, withdraw, or perhaps develop other defense systems in order to maintain himself psychologically. To understand the child's judgment of self, we must look at the whole child and study every facet of his behavior. Appraising the self concept involves observing this behavior. The human organism is fundamentally consistent in its expression. Environmental conditions as well as a temporary internal state may influence responses. However, a general consistency of behavior is maintained throughout and is discernible in every mode of expression if the observer is insight-

[5] Glasser, William. *Schools Without Failure*. New York: Harper and Row, 1969.

ful enough to interpret the meaning of the behavior accurately. Because the self image is a concept and not a concrete entity, an appraisal of this self image can be accomplished only by observing the behavior that allows insight into the system determining that behavior. In other words, the self concept per se cannot be directly measured.

Beatty[6] says that the nervous system is the basis for what we call intellect and that it is well developed at birth. As the child experiences his own body interacting directly with the environment, he begins to develop an image of what he is like. This is the self concept. Beatty further indicates that the young child reacts directly to his feelings rather than to a sophisticated interpretation of his feelings. As he grows he begins to see his feelings and reactions in terms of their impact on those around him. Thus the self concept develops. Further development stems from the feeling component generated in past encounters. The child indeed becomes that which he thinks he is. If environmental factors distort reality (e.g., parents overlooking successes and emphasizing failures), then a poor self concept results, which can inhibit his development. The child who experiences difficulty in reading may acquire an erroneous self image. Perhaps he is exposed to the task before he is developmentally or otherwise ready. Frustrated by his inability to learn, his teacher tells him he is a poor reader. To emphasize the point, the teacher reports the child's failure to his parents. Becoming anxious, they in turn tell him again that he is a poor reader. Because it has become a sensitive subject, he shuns every reading exposure. Lacking positive motivation, he dislikes the subject and practice is avoided. When he does try to read further difficulty is encountered, which serves to reinforce the feeling he had originally, "I am a poor reader." If reading had been presented so as to promote success rather than failure, the negative experience could have been prevented or reduced. The child's self concept would not have suffered a devastating blow. This example is not an isolated incident; it is a common experience in a majority of schools today for a significant number of children.

ROLE OF THE TEACHER IN SELF CONCEPT DEVELOPMENT

While the self concept is established in the early years of childhood, it remains pliable during the elementary years. At this time the teacher

[6] Beatty, Wolcott H. "The Feelings of Learning." *Childhood Education,* 45:363–369; March 1969.

plays an extremely important role in the development of the self image —both in handling the child and in reporting to his parents. Davidson and Lang[7] found that during the elementary years a significant correlation existed between the child's perception of his teacher's feelings toward him and his own self image. A positive perception resulted in a positive self image and vice versa. The academic achievement was higher and the classroom behavior more desirable for those children who saw themselves as adequate in the eyes of their teachers.

The teacher's role in the development of a child's self image is as important as are his methods of direct, cognitive teaching. In addition to noting potential and achievement, he needs to be mindful of other significant indicators, such as posture, voice quality and speech content, role in free play, conversation, drawings, and stories.

It is essential for the teacher to realize that any one of the techniques discussed in this chapter will provide merely a clue that needs to be confirmed with additional information. Behavior is a complex system which at any given moment is a balance between internal and external forces. Temporary conditions can effect a difference in both total and differentiated behavior.

A child who has witnessed or participated in a highly charged emotional scene at home can be greatly affected and appear morose, sullen, ineffective, withdrawn, or aggressive. His responses on an inventory or an instrument of projective type would likely reflect what might have been a rare experience. In fact, the rarity of the experience could intensify the reaction. If, however, emotional scenes are prevalent in a family unit, a child's daily performance probably would not be significantly distorted. As for differentiated behavior, a scratched finger could result in an awkward pencil grip or a blister on the heel could cause imbalance in posture and gait. Judging a child's self image by one sample of behavior is not a valid basis for understanding.

TECHNIQUES OF APPRAISAL

Since the importance of the self concept has been generally accepted and a more concerted effort has been made to understand it, techniques have been developed to provide some normative data. These techniques

[7] Davidson, Helen H., and Lang, Gerhard. "Children's Perceptions of Their Teachers' Feelings Toward Them Related to Self Perception, School Achievement, and Behavior." *Journal of Experimental Education*, 29:107–118; December 1960.

represent simply a point of departure. They are not intended to provide all the insight needed for a specific individual or for some particular behavior pattern. In reality, observation is limited only by the ingenuity of the observer, since all of the expressions taking place at any given moment reflect what the child is experiencing within. Once the concept of the self image is understood, the creative teacher can find numberless ways to observe its manifestations.

For clarity, the techniques of appraisal discussed in this chapter are divided into formal and informal categories. The formal techniques are those uniform methods of looking at children that are generally used. These are procedures for which research provides us with background knowledge. The same instruments have been used with many children and the responses recorded. This gives normative data and helps evaluate a child relative to his peers. In a sense, the appraisal of a child based on the formal techniques is somewhat more objective than one arrived at by using informal techniques. However, any assessment of the self concept has subjective overtones, and it is currently based on theoretical projection as much as on empirical data. Much disagreement should probably be expected for several reasons, not the least of which is the fact that there are many facets to what is generally known as the self concept. Terms such as *self-acceptance, self-esteem, self-regard, self-favorability,* among others, are not synonymous. These may represent quality gradations or subvariables within the more inclusive term, self concept.[8]

It must be remembered that even these relatively standardized techniques do not necessarily meet the criteria for accepted principles of psychometrics. Crowne and Stephens[9] cite the following major inadequacies: (1) there are no scientific data establishing the equivalence of assessment procedures used in the various techniques; (2) a clear-cut definition of the variable (self concept) being tested is unavailable; (3) the parameters of the self concept are not sufficiently defined to permit valid sampling, a procedure critical to psychometrics; and (4) it is impossible to determine whether the subject's response is based on a defensive projection or his actual self image. Despite some of the

[8] Wylie, Ruth. *The Self Concept.* Lincoln: University of Nebraska Press, 1961. P. 40.

[9] Crowne, Douglas P., and Stephens, Mark W. "Self-Acceptance and Self-Evaluative Behavior: A Critique of Methodology." *Psychological Bulletin,* 58:104–121; March 1961.

questionable aspects of the techniques used in inferring the self concept, they do provide the teacher with a functional means of evaluating the forces that motivate a given child's behavior.

The informal techniques are mainly suggestions for observation. They are categorized into verbal and nonverbal methods, encouraging the observer to look at the whole child.

There are many forms and kinds of appraisals, but the techniques presented in this chapter are those most appropriate for use in the classroom. They are easy to administer and insights can be gained readily. For a comprehensive interpretation of questionable data on specific children, collaboration with the school psychologist or a clinical child psychologist is recommended.

FORMAL TECHNIQUES

Projectives. Projective techniques refer to those evaluative methods which use ambiguous tasks to let subjects structure the situation in their own ways. Since no clear direction is to be found in the task itself, the child is forced to draw from his inner resources. He thus "projects" himself to a larger extent than is the case in tests and inventories. Within the limits of this chapter it is not possible to give a comprehensive discussion of the concept of projection. Simply stated, it deals with the aspect of personality which ascribes to something or someone a feeling or an emotion which originates from within. From the many experiences in his life, a person unconsciously selects the values, the emotions, and the behavior that he will express when called upon to draw a picture, to tell a story, or to dramatize a situation. Van Lennep[10] says that the concept of projection is "used to include all kinds of utterances and expressions of the subject as far as these are *personal* and not decided by the rules of his society." Anderson,[11] on the other hand, states:

A person is projecting when he ascribes to another person a trait or desire of his own that would be painful for his ego to admit.

[10] Van Lennep, D. J. "The Four-Picture Test." *An Introduction to Projective Techniques,* eds. Harold H. Anderson and Gladys L. Anderson. Englewood Cliffs, N. J.: Prentice-Hall, 1951. Pp. 149–180. Quoted from p. 149.

[11] Anderson, Harold H. "Human Behavior and Personality Growth." *An Introduction to Projective Techniques,* eds. Harold H. Anderson and Gladys L. Anderson. Englewood Cliffs, N. J.: Prentice-Hall, 1951. Pp. 3–25. Quoted from p. 3.

Since the act of projecting is an unconscious mechanism, it is not communicated to others nor is it even recognized as a projection by the person himself.

Figure Drawing. The projective technique generally used more often than any other with children is figure drawing. It can be used effectively with a group of children or it can be administered individually. Individual administration eliminates the possibility of copying and also provides an opportunity to observe drawing procedures and behavior mannerisms. Nevertheless, much information can be gained from group-administered figure drawings. The child is given an 8½-x-11-inch piece of white paper and asked to draw *a man* or more simply (i.e., an even less-structured direction) to draw *a person.* This last directive adds one more degree of freedom, as the child can choose to draw a male or a female figure. It is very important to give no further direction. Any question the child asks, such as "Where shall I draw it?" or "Boy or girl?" should be answered with "Any way you choose," or some other response that completely frees him to make his own decision about what, where, or how he wants to draw.

Without a thorough knowledge of personality dynamics and developmental sequence in both normal and abnormal subjects, any extended interpretation of figure drawings could be erroneous and dangerous. This task had better be left to the school psychologist or the clinical child psychologist. Nevertheless, in a group dynamic situation involving children, it is the teacher who has the greatest opportunity and primary responsibility for determining those children who should be referred for further attention. In comparing the figure drawings of his class, the teacher can readily become aware of those few drawings which are conspicuously different in detail (included or omitted), facial expression or figure proportion. These drawings as a technique do effectively provide some general clues to a subject's feelings about himself.

Machover[12] tells us that "underlying the drawing techniques is the wide and basic assumption that personality develops not in a vacuum, but through the movement, feeling, and thinking of a specific body."

---

[12] Machover, Karen. "Drawing of the Human Figure: A Method of Personality Investigation." *An Introduction to Projective Techniques,* eds. Harold H. Anderson and Gladys L. Anderson. Englewood Cliffs, N. J.: Prentice-Hall, 1951. Pp. 341–369. Quoted from p. 358.

In other words, the figure drawing is a representation of the self, or the body in its environment. The specific items that could be meaningful to a teacher would include the size of the figure, the proportion of its parts, the handling of those details included, the details deleted, the overall emotional tone of the drawing, the placement on the page, and the line quality and control. Several drawings over a period of time give much more insight than one single drawing. A very small figure usually represents the small, inadequate feelings that a child has about himself. He sees himself as of little consequence and feels lost in his environment. Many times the figures will be slanted on the page and give a drifting or floating effect. This can be symbolic of the child who feels little attachment with his environment. A very large drawing that touches or almost touches the top and bottom of the page often comes from a child who feels hemmed in or threatened by his surroundings. He is crowded, unable to expand.

The head is usually drawn first and receives the greatest amount of attention and detail. It contains the features most essential for communication. Thus social needs and responsiveness are reflected in this section of the drawing. A disproportionately large head is frequently found in the drawings of children who are having difficulty with the functions for which the head has significance, namely, mentally retarded children or underachievers. The general facial expression gives the emotional tone to the drawing. A smiling face, a sad mouth, a bewildered expression, a face with prominent nostrils and clearly defined teeth are, respectively, possible expressions of feelings of happiness, sadness, frustration, and hostility. Sometimes observable behavior is not consistent with the inner feelings revealed in the drawing. This is particularly true of hostile and aggressive feelings, which are not acceptable in our society and which the child learns early in life to repress. Hostile feelings are often expressed in devious ways, for example, teasing, sneaking, irritating activities. Sometimes only in a drawing or a story will negative feelings be revealed.

The eyes, mouth, hands, and feet are the main points of contact with the environment. The majority of children seven years old and older include all of these features in their drawings. Their omission suggests that the subject may have difficulty interacting with his environment and the people in it. The inclusion of certain details at an early age infers an emotional impact involving the particular body part. The writer observed in the drawing of a seven year old what appeared to be knees, or kneecaps. This is a detail not usually seen in the drawings of children under ten years of age. Upon questioning, the subject said he had been hospitalized with a knee injury a few years before. The average child does not include ears in his drawing until he is eight or nine years old. Yet in working with deaf children the writer finds ears to be prominent in their drawings at a much younger age. The striving child tends to place his picture near the top of the page, while the dependent, family-rooted child will place his at the very bottom, generally adding grass or some detail in the environment to provide a feeling of attachment or security. A light, stroking line is often drawn by the insecure child. The light line quality can also be indicative of a low energy level. This in turn could possibly suggest depression resulting from feelings of inadequacy. Erasures and "work-overs" indicate dissatisfaction, while shading tends to denote anxiety. The initial response to the request and the sequence used by the child in drawing the figure are both highly significant. The hesitant, uncertain child who has to ask several questions before starting the task may be revealing his insecurity and need for reinforcement. Most children start with the head and proceed downwards. Some children, however, start with the feet and proceed upwards. Since the head is our most significant contact with our environment, this procedure can suggest that the child is avoiding this contact.

Another version of the figure-drawing technique is the request to "draw a family." Here it is important to note whether or not the child includes himself in the group. In addition to the points mentioned above, the relative size of the figures in the group may be of importance. If the child sees himself as isolated, rejected, or insecure in his family, the teacher can feel quite sure he will carry these same feelings into the classroom. Other drawings that provide insight into the feelings of children are their drawings of houses and trees.[13]

THE CASE OF VIC

Vic's grandfather was illiterate. His father is a large man with a strong, commanding voice and personality. He is successful financially and active in community politics. He is proud of his achievements and feels that anyone can succeed with enough hard

[13] Buck, John N. *The House-Tree-Person Technique.* Beverly Hills, Calif.: Western Psychological Services, 1956.

knocks. A child who does not achieve is "mentally lazy" and has not been beaten enough. Vic's mother hovers over him. In the sixth grade she was still tying his shoes. Vic was first referred to the school psychologist in the second grade for hostility, hyperactivity, and disturbing habits. He was referred again in the fourth grade for underachievement and severe acting out behavior. His teacher said he needed friends and was seeking them by punching, pushing, and bickering. In the sixth grade he was referred for underachievement and for direction in determining junior high placement. There were no problems of hostility in the sixth grade.

Following are Vic's figure drawings at the time of each referral. When drawing the first one he said he was drawing his sister. This figure suggests some anxiety and insecurity, but depicts a basically happy boy. The amount and kind of detail included were average for his chronological age. Intellectually, he measured average on an individual intelligence test. The smile is smaller on the fourth-grade drawing, there are no pupils in the eyes, and there is less detail than in the second-grade drawing. His difficulty in interpersonal relations is suggested and withdrawal tendencies are indicated. Stories in response to pictures in the fourth grade indicated that Vic saw adults as powerful and mad. The father characters in his stories were capable and to be respected. The small characters were sad most of the time and resolved their conflicts by running away or setting fires.

It is interesting to note that the sixth-grade picture has basically the same amount of detail as the second-grade picture. According to Harris,[14] some indication of intellectual ability is given by the amount of detail a child includes in his pictures. As the child develops, the details increase. If scored by the Harris-Goodenough scale,[15] Vic's sixth-grade picture would indicate lower intelligence than the second-grade picture and thus could suggest a deterioration in intellectual functioning. The later drawing probably reflects accurately his functioning ability, not his innate potential. The facial expression in the second-grade picture suggests a happier feeling than the expression in the sixth-grade drawing.

[14] Harris, Dale B. *Children's Drawings as Measures of Intellectual Ability*. New York: Harcourt, Brace and World, 1963.
[15] Ibid., pp. 294–301.

Fig. 1. Second Grade

Fig. 2.   Fourth Grade

Fig. 3. Sixth Grade

Over the years, with family and school pressure, Vic's acting out behavior changed to withdrawal behavior, which is easier to live with and more acceptable. Although repeated recommendations for professional help were made, the parents continued the same pattern four years after the original referral while "looking for him to get out of his lethargy." The steady deterioration of the intellectual functioning level and self concept are well depicted in these three figure drawings made over the four-year span.

Sentence Completion. A projective particularly applicable to classroom use is sentence completion. This is a semistructured technique which requires the subject to complete sentences for which a stem of one or more words is supplied. He is instructed to answer quickly with the first thought that comes to mind upon hearing or reading the given stem. The technique is flexible and can be adapted to a variety of purposes. Teachers can construct their own forms to tap feelings about classroom procedures and personal attitudes. An innovative teacher trying new approaches can note changes in student reactions by using a sentence completion form periodically during the year.

Administration and scoring time are shorter than for most projectives. Multilevel interpretation is possible depending upon the examiner's clinical experience. In studying the responses of a class, the teacher can readily spot the unusual or bizarre answers. Group administration from the third grade on is relatively efficient. Prior to the third grade, individual administration is necessary since undeveloped language skills and the sheer mechanics of writing interfere with the child's ability to get his thoughts on paper. Disadvantages of the technique include the possibility that precocious subjects will recognize the purpose of the task and respond with silly or defensive answers.

The technique mainly reveals the subject's conscious concerns, fears, wishes, attitudes, and feelings. For both children and teen-agers these can be greatly influenced by immediate circumstances. The same projective given at intervals will quickly designate which concerns are the result of fluctuating circumstances and which are fixed in the personality structure. The following examples are taken from the record of a high school girl who was very emotional about home problems. The instability of the home affected her grades, her friendships, and her own general well-being. With the help of an agency and two professional workers, some major decisions were made which provided some strength and constancy in the home. Three months later the girl responded to the same test. The responses on numbers two, three, four, five, eight, and possibly twelve are quite similar and tend to reflect feelings that were maintained over the three-month period. This is a good example of the consistency of the internal phenomenal state in expression. The other responses are quite different and seem to deal with vacillating feelings which are affected by immediate concerns and circumstances.

1. I want to know ..... how to make more friends.
  how to play the guitar.
2. People .... are usually nice but sometimes are unfriendly.
  can be cruel without knowing it.
3. A mother .... should take time to understand her children.
  is supposed to love her children.
4. My greatest fear ..... is a fear of heights.
  is a fear of heights.
5. I can't .... seem to improve my grades.
  seem to get the hang of memorizing.
6. I suffer .... when I talk to my mother.
  when I see children growing up in the slums.
7. I failed .... biology and math.
  to enjoy myself when I was at camp.
8. Reading .... is my favorite hobby.
  is one of my favorite hobbies.
9. I am best when ..... I can be left alone.
  I am with other people.
10. I am very .... upset.
  quiet when I am around people who don't like me.
11. I wish .... that I was born to a different family.
  I could play the guitar.
12. I secretly .... wish I was a different girl.
  wish I could lose 23 pounds.
13. I .... can't wait until I am old enough to be on my own.
  am going to learn how to sew.
14. My greatest worry ... is that I'll have to go home.
  is that I won't be able to be a nurse.

This subject cooperated by responding quickly on both occasions. When questioned about her previous responses, she did not remember what she had written and was surprised at the differences when the responses were read back to her. There were notable differences in her figure drawings and handwriting also. She knew she felt better and that her grades had improved, but she did not realize the improvement would be evident in these more subtle response patterns. A sample sentence completion form follows.

Incomplete Sentences

Name_____Date_____

Here are some sentences that are not finished. Finish each sentence as quickly as you can. Write down the first thing that comes to your mind. Be sure to express your feelings.

1. I'd like to_____

2. I am best when_____

3. I wish my family would_____

4. When I take my report card home_____

5. My father_____

6. Some day I will_____

7. A good mother always_____

8. I hope I'll never_____

9. I feel bad when_____

10. Children would be better off if_____

11. When I was little_____

12. I don't know why_____

13. If no one helps me_____

14. Some teachers_____

15. A sister_____

16. Instead of reading, I would rather_____

17. It makes me mad when_____

18. Some brothers_____

19. If my mother only would_____

20. At school_____

21. I am happy when_____

22. Most people don't know that I_____

23. I'm tired of_____

24. If I only had_____

25. I would rather_____

26. In a fight_____

27. I am good at_____

28. What I hate most is_____

29. I can't_____

30. Books are_____

31. I wish my father would_____

32. I believe that_____

Picture Stories. Another projective which is dependent upon a child's perception of his environment and is influenced by his judgments, values, attitudes, and feelings is the story he will tell when stimulated with a relatively ambiguous picture. Some stories will be rote repetition of something recently heard or read, but if imagination is stressed, most children are agreeable to creating a story of their own based on experience. Once started, children are motivated by the ideas that come to them and often express surprise at the results.

The Thematic Apperception Test (TAT), the Children's Apperception Test (CAT), both human and animal forms, and the Michigan Picture Test (MPT) are the clinical tools frequently used for this purpose. These instruments must be used individually and a series of stories is necessary to gain insights for clinical evaluation. This is a time-consuming task and it is possibly better oriented to a clinical setting. However, there is a place in the classroom for this technique. Suitable pictures for stories may be found in magazines, picture books, and coloring books. It is important to find an action picture, a conflict if possible, pertinent to a child. The resolution of the activity depicted should be unpredictable. This frees the imagination of the subject to develop his story from his own intrinsic motivations. The story technique is appropriate throughout the elementary grades. The response may be either verbal, written, or depicted in drawings. The children are instructed to begin their story with events prior to the picture and then to develop an ending. At the upper-grade levels the technique can be elaborated by requesting comments about the attitudes of the various characters in the story. At the kindergarten and first-grade levels a group approach has been successful. The children are asked to draw pictures which give their ideas of what happened before and right after the action in the picture.

Identification by the child with the small figure in the picture is usually assumed. The action precipitated and the role of the small figure in the story are indicative of the child's feelings regarding adult-child relationships, peer relationships, or his ability to relate to authority figures and conflict situations. In a study[16] of first-grade children whose reading achievement was below that predicted on the Metropolitan Reading Readiness Test, there was a definite trend toward submission and feelings of inadequacy in their CAT stories. Achieving children told stories about small figures who became winners in a variety of ingenious ways.

[16] Bourisseau, Whitfield. "A Study of Non-Intellectual Factors in Relation to School Achievement of Primary-Grade Pupils." Unpublished Master's thesis, Kent (Ohio) State University, 1964.

Children with expressive language problems or motor problems will probably have difficulty with this method. Cognitive involvement is limited when the mechanics of writing tires the child to the point of limiting his motivation. For the best results, emphasis should be placed on story content and development rather than spelling, punctuation, and handwriting. An advantage of this technique is its use in emphasizing story sequencing—an important adjunct to reading comprehension.

Self vs. Self-Ideal Inventories. Based on the assumption that the stable, well-adjusting child is one that is satisfied with himself, inventories have been devised to determine to what degree a subject meets this criterion. A list of characteristics is given to the child, and he rates himself on a scale (three to ten points) that represents the degree to which he is like the quality named. He is then asked to respond to the same list a second time, recording to what degree he would want to possess the quality named. If there is a wide discrepancy between his rating of himself and his self ideal, it follows that he is unhappy with himself and hence has a poor self image.

A survey of the research literature discloses that when the self concept is measured, this is the type of device most generally used. As a research tool it can be quantified, and so it meets the requirements of a statistical study. Another advantage is that it is a simple paper-and-pencil, almost self-explanatory task that can be administered to a group. No special skill is necessary for either administration or scoring. A disadvantage is the structured format, which forces the child to respond only to those characteristics named in the inventory. Despite this limitation, it is a good measure for the teacher to use along with some of the other suggestions in this chapter.

Lipsitt[17] devised a form of the self vs. self-ideal inventory that can easily be used in the classroom. Inventories similar to the ones he devised and based on his descriptions are found on pages 100–101. This inventory is scored by giving a value of one to five for each characteristic depending on the degree that the child indicates. Note that there are three negative characteristics included: "lazy," "jealous," and "bashful."

[17] Lipsitt, Lewis P. "A Self-Concept Scale for Children and Its Relationship to the Children's Form of the Manifest Anxiety Scale." *Child Development,* 29:463–472; December 1958.

HOW I FEEL ABOUT MYSELF

For each question draw a circle around the number that best states your feeling.

	Not at all	Not very often	Some of the time	Most of the time	All of the time
I am friendly	1	2	3	4	5
I am happy	1	2	3	4	5
I am kind	1	2	3	4	5
I am brave	1	2	3	4	5
I am honest	1	2	3	4	5
I am likable	1	2	3	4	5
I am trusted	1	2	3	4	5
I am good	1	2	3	4	5
I am proud	1	2	3	4	5
I am lazy	1	2	3	4	5
I am loyal	1	2	3	4	5
I am cooperative	1	2	3	4	5
I am cheerful	1	2	3	4	5
I am thoughtful	1	2	3	4	5
I am popular	1	2	3	4	5
I am courteous	1	2	3	4	5
I am jealous	1	2	3	4	5
I am obedient	1	2	3	4	5
I am polite	1	2	3	4	5
I am bashful	1	2	3	4	5
I am clean	1	2	3	4	5
I am helpful	1	2	3	4	5

WHAT I WANT TO BE LIKE

For each question draw a circle around the number that best states your feeling

	Not at all	Not very often	Some of the time	Most of the time	All of the time
I would like to be friendly	1	2	3	4	5
I would like to be happy	1	2	3	4	5
I would like to be kind	1	2	3	4	5
I would like to be brave	1	2	3	4	5
I would like to be honest	1	2	3	4	5
I would like to be likable	1	2	3	4	5
I would like to be trusted	1	2	3	4	5
I would like to be good	1	2	3	4	5
I would like to be proud	1	2	3	4	5
I would like to be lazy	1	2	3	4	5
I would like to be loyal	1	2	3	4	5
I would like to be cooperative	1	2	3	4	5
I would like to be cheerful	1	2	3	4	5
I would like to be thoughtful	1	2	3	4	5
I would like to be popular	1	2	3	4	5
I would like to be courteous	1	2	3	4	5
I would like to be jealous	1	2	3	4	5
I would like to be obedient	1	2	3	4	5
I would like to be polite	1	2	3	4	5
I would like to be bashful	1	2	3	4	5
I would like to be clean	1	2	3	4	5
I would like to be helpful	1	2	3	4	5

The responses on these serve as some check on the child's understanding of the task and his ability to mark these in reverse. The scoring should also be reversed—a circle around number one following "lazy" should be scored as five rather than one. This same procedure is used for the self-ideal scale.

Q-Sort. An individual technique somewhat more complicated than the inventory is the Q-Sort, a valuable and insightful aid. The format most generally followed is that developed by Butler and Haigh.[18] (A thorough discussion of twenty-seven types of Q-Sorts, ranging from single adjectives to brief phrases or sentences, is given by Wylie.[19]) Basically, the procedure is to ask the subject to sort a large number of cards on which items descriptive of personality traits have been individually written. Once the cards are devised, as many children as there are sets of cards can work simultaneously. The cards will include an equal number of positive and negative characteristics and a smaller group of items which are neutral. A list of single words could include such descriptions as shy, confused, a failure, unreliable, sad, without friends, generous, happy, poised, tolerant, optimistic, tall, and strong. Whole sentences might include statements like "I am a happy person," "I am liked by most people who know me," "I am stronger than most of my friends." A comprehensive Q-Sort will consist of 80 to 100 items. The cards are to be sorted into nine (or eleven or seven) stacks which range from those descriptions he feels are most like him to those which are least like him. Those traits most like him are given a value of one and those items least like him a value of nine (or eleven or seven), with the others falling in between. When this is done and recorded, the same cards are arranged again according to the degree that the traits match his self-ideal. In both instances he is instructed to distribute the cards in a certain manner among the piles (larger numbers of cards in the center piles) to help later computations.

A correlation coefficient is then calculated between the two sets of scores. This coefficient indicates the relation between the subject's

[18] Butler, John M., and Haigh, Gerard V. "Changes in the Relation between Self-Concepts and Ideal Concepts." *Psychotherapy and Personality Change*, eds. Carl R. Rogers and Rosalind F. Dymond. Chicago: University of Chicago Press, 1954. Pp. 55–75.

[19] Wylie, op. cit. (n. 8), pp. 41–64.

self description (how he sees himself) and his self ideal (how he would like to be). The higher this correlation, or the closer the subject is to his ideal, the better he feels about himself, which suggests a good self concept. The lower the correspondence, the poorer his self concept.

As with the incomplete sentence technique, the type of information gained from the Q-Sort is determined by the teacher's skill in devising the Q-Sort items. Depending on the information desired, the items can be designed to elicit information about peer relationships, academic achievement, or how the student perceives himself generally. The Q-Sort is best used with second-grade children and older. The subject needs to be able to read the cards and to have a good concept of the characteristic listed if he is to evaluate himself relative to it. It is possible to use the technique with younger children, but considering the time involved in individual administration as well as the necessity of limiting the number of items, other techniques would be more appropriate at the kindergarten and first-grade level.

Personality Adjustment Inventory.[20] A large section of this inventory uses a form of the self vs. self-ideal method. Eighteen characteristics are attributed to fictitious children by name (boys or girls depending on the sex of the subject). The subject responds to these characteristics both in terms of his self image and his self-ideal. Additionally, he is asked which fictitious child would be most acceptable to his father and to his mother individually. The responses indicate if the child is satisfied with himself and provide as well some insight into the compatibility of his feelings about himself with his parents' aspirations for him. If the child's interests and ambitions are different from those of his parents, conflict and its emotional concomitants can be suspected.

The Semantic Differential Technique. The semantic differential technique polarizes attitudes and attributes. The subject is asked to determine where on the continuum between negative and positive poles he sees himself.

The Hodgkiss Self-Concept Scale for Children.[21] The HSCSC uses a pic-

[20] Rogers, Carl R. *A Test of Personality Adjustment.* New York: Association Press, 1931.

[21] Hodgkiss, Eleanor B. (25750 Melibee Drive, Westlake, Ohio) "Hodgkiss Self-Concept Scale for Children." Unpublished test. © 1969.

torial form of the semantic differential model. The format is an attractive blue plastic board with pictures of boys (or girls, depending on sex of the subject) in activities depicting such polarized concepts as boy-girl, happy-sad, sharing-selfish, pretty-ugly, and kind-mean. There are fourteen such characteristics represented. By placing pegs in designated holes the child indicates if he sees himself as being "just like," "almost like," or "a little like" the chosen picture. The holes are numbered from one to seven with the completely negative aspect receiving one point and the completely positive aspect receiving seven. These points are added and a good self concept is represented by a high score. Small children are particularly delighted with the "choosing game" and respond readily. The scale is applicable at the nursery school, kindergarten, first- and second-grade levels. It does have to be administered individually, although once the child understands the task, the teacher can leave him to work by himself.

Preschool Self-Concept & Picture Test. Using the same basic technique, Woolner[22] has designed the PSCPT. This test was developed with the preschooler in mind; however, the author believes it to be equally effective at the kindergarten level. The PSCPT consists of ten plates with paired pictures on each plate which represent personal characteristics inherent in the cultural environment of each preschooler. The rationale for selecting the characteristics which are depicted on the ten plates is related to the needs, concerns, characteristics, and developmental tasks of preschool children, their parents, and teachers. A unique feature of this test is separate but comparable subsets for Negro and Caucasian boys and girls.

The children are shown the pictures and asked, "Which boy (girl) are you?" A second time they are asked, "Which boy (girl) would you like to be?" Answers to the first question represent the child's self concept. Answers to the second question represent his ideal self concept. The greater the agreement between these two sets of answers, the greater the degree of satisfaction the child has with himself.

Sociometrics. Within the formal structure of every classroom there is an informal social structure which is significant in terms of class manage-

[22] Woolner, Rosestelle B. "Kindergarten Children's Self-Concepts in Relation to Their Kindergarten Experiences." *Dissertation Abstracts,* 27:9; 1967.

ment and group standards and values. This social hierarchy is determined by personal attractions and repulsions existing among members of the group. A student's position, and changes of position, in the social structure influences his progress and development. A method for understanding this structure is the sociogram, which determines the "stars" and "isolates" in any given group. The "stars" are those children selected as friends by many of their classmates. The "isolates" are those rejected children who are not regarded as desirable friends in a peer choice situation. To get this information, the teacher asks the children to check from a prepared class list those classmates they would like to be with in a social situation and in an academic situation. For less than three dollars a complete kit entitled *Classroom Sociometric Analysis* can be obtained from the Educational Research Council of America.[23] This kit includes documented research, a bibliography, detailed information about how to administer and score the sociogram, printed forms for graphing the results, and excellent suggestions for interpretation and use of the information acquired.

Most teachers soon get to know the children in their class and feel they can identify the cliques, the most popular and the least popular children. However, research and this writer's experience indicate that while the teacher is correct in many cases, some subtle and surprising relationships always become evident through the use of a sociogram. This highly significant and informative technique has not been used nearly enough. It is easy to administer, readily adaptable to various situations, and applicable to every age level. Side remarks of the children are often revealing. Recently, kindergarten children were asked to choose those class members they would like to have sit at their table. One little boy, in choosing an especially hyperactive, difficult child (one both the teacher and the examiner thought would be an isolate), made the qualifying remark, "But make him a little bit further from me, okay?"

Like any technique, it is not 100 percent effective. A child can be socially amenable and accepted in the group and still have inadequate feelings about himself. However, it is relatively impossible to feel good about one's self while being isolated and rejected. If a child is an isolate on a sociogram, it is almost certain that he has a poor self concept.

[23] Myers, Eddie. *Classroom Sociometric Analysis.* Cleveland: Educational Research Council of America, 1970. (Rockefeller Bldg., Cleveland, Ohio 44113)

The teacher can thus identify some of the children needing help in social development. Periodic administration of the sociogram through the year is desirable in distinguishing trends in temporary and permanent social attitudes.

Although there may be some overlap, children usually differentiate between those classmates they choose as friends and those they choose to work with in some academic project. The first relationship is formed mainly for pleasure and enjoyment; the latter is determined by an objective to be accomplished, and the abilities of the peer are taken into consideration. A better analysis of the classroom social structure results when both socially and academically oriented questions are used. Depending upon the age level, examples of two questions are: (1) "If you could invite a friend to spend the night with you, which three [three to five] class members would you choose?," and (2) "For the purpose of grouping in the coming social studies project on transportation, with whom would you like to work?"

The success of the technique depends first upon the relationship between the teacher administering the sociogram and the children, and, secondly, upon the implementation of the results obtained. There must be friendliness and mutual trust, and the child must recognize some purpose for the question.[24] If the results are not used for the prestated purpose, the children will tend to be less cooperative another time.

The sociometric data provide the teacher with a basis for counseling students and with insight for better group management. For example, if the enthusiasm of the sociometric stars can be enlisted for some given project, the chances of its being accepted by the class are greatly enhanced. In grouping, it is best to put no more than one isolate in any one group and to place every child with at least one class member of his choice. Rather than separating cliques, a better procedure is to expand them by bringing in additional children who were named by one or more members of the clique. The subgroup should be sizable enough to resist pressure from the clique.

Scoring the sociogram is a simple process of recording the choices on graph paper. Once plotted, it is easy to see the number of choices each student has made, how many choices each has received, and which

[24] Dinkmeyer, Don C. *Child Development: The Emerging Self.* Englewood Cliffs, N. J.: Prentice-Hall, 1965. Pp. 60–64.

choices were mutual. When two students select each other a mutual choice is said to exist.

Periodic administration of the sociogram will indicate trends in individual and class development. According to Bonney,[25] some indications of class growth are: (1) an increase of mutual choices, (2) a more equitable distribution of choices of girls by boys and vice versa or between races or any other subgroup within the class, and (3) an increase in the relationship between more choices received and better academic achievement scores. A student who is achieving well and becoming increasingly popular in the classroom has identified with the objectives of the school and thus feels secure and accepted. Probably the most significant sign of class growth would be an increase in the number of students receiving mutual choices. In building a better self concept the value of one mutual friend where previously there was none is immeasurable.

Following are figure drawings by three sixth-grade boys (pp. 108–110); one was determined a star and the other two were isolates on a sociogram. The pictures are good examples of how the self concept is affected by social status (or social status affected by self concept) and is reflected in human figure drawings. The first figure was drawn by a well-adjusted, accepted, popular boy with an IQ 132. The second and third figures were drawn by boys with problems who had been rejected by the group. Their IQ's were 114 and 121, respectively. The exact ages of these boys at the time of testing were eleven years seven months, eleven years five months, and eleven years three months.

INFORMAL TECHNIQUES

Verbal Techniques. The younger the child the more open and willing he usually is to express feelings about himself. By listening to comments made to the teacher and verbal interaction with peers, the listener obtains insights into the child's perception of himself. Unsolicited, they offer many such statements as, "I don't do that very good," "I can't do that," "Susan's better than me." Some remarks can be candid and very poignant. One little child revealed to the writer, "They don't like me, they don't say, 'Hi'."

[25] Bonney, Merl E. "Report of Research in Three Schools." Unpublished paper. Denton, Texas: North Texas State University, 1968.

Fig. 4.   Star—Sixth-Grade Boy

Fig. 5. Isolate—Sixth-Grade Boy

Fig. 6.   Near Isolate—Sixth-Grade Boy

Conversation. When a child is engaged in conversation and asked, "John, do you think you read better than most of the children in the class, as well as most of them, or do you think many of the children read better than you?" he can usually come up with a valid concept of his ability. The child who has a distorted concept of his ability is the one with problems. The writer was recently conducting some simple screening measures with a group of children. It was obvious that one little boy was uncomfortable; his face was flushed, he responded hesitatingly, and he looked in general very insecure. He was doing well on every request but seemed to be unaware of his success. When asked how he thought he had performed, he was sure he had not done well on anything. Yet in reality he was performing with other children who were not able to respond as satisfactorily as he. His general feelings about himself were so poor that he was unable to judge correctly in a successful situation. The examiner looked him right in the eye and said, "Bobby, you did very well—in fact, better than anyone else!" He was an inch taller as he walked out on a fleece-lined cloud.

With some children a structured interview will prove to be more profitable. Most children are quick to fantasize and thoroughly enjoy the magical aspect of making three wishes. These wishes may deal with material things, family relationships, or hostile desires. Expansion and clarification of the statements is a good means of getting a child to talk about himself. Another device is to ask him to fantasize being an animal for one day and to name the animal he would like to be. In using this approach the teacher must be sure to ask why the child has selected some particular animal. One little boy said he wanted to be a dog because everyone liked dogs; another wanted to be a tiger so he could pounce on other animals. Equally effective is asking them what animal they do not want to be. One child answered that he did not want to be a snake because snakes are stepped on. One might wonder from such a response if the wisher had some feelings of being stepped upon.

Following are several other questions which naturally lead into a productive conversation. These questions can be asked casually of lower elementary children in individual conversation, or they can be used in written form for a class of upper elementary children.

What is the best or nicest thing that ever happened to you?
What is the worst thing that you can remember ever happening to you?

Would you rather be a boy or a girl? Why?

If you could be changed and be different from what you are, if you could be changed anyway you wanted to, how would you want to be changed? What would you want to be like?

Would you rather go to school or stay home?

When you daydream, what do you daydream about?

What things scare you or frighten you?

If you were going to a Halloween party what kind of costume would you like to wear?

How would you change your home or your family or yourself so that you could be happier?

Dreams are an important part of the lives of children and to some children they are very frightening. Given an opportunity to talk about their dreams, these children often come to see the unrealistic aspect of their fears. This also provides the teacher with more information about the class. An analysis in depth is inappropriate and unnecessary. In a general discussion the teacher might want to make such comments as "That was a happy dream," or "That was a spooky one." As he listens to the dreams over a period of time, he can identify by comparison those children whose dreams are sufficiently different or bizarre to suggest problems. If such is the case, consultation with the school psychologist or a clinical psychologist would be appropriate.

Puppetry. Except for a relatively few withdrawn, nonverbal children, the majority delight in the dramatic, make-believe quality of puppets. Often, the self-conscious, threatened person who finds it difficult to talk about himself communicates freely through the personage of a puppet. Hand puppets, rather than marionettes, are better for classroom use. These can be purchased or made by the children with socks or paper bags. In order to keep the puppeteer out of sight and the attention of the audience focused on the puppets, some kind of stage must be devised. One improvised from a cardboard carton, a high-backed chair, or a blanket nailed between two posts will work well.

To get the best results, characters should represent persons pertinent to the child—parents, teachers, and peers. The stories must be in the simple language of children, related to their ideas, and should be direct, forceful, and obvious. The action can be initiated by asking the children to enact the ending to a conflict situation posed by the teacher or to make a story entirely from their own imagination. If other behavior patterns indicate that a child may have a poor self concept, the teacher can further his understanding by suggesting roles for the child to play. This technique can be used successfully at all grade levels.

Autobiography. In the upper elementary grades an autobiography can be useful in providing clues about behavior. To be effective, it is essential to assign it as an exercise in creative writing, without regard for spelling, punctuation, or sentence structure. The same basic information can be obtained from the school records. However, the way the facts are perceived by the child gives information that cannot be found in the records. To get the best results, the teacher should specify the topics to be included, such as the child's description of himself, his parents, siblings, and anyone else who lives in the home; the type of family activities in which they participate; how he spends his time; what he likes to do; and what his ambitions and dreams are.[26]

Nonverbal Techniques. *Teacher Observation.* There are many seemingly unimportant aspects of behavior that can make a significant contribution to the teacher's understanding of the child's self image. Very often they go unnoticed or are accepted as an idiosyncrasy. Hence the observer is unaware of significant aspects of the fabric that is the whole child. A relationship has been established between children's drawings and their feelings about themselves. We know these feelings emanate from a system that is basic to all behavior. However, the relationship between this system and other modes of behavior is not as well defined. The same basic feelings that result in an inadequate figure drawing are determining all expressive (and nonexpressive) behavior to a greater or lesser degree depending upon the circumstances confronting the child. Any isolated bit of behavior may or may not be significant to the whole but it can be a clue that indicates a need for subsequent observation using both formal and informal methods.

Handwriting. Very often the child with a poor self concept will be depressed and his handwriting may be affected accordingly. Emotional

[26] Dinkmeyer, op. cit. (n. 24), pp. 66–67.

involvement may be energy draining and this in turn may be reflected in limited output. Line quality is sometimes light, sketchy, and indecisive. Koppitz,[27] in interpreting the Bender Gestalt Test, and Machover,[28] in interpreting figure drawings, both refer to line quality as significant. Depressed feelings can also interfere with a child's ability to maintain a consistent level of effort. He may start with a firm strong stroke that disintegrates into smaller, more poorly formed letters. The child who exhibits such a tendency may be one who cannot or will not complete a given assignment. Even though he may start well, often he will lose motivation and fail to complete the task.

Speech. Speech content and volume can be affected if a child for some years has held the conviction that he is inadequate. Meerloo[29] comments that "inflection, choice, and order of words are all related to variations of human behavior, variations of feelings and of thinking." Attempts to compensate for feelings of inadequacy may result in different speech patterns. Eisenson, Auer, and Irwin[30] relate the limited conversation of the "under-talker" to deep feelings of inadequacy and a basic feeling of a lack of self-worth stemming from childhood. They associate the "over-talker" with anxiety. A child may be reticent to speak or may speak slowly with limited and immature speech content. Conversely, the same feelings of poor self-worth may trigger anxiety, evidenced by a great need to reach out to peers and adults. This child gets attention in any way that he can, negatively or positively. He responds to any subject mentioned, and some not mentioned, with a verbal frothing that has little regard for the interest or fatigue of his listener.

Role in Free Play. In the elementary grades particularly, observation of the child in free play is productive. A periodic notation of each child's activity is a good technique for evaluating trends in social development. Only a few minutes are necessary to record such observations as: "Billy, father in housekeeping corner"; "Mary, the dog"; "John, watch-

[27] Koppitz, Elizabeth M. *The Bender Gestalt Test for Young Children.* New York: Grune & Stratton, 1964. Pp. 138–139.

[28] Machover, op. cit. (n. 12), p. 353.

[29] Meerloo, Joost A. M. *Unobtrusive Communication.* Assen, The Netherlands: Koninklijke Van Gorcum & Co., 1964. P. 48.

[30] Eisenson, Jon; Auer, J. Jeffery; and Irwin, John V. *The Psychology of Communication.* New York: Meredith Publishing Co., 1963. Pp. 350–351.

ing block activity"; "Susan, with puzzles alone." If over a period of time Mary is always an insignificant figure, John usually watches, and Susan consistently chooses individual activities, difficulties in social development might be suspected. A child who consistently plays alone usually does not know how to become involved with other children. When questioned, he will defend his position in terms of not liking the other children, or preferring to play alone. A child who readily dislikes many children is having difficulty in interpersonal relationships. This may reflect a basic rejection of self.

The same kind of observations can be made of older children during recess. Quickly note who they are playing with and what they are doing.

Conversation between children can also be enlightening. Comments such as, "Don's the biggest and I'm the next biggest," reflect a child's view of himself relative to one of his peers. The comment may correctly estimate the physical size of his friend, or it may refer to feelings he has about the relationship. If the latter is the case, and if this same attitude is prevalent toward many children and in different activities, then the frame of reference for most of this child's behavior is one of being second-best.

Muscle Coordination. Educators have become increasingly involved with those children who have difficulty learning by methods that are generally effective with the majority. To some degree, approximately 20 percent of all children have some learning problems, manifested usually in the language arts. One of several characteristics of children in this group is that they have difficulty in body management. In varying degrees, they have an impaired sense of right and left; they have difficulty in judging space and consequently they run into desks and stumble over their classmates; they have an impaired sense of spatial concepts such as up and down; their arms and legs seem to be extraneous appendages rather than coordinated parts of a working unit; and more often than not they have difficulty screening out visual and auditory stimuli, and hence they are distractible and hyperactive. They are clumsy, trying, and frustrating, but not unintelligent. Some of them score in the superior range of intelligence. They have difficulty with reading, writing, and spelling but often perform well in arithmetic.

As adults we have learned to accept our physical limitations. It is difficult for us to comprehend the consternation of and the problems encountered by the child who is unable to compete in the physical activities of childhood, and who is the object of laughter or ridicule when he awkwardly tries to join the group. By recalling the momentary panic experienced when we misjudge space in descending stairs, we get some inkling of the insecurity felt by the child who experiences spatial misjudgment daily. Accelerated reasoning development and vocabulary and greater development in other aspects of higher cognition generally do not compensate for poor body management at this age. For the poorly coordinated child with less intelligence the problem is magnified.

Bryant Cratty, Director of the Perceptual-Motor Learning Laboratory at the University of California, said that almost without exception, the child who has difficulty managing his body has a poor self concept.[31] For the teacher interested in learning the feelings of pupils toward themselves, a very good first step is the observation of gross and fine motor performance in the gym, on the playground, in competitive games, and when writing. The majority of children having difficulty in physical coordination need help in both developing these skills and recognizing their strengths and weaknesses so that a general feeling of inadequacy does not erroneously permeate all areas of endeavor.

SUMMARY

Increased study and concern regarding the failures in today's society (misfits, underachievers, delinquents) have developed an awareness of the great importance of the feelings that we have about ourselves. These feelings are as significant in determining behavior and success as intelligence, education, opportunity, or money. The concept of self stems from early physical and mental experiences. Home and school and their associated environments are the major forces in the development of the concept. These findings have made it imperative for the teacher to seek a more comprehensive understanding of the individual child in addition to teaching the traditional curriculum.

The self concept is difficult to discern because it cannot be measured. It is an inner system of feelings which is manifested in behavior. Hence the teacher is challenged to look at behavior in terms of what the child

[31] Cratty, Bryant J. "Movement and the Maturing Child." A talk given at Parkwood Elementary School, Cleveland, Ohio, February 25, 1970.

is trying to express rather than in terms of the positive or negative qualities of the behavior itself. The human organism is consistent in its expression, which means that feelings are indicated in the totality of the individual. Research, skilled observation, and developmental insights provide some tools for understanding. Because behavior is exceedingly complex and represents many things at any given moment, no one technique or single observation provides enough information. As in a detective game, each piece of evidence or information is a clue to be followed and substantiated by various other methods. Behavior can be the result of both temporary and more permanent attitudes. Periodic assessments over a period of time give the most valid information. Any assessment of the self concept should, however, be made with caution, for it is difficult to define and thus hard to quantify.

In this chapter appraisal techniques have been divided into formal and informal methods. Formal methods are the partially structured techniques for which there is some background information and normative data. Informal methods involve the observation of specific unstructured behavior. The informal methods result in more subjective appraisals than do the formal ones; however, any appraisal of the self concept tends to be relatively subjective.

The formal methods include several projective techniques, for example, the self vs. self-ideal inventory and sociometrics. The informal methods include suggestions for focusing on, and giving more meaning to, typical teacher-child encounters. They promote awareness of the whole child. This awareness is achieved by direct contact with the child in his environment. Interviewing, listening to his conversation with his peers, asking him to write about himself, and generally observing him in action in the room, on the playground, and in the gym, are among the apt procedures. The language of the body (eye expression, muscle tension, distance to others, etc.) also reflects a child's feelings sometimes more accurately than his verbal expressions.

Responsibility for the self image construct does not end with diagnosis or evaluation alone. The elementary teacher is instrumental during the years most critical in the formation of the self concept. He may be faced with the difficult task of compensating for a negative concept originating from the home environment. The teacher's responsibility then is to provide the parents with the advice and guidance necessary to bring about positive changes in the home situation. The following are some suggestions useful in both the home and the classroom for helping a child attain a positive orientation to himself.

1. Realistically assess strengths and assist the child in becoming aware of his assets.

2. When it is necessary to correct or discipline a child, do so individually, never in front of others.

3. Call attention to a child's strengths not only individually but also before others.

4. Establish an environment in which the child is genuinely respected, in which he is heard, his ideas are tried, and he has opportunities to share in real responsibilities, not tasks created to keep him busy.

5. Establish a permissive atmosphere which encourages the shy and withdrawn child to participate and which gives him the freedom to express himself openly. The classroom environment should be under continual examination.

6. "Methods of developing feelings of adequacy in the child through encouragement, love, and guidance should be utilized at all levels, and particularly in the elementary school grades."[32]

7. "Parents should be helped to recognize that each child is unique and functions in terms of his self concept. Ways to create better relationships between parents and children should be devised so that true understanding is promoted."[33]

8. Avoid abnormally dependent relationships with one or two socially isolated children by integrating the child into a group. Accept him, but don't adopt him.

9. Group participation rather than individual exhibition of skills is important for the isolated child.

10. Look, nevertheless, for opportunities for the isolated child to help another successfully in a skill, game, or school subject.

11. With concern and consideration, evaluate the suggestions of class members in helping the isolated child toward better adjustment.

12. The development of at least one mutual friendship is exceedingly important. An equal relationship rather than an unequal, dependent one should be encouraged.

13. Solicit the help of the parents in developing friendships by suggesting that they include other children in family activities and trips.

[32] Dinkmeyer, op. cit. (n. 24), p. 215.
[33] Ibid., p. 215.

14. Attempt to develop in the child a willingness to accept help from others.

15. Lastly and most important, a child's feelings for others is determined by his feelings toward self. Help him to accept and care for himself, his school work, and others.[34]

SUGGESTED READINGS

Bonney, Merl E. *Mental Health in Education.* Boston: Allyn and Bacon, 1960. Directed to teachers, this book attempts to provide for them a wide variety of materials that bear on the total development of children from kindergarten through high school. All areas of mental health are covered well.

Combs, Arthur W. (ed.). *Perceiving, Behaving, Becoming.* Washington, D.C.: Association for Supervision and Curriculum Development, 1962. Earl C. Kelley, Carl R. Rogers, Abraham H. Maslow, and Arthur W. Combs have contributed articles to this yearbook. In the fields of education, psychology and psychiatry these men are outstanding. Their professional lives have been devoted to an attempt to understand how we can function better as human beings. In this book they present their insights and knowledge about how we can become more self-actualizing.

Combs, Arthur W., and Snygg, Donald. *Individual Behavior.* Rev. ed. New York: Harper and Row, 1959. The perceptual approach to behavior is seen as necessary to a better understanding of human behavior.

Dinkmeyer, Don C. *Child Development: The Emerging Self.* Englewood Cliffs, N. J.: Prentice-Hall, 1965. An overview of child development emphasizing both internal growth forces and external adjustment processes. A unique feature of the format is the interspersion of questions within the paragraphs to direct attention to the important points.

Dreikurs, Rudolf. *Psychology in the Classroom.* 2d ed. New York: Harper and Row, 1968. Part I presents a theoretical premise for the application of the psychological approach in the classroom. Part II describes

---

[34] Myers, op. cit. (n. 23), pp. 21–22.

actual everyday classroom problems and correct and incorrect attempts to solve them. Many effective procedures are presented.

Glasser, William. *Schools Without Failure.* New York: Harper and Row, 1969. A critical analysis of the role that education itself has played in causing students to fail. Glasser gives definite suggestions and examples for establishing classroom environments in which learning can take place in a positive atmosphere.

Raths, Louis E., and Harmin, Merrill. *Values and Teaching.* Columbus, Ohio: Charles E. Merrill, 1966. For the teacher who is interested in helping her children learn more about their values, this is an excellent book. It includes both a discussion of values and many practical suggestions for implementing this learning. An outstanding book on a difficult subject.

FIVE · THE BRUISED SELF:

MENDING IN EARLY YEARS

Robert and Evelyn Kirkhart

We have met the enemy, and he is us!

POGO

Skinned knees, cuts, even a hard bump on the head or a broken arm are more or less tolerated by concerned adults as part of the process of growing up. When the necessity arises, we tend to feel able to respond promptly to youngsters' problems of this nature on a surprisingly large number of occasions. Either our own past experience tells us that intelligently administered tenderness plus soap and water is all the assist the child needs, or we hurry him off to the doctor for the specialized treatment we are unable to provide by ourselves. We usually can assess need appropriately in such physical problems of childhood. Not only have we "been there" ourselves, in many cases, but our society educates us fairly specifically in first aid to the physically injured. What is more, a pragmatic test reinforces what we have learned. That is, it works: the skinned knee stops hurting after it is treated and begins to heal; infection is limited; bones grow straight again after we see to it that they are set properly; and so on. Conflicting theories of disease or injury which would confuse our immediate response do not bother most of us. Thinking that perhaps an angry god was being appeased or that the child was being punished for prior wickedness for which suffering should be encouraged is not part of our way of life. We do not even allow our guilt feelings, over how we may have unwittingly contributed to the injury, impede us. We simply recognize the problem as it arises and act to restore wholeness of body to the child as quickly as our resources permit.

Think now, for a minute, how you would respond in the following situation: you are a teacher of a fourth-grade class. A child comes running to tell you that Danny, who is in your class, has just set fire to a wastebasket full of paper in the rest-room! What are you going to do, you wonder as you run out to find Danny, to deal effectively with this troubled situation? Are you as sure of yourself as if he had, say, tripped on the stairs and loosened some teeth? Most of us may not have too much difficulty in knowing what we might *feel* like doing to Danny! However, the appropriateness of our actions in terms of the child's inner problems may be something vastly different, and something of which we are quite unaware.

As the previous chapters of this book have demonstrated, identifying a young person's self concept is considerably more complicated than describing his surface, physical appearance. Correspondingly, it is not difficult to understand why manuals of psychic "first aid" have been slow in appearing. Modern psychology is about one hundred years behind physical medicine in making an impact on the decisions of the average person. Furthermore, competing theories, fads, and terminology evolving from this relatively recently organized body of knowledge have confused and bewildered almost as often as they have provided answers to problems. In fact, some professional psychologists have felt so keenly the limitations due to the huge gaps in knowledge about people they have strongly urged psychologists to "stay in the lab" for quite a while yet. It is with remonstrations of this type in mind that the prescriptions for dealing with "bruises" to the self in young children are presented in the following pages. The necessity for maintaining openness to new findings regarding some of the specifics which we will be discussing cannot be emphasized too much. Considerable research support is available for some of the assumptions and recommendations which we have incorporated. However, we have relied primarily upon actual work with children and the significant others in their lives to present a sketch of what can be done to help troubled people. To withhold knowledge of techniques and insights which have been found to be effective because "the data are not all in yet," seems as foolhardy and insensitive as allowing a child to bleed to death because the most sanitary and technologically sophisticated materials are not at hand to stop the bleeding.

The fact of the matter, of course, is that all of us who are grown bear scars of psychological wounds inflicted in early childhood. We have been lucky. Events somehow occurred along the way which enabled us to heal over and grow up enough to function reasonably well in the adult world. Perhaps you have visited a mental hospital or have relatives or know of individuals who were not so fortunate, however. The early bruises were allowed to fester and be compounded and have become such a source of difficulty for these individuals that the stress of normal living is intolerable. One of the most impressive aspects of clinical psychological work is the much greater ease with which psychic wounds can be treated and helped to mend in children during their early years of development, as contrasted with adolescents or, especially, older adults. Not only are the wounding conditions more easily isolated, but the environment is generally more flexible and simple, and the drive toward wholeness and growth appears maximal.

PSYCHOLOGICAL PATHOGENS

In viewing the matter of mending bruises to the self system, of which the self concept may be regarded as a reflection, it seems helpful to pursue the analogy to physical trauma a bit further. We know, for instance, that certain conditions predispose a child to injury. They are what the physician refers to as *pathogenic* conditions. For example, a youngster's chances of being struck by a car increase in proportion to the amount of traffic on the street in which he is playing; he is more likely to fall prey to disease germs if he is kept chronically ill-fed and fatigued; solitary play around deep water when swimming skills have not been mastered increases the chances of the child's falling victim to a drowning accident. Similarly, it has been noted that certain conditions which occur in the lives of children produce psychic distress, with the amount of distress corresponding to the severity of the pathogenic conditions. To be sure, the child has resources within himself which attempt to restore health to his environment. Very frequently, however, these resources are simply inadequate to deal with the crush of the events around him. It is for this reason that we have chosen to approach the

problem of "healing" by first taking a look at some of the more common predisposing factors to psychological suffering in a child's world.
When we want to think in terms of helping psychic bruises mend, we
begin by determining the cause of the distress that the child is experiencing and manifesting in symptoms. Therefore, some of the specific
pathogens typical in contemporary American life will be considered in
the next few pages. It should be noted at the outset that these pathogens
cut across social, economic, and ethnic boundaries. Some more than
others may be characteristic of certain elements in our society. However,
it is generally more useful to concentrate on specific features of a
child's life space when attempting to help him than to think in overgen-
eralized terms such as *disadvantaged* or *abnormal,* and the like. We
need to know what specific troublesome conditions our efforts can help
alleviate.

LACK OF CONSISTENCY AND LIMITS

One of the most widespread complexities which children encounter is
inconsistency. Adults are very often not consistent in their demands,
nor are they consistent in all cases with other adults. Mother and dad
and teacher and everyone else express their uniqueness as individuals
in a wide variety of ways which simply do not coincide with each other.
A certain amount of this is healthy and helps children see the pattern
for also developing as unique individuals. However, as with salt in one's
diet, because some is good for you does not mean that a steady dose
of a lot of it is better. In fact, chronic inconsistency is a highly damaging
interactive pattern which has led families, and teachers as well, into deep
trouble. Adults are often hypocritical in their behavior, and "Do as I
say, not as I do!" is the teaching technique attempted. Some make
threats in such an extreme or extravagant fashion that they feel they
cannot really carry them out, and the child is actually left with no
limits at all. Too frequently, adults do not share similar goals and
expectations for the children under their care. What tends to happen is
that when one sets limits for the child, the other tries to be a "nice guy"
and reduces or undoes the expectancy which the first adult had set up.
For example, mother tries to make up for father's harshness and "babies"
her son—and so father becomes more and more punitive to make up for
mother's "softness." Discrepancies between the values held by parents

and by their child's teachers are also common. School activities and requirements are openly criticized in many homes. At the same time, some teachers tend to consider parents more of a bother than anything else.

Adults frequently do not work together to clarify roles and to set goals and limits for themselves and the children in their care. The distress which the child experiences as a result of such inconsistencies in adult expectation is then compounded by the anger directed toward him for his failure to please all these different people.

Children do need limits, and they will test and probe to find where the limits will finally be consistently placed in their lives. If this point cannot be found, their own behavior becomes increasingly disorganized; and they grow more and more anxious, insecure, and angry. As Fritz Redl and David Wineman have argued in *Controls From Within*,[1] a child can develop internal controls, that is, can work and limit his own behavior along appropriate lines, only after he has learned limits by incorporating and identifying with external controls placed upon him by consistent adults.

OVERCOERCIVENESS

Some parents tend to be too controlling with their children. Usually these parents think the child needs their constant attention and supervision in order not to make mistakes and get hurt or waste time. Reasonable care gets carried to extremes. Nearly everything the youngster says, does, and experiences is checked and double checked. When mistakes are made by the child, a long lecture follows pointing out how much better it would have been if mother or father had been heeded or asked, since they always know what is best. The child soon learns that his own attempts to make decisions and to act independently must first be sanctioned by some adult. He becomes unsure of himself, fearful of novel situations, and constricts his efforts to reach out in his environment.

As a pathogen, such excessive behavior has tended to diminish in this country over the years. Glaring examples are still seen, however, especially with children of immigrant parents who are attempting to adapt to a new situation themselves, and with first-born children whose

[1] Redl, Fritz, and Wineman, David. "Controls From Within." *The Aggressive Child.* New York: The Free Press, 1957. Pp. 251–557.

parents feel extreme concern about making mistakes with their new responsibility.

PERFECTIONISM AND CRITICALITY

Carl Jung once pointed out that the best is the enemy of the good. Life calls for completion, not perfection.[2] Nevertheless, parents and teachers do tend to impose high standards for achievement on children. The goals which we hold up are often ill-defined and constantly accelerating. These vague goals aiming toward perfection are what Wendell Johnson refers to as "idealization."[3] However, since perfection is an elusive will-o'-the-wisp, its pursuit leads to chronic frustration. This, in turn, causes ever-increasing demoralization, depression, and despair. It becomes hard for a child to acquire a really good feeling about himself. He "knows" he should have "tried harder" or done "just a little better." He becomes a joyless child, always feeling that he has fallen short of the goal. Nobody else, especially inferiors, pleases him—and he is not pleased with himself. Unless the pattern is changed, the self-fulfilling prophecy might well be realized: he feels like a failure, and a failure he will be. The estimation of personal self-worth and social relationships suffer correspondingly. Julian Rotter has empirically demonstrated that a child whose expectancy of success is very low because of extremely high goals will predictably fail.[4]

Adults who are inclined to be perfectionistic are usually too critical, always expecting too much too soon. Hence, they find it difficult to praise. They tend to overlook the many small, positive accomplishments a child performs, and to focus too much on his deficiencies. This, of course, only serves to augment the youngster's feelings of inferiority and inadequacy, as well as builds up angry, resentful feelings toward the critical adult, whom the child perceives as demanding and withholding.

FAILURE TO ACHIEVE SUCCESS IN RESPONSIBILITY ASSUMPTION SKILLS

In all cultures children receive some form of systematic instruction in how to work and in how to be a potential contributor and provider

[2] Jung, Carl G. *Memories, Dreams, Reflections.* New York: Random House, 1963.

[3] Johnson, Wendell. *People in Quandaries.* New York: Harper and Row, 1946.

[4] Rotter, Julian B. *Social Learning and Clinical Psychology.* Englewood Cliffs, N. J.: Prentice-Hall, 1954.

as defined by the culture. Work, and the meaning of work, has changed so much for both sexes recently that even adults are confused regarding what direction children's instruction should take. Nevertheless, a great deal of a child's sense of adequacy hinges on his understanding of what his role in life is to be and how well he is able to master the specific skills which make up that role. Inability to comprehend and to play "according to the rules of the game" results in massive feelings of inferiority and inadequacy for children. Too often, parents and teachers expect performance from youngsters when not nearly enough structure, adequate teaching, and sufficient practice have been provided to assure the child of success. This sink or swim approach has presented some children with failure after failure in their efforts to cope with adult demands and goals. As Alfred Adler pointed out, no one takes to the worthless side of life unless he has first become convinced that he cannot make a go of the worthwhile side.[5] Lack of a sense of mastery and adequacy also results in inability to frustrate the whims of the moment for the sake of long-term goals. This was demonstrated in a study in which neurotic and ghetto children chose one candy bar "today" instead of the offer of five "tomorrow."[6] Success in school and in life generally, however, is associated with the mini-max principle: the adoption of a strategy in which loss is minimized and gain is maximized.

OVERINDULGENCE

One very common way to arouse feelings of inadequacy is to cater too much to a child's desires and whims. The insidious aspect of overindulgence is that the adult doing the harm is so oblivious to his error. Everyone knows when a child is being pampered and spoiled except the person doing it. Most typically, it is a good-hearted effort to be generous. What is being reflected, however, is the adult's desire to keep the child dependent and relatively helpless in order to increase his own power. This is, unfortunately, a very common motive of many people who work with small children. The goal of human interaction

[5] Ansbacher, Heinz, and Ansbacher, Rowena. *The Individual Psychology of Alfred Adler.* New York: Basic Books, 1956.
[6] Mischel, Walter. "Delay of Gratification, Need for Achievement, and Acquiescence in Another Culture." *Journal of Abnormal and Social Psychology,* 62: 543–552; May 1961.

should be *adult* to *adult*, as Eric Berne stresses.[7] This means that the superior "parent" role needs to be played down whenever possible in dealing with children in order to help the child come up to the adult level. This does *not* mean that the grown person should try to come all the way down to the child's level! Regrettably, many adults feel comfortable with children only when acting out one of these extremes.

REJECTION BY SIGNIFICANT ADULTS

Children experience rejection in many ways which do not "make sense" to some of the rest of us. A death, divorce, serious illness of a parent, even arguing between people important to the child—all these can be experienced by a child as severe personal rejection. Probably the most prevalent felt rejection is that of simply being ignored, which is the plight of many children a good bit of the time. Another common source of this problem, arising from the life style of even well-intentioned parents, has been identified as the "absent father" syndrome.[8] This has produced a pattern of difficulties which is shared by both the father-less ghetto child and his affluent cousin in the suburbs whose business or professional father is always away at the office or lecturing or attending meetings.[9] Optimal development requires the active participation of both parents, as Sears, Rau, and Alpert have amply demonstrated.[10] When this is lacking for any reason the child's efforts toward appropriate sex-role identity and his feelings of security are negatively affected. When mother is unable to feel warm toward her child, the outlook is particularly bleak. A disguise of overconcern or busyness will not fool the youngster, who feels so dependent on her for basic nurturance.

One of the big problems in this regard is that there are not many "substitute" parents available to children at the present time. Formerly, wrong or inadequate parenting often was counteracted by some other adult nearby. An aunt or uncle or grandparent, or even neighbor, might

[7] Berne, Eric. *Games People Play.* New York: Grove Press, 1964.

[8] Lerner, Max. "The Vanishing American Father." *Readers Digest,* 87:116–118; May 1965.

[9] Nash, John. "The Father in Contemporary Culture and Current Psychological Literature." *Child Development,* 36: 261–295; March 1965.

[10] Sears, Robert R.; Rau, Lucy; and Alpert, Richard. *Identification and Child Rearing.* 2d ed. Stanford, Calif.: Stanford University Press, 1967.

develop a special interest in a child and more or less serve as a mentor during his growing-up years. Mobility patterns being as they are, however, few children are so blessed today. Not many teachers and Scout leaders, with their numbers of children and annual turnover, can maintain a truly special relationship with any one child. In the vacuum of concern that is often the result, the peer group tends to take over as the dominant influence in the young person's life. As we have been observing over the past thirty years, this has been occurring at an increasingly early age.

IDENTIFICATION WITH ADULT NEUROSIS

It sometimes happens that children and their parents get along *too* well. Like father, like son is fine—unless father is in trouble himself! As a child's efforts toward growth and development continue to be affected by those around him, the neurotic qualities of the important adults can be, and often are, directly incorporated. This is a straight-line learning process whereby the child acquires or "picks up" the problem from the parent or influencing adult. In the clinic, we will often see a thin, tense, nervous mother—with a thin, tense, nervous daughter. The playground bully is frequently the son of a blustery, aggressive father who has defined his own masculinity in terms of physical power and violence, rather than work. Many boys will watch their fathers become intoxicated and then be physically abusive to mother, and will feel sorry for her and angry at father. Tragically, however, as adults they repeat their fathers' model with their own wives. Those concerned with the growing problems of drug abuse have stressed that the adults first turned to drugs in increasing amounts: to sleep, to stay awake, to keep from feeling pain, to relax—and as a result their children have accepted marijuana and other such drugs, which they view as "their own" to misuse.

PRIMARY IDENTIFICATION WITH OPPOSITE SEX ADULT ROLE

Establishment of one's sex-role identification is probably the keystone of the self system. This should be well under way in childhood with an ever-increasingly appropriate view of and desire for the adult role for which the young person is biologically destined. Nearly all small boys experience too much dominance by women at home and at school and too little time with men to feel gracious about pulling away from the feminine role. Still, most learn that they must do this, and so they "hate girls" for a while. Some boys are not able to effect this pulling away toward the masculine world nearly as well as others: mother is too strong, or too seductive, or father is too weak or remote or away. Pressures related to this inability can make life increasingly difficult for the "sissy," effeminate boy. Girls usually have an easier time of understanding and accepting the feminine role while they are young. However, a disturbed relationship with mother while being "daddy's best girl" can set the stage for trouble. Insufficient attention can leave a child feeling so rejected and hungry for affection from the opposite sex parent that he is nudged into seeking it elsewhere and becomes promiscuous in adolescent years. Unquestionably, the delicate balance between providing special love for opposite sex children and not over-doing it, and thus encouraging inappropriate sex-role identification, is not easy to achieve. It is apparent from the amount of discomfort and hostility felt by many adults toward members of the opposite sex or their own sex that this problem has widespread ramifications for a great many children. Some men still basically "hate females," and some women really hate men. Unfortunately, these same people may be, and often are, parents and teachers.

DISHONESTY AND DECEPTION

Someone once observed that only adults are permitted to tell false-hoods and half-truths with impunity in our culture. If father buys ice-cream cones on the way home with the children before supper and no one "remembers" to tell mother, the matter will likely be ignored. On the other hand, the wrong answer from young Mary to the question, "Did you eat cookies before supper again?" may very well result in a long lecture or a paddling. This adult tendency to maintain a double standard justly infuriates children. No one is fooling Johnny when he finds the empty whisky bottle mother hid so father wouldn't see it, or when grandma says, "Here's an extra quarter, but don't tell your mamma." The values of honesty and facing difficult situations without duplicity are badly undermined by adults in a great many situations. They rationalize it as "not wanting to cause trouble," "being polite," "saving money," "just wanting to get ahead," and so forth. Even though grownups do not like it when children become adept at making up excuses and being "sneaky," they often will engage in such behaviors themselves as they attempt to sort out the shades of gray in the adult world. The fact that dishonesty and deception are so widespread is evidence that they have much immediate reward value for people. Unfortunately, the high price of these practices often is ignored: decreased ability to cope with the difficult realities of life, involvement in an ever-increasingly complex web of deception in order to keep the story straight, and for some, an increasing confusion of reality with the fantasies of rationalization and self-justification. Depending on the kind and amount of stress in a youngster's life, the damage produced by this kind of behavior may vary from occasional guilt feeling over "white lies" to acute, psychotic, delusional states.

FAMILY STRESS

Sibling Rivalry and Competitiveness. When two fairly evenly matched players highly value the prize, the race is on. In families, the children may not be evenly matched at all, but if love, recognition, and attention are so sparingly provided that the children feel the need to compete for what little there is, the race is on anyhow. This is a primary basis for excessive rivalry, envy, jealousy, and similar behaviors destructive to family cohesiveness. Some children will begin to feel that they have lost out early in the game. They become overwhelmingly discouraged and refuse to try much of anything anymore. The viciousness of the rivalry between more evenly matched children can become almost incredible. It can also become a way of life. An only child with excessively aloof or ambitious parents will also suffer in this manner. One-upmanship is practiced and refined all during childhood by youngsters who feel driven to prove their worth as individuals. Our culture has tended to put a stamp of "OKAY" on these efforts and provides external rewards for competitive achievement. The blows to the self concept produced by failure, however, come hard. Another casualty, frequently, is the ability to work with others in cooperative enterprises. When one is on the top of the heap, others must be kept down. If your concern is "making it big," people in the way get shoved aside. This is not a pretty situation; neither does it produce pleasant children or adults.

Valid questions have been asked in educational circles about what kinds of competitiveness should be encouraged in school.

Communication Breakdown. Some parents never learn how to talk with their children. They give directions and orders, say "good night," and that is about it. Little wonder, then, that the children stop trying to talk to them after a while and a real communication breakdown occurs. The child who leaves his parents out of everything at ten is often the child who was told regularly to "keep quiet" when he was younger and more talkative. Good communication is basic to constructive problem solving and the working through of difficulties. Parents who do not give their offspring a model for communicating and talking out the problems that inevitably arise between parent and parent, and parent and child, do not give their children the basic skills needed as adults for marriage and effective living with others. Quarreling and bickering represent a breakdown in communication almost as self-defeating as silence. No problems are resolved when opponents attack each other rather than the issues.

Marginality. Children who feel less privileged than others come to think of themselves as being "out of it," and often for good reason: they *are* left out of things. Being black, Jewish, an American Indian, or "just a girl," are some obvious reasons for being left out. Economic insufficiency can produce a similar feeling. Beyond the level of reasonable necessity, preoccupation with getting and having money becomes largely a psychological matter. When a specific standard is very important to a family or to a child's subculture, objective standards are irrelevant. A child concerned about being poorer than his peers may be excruciatingly self-conscious. Social isolation can be painful whether self-imposed or caused by the actions of others. Many a child has been reduced to stealing something he valued because he had no means of obtaining it legitimately.

Instability and Breakdown of Family Unit. Some mothers and fathers have such a poor relationship with each other that they threaten divorce or separation constantly. A youngster in a home like this predictably will be nervous, insecure, and chronically worried. Alcoholism on the part of one or both parents, with its many and varied deleterious effects on family life, is widespread. Serious disabilities of parents, and severe mental problems in particular, mitigate against wholesome development. Psychological disturbance in any one member of the nuclear family disturbs the psychological equilibrium of the entire family.[11] Children are especially vulnerable. When family breakdown does occur as a result of divorce, separation, death, or institutionalization of a parent, stress and emotional difficulties for the children frequently become severe.

PHYSICAL ABNORMALITIES AND DEVIATIONS

Alfred Adler was the first to delve into the effects of imperfect or exceptional physical growth on emotional development. He pointed out how massive feeling of inferiority and lack of healthy interest in other people tend to accompany such phenomena.[12] Something as slight as a mole on the forearm can be the source of much concern even to a very young child. Pronounced physical differences need to be interpreted very carefully to children if serious personality side effects are to be limited. This is especially true of unusually high or low intelligence. A very bright or an especially handsome child often comes to expect that the good things of life should be his without much personal effort or investment and he becomes demanding. His counterpart, the dull or homely child, frequently expects—and gets—little in the way of rewards. Listlessness and apathy are common in such a child.

Improved medical technology has resulted in more babies with congenital defects surviving into the childhood years than formerly. At the same time, the depressive effects of malnutrition on physical, intellectual, and emotional development are widely known but have not, as yet, been removed as a serious pathogen in this country.

GUILT

One of the by-products of anger and resistance is guilt. All children are bound to experience these feelings eventually, of course, as they

[11] Berelson, Bernard, and Steiner, Gary A. Human Behavior: An Inventory of Scientific Findings. New York: Harcourt, Brace and World, 1964. P. 316.
[12] Ansbacher and Ansbacher, op. cit. (n. 5).

come in contact with other people. When anger is directed in an intense way toward one person, such as father or mother, the child may find himself wishing that person harm or even death. Should harm or death actually occur, the guilt over these fantasies can become devastating.

Guilt stems not only from angry feelings but also from sexual feelings, which tend to be inhibited in our culture. In children under ten, guilt is especially related to masturbation and exploration of genital parts to which adults have overreacted. Guilt also frequently accompanies other culturally tabooed activities, such as stealing, dishonesty, vanity, and envy.

Some guilt is a normal part of growing up. Anthropologists point out that every known society has restrictions in the areas of hostility, sexuality, and dependency. Only limited amounts of these behaviors can be tolerated if the culture is to survive. The restrictions on these areas make up the morality of a society, that is, the code of rules which each child must learn if he is to become socialized in that society. The moral code has been likened to an anvil and the individual conscience to the hammer, with which a truly human individual possessing feelings for others, altruistic concern, frustration tolerance, and unselfishness is fashioned. Hence, the child who experiences no guilt will not mature as he should. An excess of guilt can become a serious problem, however, and the source of such symptoms as accident-proneness, self-induced failures, depression, unwarranted feelings of inferiority, and irrational fears.

SOCIO-CULTURAL PROBLEMS

We are currently undergoing a transitional period in all three of our major social institutions: the family, the school, and religion. The security and stability provided formerly by the limited changes in people's lives simply do not exist for most families today. Parents are desperately trying to sort out the important from the trivial in life, and the heightened confusion which they experience is passed directly on to their children. Moral direction has become increasingly vague, and many people have lost a sense of meaning in their lives. Anthropologists who have studied personality breakdown resulting from the weakening of group structure that accompanies rapid social change have observed heightened rates of mental illness, alcoholism, and delinquency.[13] This process of social reorganization is happening in this country now, and it is taking its toll in terms of generation gap problems, feelings of isolation and alienation, as well as antisocial behaviors. Erich Fromm asks about the mental health of our culture as a whole in his book *The Sane Society*.[14] He suggests that our culture has become neurotic in some areas because of its focus on consumerism and the tendency of people to relate to each other as objects to be used instead of appreciated and loved. He asks if it is possible that man, through mass production techniques, has become alienated from his tools, his skills, and his own sense of adequacy. Erik Erikson raises essentially the same issue in *Identity: Youth and Crisis*.[15] He feels that a society should provide young people from an early age with viable channels for their idealism. Otherwise, they will never develop fully into maturity and will not be able to focus on "generativity" and integrity. At the present time, little attention is given to providing young children with such channels.

Boredom has become a common feature of our times. This wears away feelings of initiative, dignity, and adequacy even in children. They are entertained with television and elaborate toys in the development of which they have had no part. Youngsters no longer tend to feel much pride in their own efforts to produce artifacts, for they learn that "nicer" ones are always available at the store. Time is usually scheduled for them, and when left alone they don't know what to do with themselves. They live in a world almost completely apart from the adults whom the parents would like them to emulate. Too often children feel like a nuisance to the busy people around them, and they are. Few opportunities exist for most children to feel much pride in accomplishment and adequacy in fulfilling a useful role.

As children mature away from the narrow confines of home and begin seeking friendships elsewhere, they might come to identify with a deviant individual or group, such as a delinquent street gang or a drug

[13] Hallowell, A. Irving. "The Sociopsychological Aspects of Acculturation." *The Science of Man in the World Crisis*, ed. Ralph Linton. New York: Columbia University Press, 1945. Pp. 171–200; and "Values, Acculturation, and Mental Health." *American Journal of Orthopsychiatry*, 20:732–743; October 1950.

[14] Fromm, Erich. *The Sane Society*. New York: Holt, Rinehart and Winston, 1955.

[15] Erikson, Erik H. *Identity: Youth and Crisis*. New York: W. W. Norton, 1968.

peddler. Much more numerous than in former years, such antisocial persons can have an insidious, rapid, and extremely dangerous influence upon the healthy development of young children.

The deleterious effects of population increase merely in terms of crowding are being suggested by the work of investigators such as Konrad Lorenz. His animal studies repeatedly show a rise in anger, aggressiveness, and biological breakdown as greater and greater numbers of individuals are confined in limited areas of space.[16] Edward T. Hall has summarized the implications of these studies for man if overlapping personal distances are ignored by social planners.[17] The effects of persistently being in a group situation are also being investigated. For example, Bruno Bettelheim has found evidence in studying kibbutz children that the price of greater social cohesiveness may be a reduction in the sense of personal identity and creativity.[18] Furthermore, the phenomenon of segregation by age and decreasing involvement in the adult world characteristic of American children—coupled with television's violent, callous, and superficial modeling effects—is producing increased alienation, indifference, and violence in the younger generation. This is markedly affecting all segments of our society, the middle-class children as well as the economically disadvantaged.[19]

Sudden, situational factors may further overwhelm a child. Examples would include involvement in a severe accident, extensive hospitalization, rape, or witnessing violence, such as murder or acts of war. Fortunately, at present most children do not encounter these problems, but the psychological devastation can be acute for those who do.

SYMPTOMS OF PSYCHOLOGICAL DISTRESS

It is readily apparent that the degree of wounding that occurs because of the presence of psychological pathogens will reflect the severity and compounding of the pathogens. Hence, predicting how likely it is that a child will suffer from a certain environment is similar to predicting

[16] Lorenz, Konrad. *On Aggression*. London: Methuen, 1966.
[17] Hall, Edward T. *The Hidden Dimension*. Garden City, N. Y.: Doubleday, 1966.
[18] Bettelheim, Bruno. *Children of the Dream*. New York: Macmillan, 1969.
[19] Bronfenbrenner, Urie. *Two Worlds of Childhood: U.S. and U.S.S.R.* New York: Russell Sage Foundation, 1970.

the outcome of a highway traffic situation: when the pavement is wet on a specific curve and the density of traffic is high, the chances of any one individual maneuvering through the spot without an accident are reduced by a known percentage. Just which specific individuals will become involved in accidents is not generally ascertainable, but as the factors predisposing to trouble increase, so does the likelihood that the person for whom you are concerned will be the next one confirming the statistics.

Let us now take a look at the symptoms of pathogens such as those we have been describing. What are the predictable outcomes of these situations? It is frequently noted that *symptoms* tend to be confused with *causes* in cases referred to a professional mental health worker. This causal inaccuracy on the part of parents, teachers, and other concerned adults confuses and clouds the contributions they could be making toward helping the child out of his trouble. For example, Danny's problem is not *basically* that he sets fires at school. Rather, this is a serious symptom of deep emotional distress associated with school, home, and the total world in which he finds himself. His needs for limits, recognition, security, and the like have been radically thwarted; and he is acting out in a dangerous but dramatic way, since other methods of calling attention to his anguish appear to have failed for him. This is not to say that the fire setting does not present a real problem for the child in terms of his future in school, other people's attitudes toward him, and so forth. That is precisely his neurotic paradox. The symptomatic behaviors that bring him tension release, escape, or short term gratification only serve to make him more unhappy in the long run due to the maladaptive nature of the symptom itself. A symptom must be viewed as a pull from the front as well as a push from the rear, as it were. Thus, a given symptom can be caused by historical experiences that push the child to give vent to frustration, tension, and anger; but at the same time it is purposive and future-oriented in terms of attention-getting, reduction of expectancy, or other types of secondary gain.

As in the realm of physical problems, we are usually unaware of the extent of stress to which a person has been subjected until his own defenses are no longer able to contain it, and he becomes obviously injured or sick. Psychological behavioral symptoms serve the same purpose as the symptoms of physical illness. They are like the warning lights on a car's dashboard indicating that the engine is being overtaxed for some reason or is suffering from a serious insufficiency.

A list of some of the more typical symptoms of psychic stress in childhood includes:

Accident proneness	Passive resistance
Attention-getting behavior	Perfectionism
Bad dreams	Poor peer relations
Bed-wetting	Psychosexual disturbances
Cleanliness compulsion	Psychosomatic problems
Cruelty	School phobia
Daydreaming, fantasizing	Self-abasement
Depression, apathy	Sexual disturbances
Defiance, sullenness	(exhibitionism, peeping)
Excessive emotionality	Sibling rivalry
Feeding problems	Shyness, introversion
Fears, phobias	Sleep disturbances
Hair-pulling, eyebrow plucking	Social withdrawal
Health or physical	Soiling (bowel)
preoccupations	Stealing, delinquency
Hyperactivity	Stuttering
Joylessness	Superiority complex
Lying	Temper tantrums
Nailbiting	Tenseness
Nervousness	Thumbsucking
Muscular spasms (tics)	Underachievement
Obesity (nonglandular)	Worry
Obsessive interests	

Please note that such a list should not be cause for psychological hypochondriasis! *Most children will manifest some of these symptoms at special times when things have temporarily gone poorly for them. The sign that the child is really in trouble is when several symptoms begin to occur together and they become time-spanning and situation-spanning, that is, when the symptom crops up again and again over an extended period and in several different contexts.* Some examples of actual cases in which a child has experienced so many pathogenic difficulties that symptoms of this kind have become serious may be helpful at this point.

CASE A

A child on the verge of withdrawing from reality into childhood autism. Kathy is five years old, a pretty, blond little girl of lower-income parents. She has four siblings, all several years older. Although the family was never able to get ahead financially and Kathy's birth was not planned, both parents appeared to have a genuine affection for her. Many areas of tension existed between the parents, however, and arguments were loud and frequent. Father, at times, was physically abusive to mother during their quarrels. Divorce had been considered but was rejected because of the children and especially the difficulties which Kathy had experienced. Both parents and siblings tended to overindulge Kathy and give in to her demands.

As a baby, Kathy spent nearly half of her first twenty-four months in the hospital because of a congenital hip deformity. During this period she was often confused as to who mother really was, the nurses in the hospital or the woman at home.

Her parents had been referred to the psychologist by a welfare agency, which helped supply funds for therapy when Kathy was four years old. She had been withdrawing from all social situations, showing increased reluctance to talk with anyone, even her sister and brothers. Although she had been toilet-trained completely by the age of two years and six months, she had regressed in this area and was again beginning to wet and soil herself day and night. She was extremely irritable, crying easily and having temper tantrums when not given her own way. She was also very fearful of new situations and people. She seldom laughed, smiled, or seemed to enjoy anything.

Attempts by the parents to enable mother to work outside the home and to help Kathy overcome her shyness and lack of sociability by enrolling her in a day nursery resulted in complete failure: she would either gaze vacantly at a fixed spot, not responding to any aspect of the environment, or cry frantically the entire period.

At home, increasing amounts of her daytime hours were being spent in a kind of daydreaming and vacant staring. At night she would have extremely bad dreams that involved people or animals chasing and hurting her. Nearly all of Kathy's symptoms had been in evidence for over a year and were increasing in severity month by month.

Note some of the more prominent pathogens in Kathy's life: her early lack of consistency in mothering and expectancy as she was shunted back and forth from home to hospital; early trauma involving pain and fear of repeated operations and body casts; feelings of rejection by parents when she was left in the hospital; tensions in the home; over-indulgence with consequent lack of skill in mastering her environment; identification with father's temper outbursts.

The treatment plan for Kathy consisted of helping her act out and talk over her feelings with the psychologist in a playroom. Although it was difficult for her to leave her mother when she came to the playroom, she slowly began to build up a relationship of trust and confidence with an adult outside the family. She was initially attracted to the nursing bottle and the toy guns, which she used to pretend she was shooting the therapist. After the third weekly session, she told the therapist in a very serious, confidential way, "You know, I don't *really* want to kill you when I shoot you with the gun." Her interest soon began to increase in other toys in the room. The goal in the early sessions was to help her feel comfortable with a new situation and adult by not causing her fear in any way, and to be gentle but very consistent. This was to counteract the trauma and inconsistency which she had experienced previously in her life.

After each of Kathy's weekly half-hour sessions, the next half-hour was spent with the parents discussing Kathy's need for consistency, limits and success in assuming responsibilities at home, and most of all, trying to alleviate the arguments between the parents. The toilet training regression was considered to be a reflection of Kathy's increasing lack of mastery over herself and her environment and an expression of anger toward her parents. The mother and father were advised to ignore this symptom temporarily and to try to remain as neutral as possible about these acts.

Mother was able to alter her ways of relating to Kathy and her husband rather quickly. As Kathy improved, mother was able to find paid employment and help ease the family financial situation. Father found it much more difficult to alter his behavior patterns because of his own very disturbed family background. Consequently, he entered therapy himself for a while in order to better understand his uncontrollable outbursts at his wife and to try to deal with his felt inferiority, which kept him from seeking better-paying work successfully.

Within a period of three months all of Kathy's original symptoms had disappeared. She began looking forward to the psychotherapy sessions, asking her parents when she could go to visit her "friend" again. Periodic regressions occurred when some crisis took place at home, but both the crises and regressions became further and further apart as a corrective emotional experience was maintained for Kathy and as her parents learned more adaptive ways of dealing with their personal and marital problems. Kathy began school a year later without incident and was described by the kindergarten teacher as a "friendly, well-adjusted little girl."

Kathy's great cluster of symptoms, heeded at this time in her life, served to alert those concerned about her that she was likely headed for severe mental illness. Had they been ignored, the prognosis for Kathy's ability to adjust to a normal life would have grown increasingly dim.

Let us now consider another kind of problem situation, this time less acute, but nonetheless one that can be pivotal to a child's future: underachievement in school.

CASE B

A child experiencing disabling difficulties in school. Ten-year-old Ricky is in fifth grade. He is the younger by about a year in a family with two boys. His brother is a very capable and conscientious student who does well in school. Ricky received a Wechsler IQ score of 130 which places him in the upper 3 percent of general intelligence, but for several years he has been getting mainly D's and F's on his report card. At school the teachers complained that he wanted to be the center of attention constantly.

Ricky stated that he thought his mother preferred his brother to himself, and the two boys fought a lot. Mother did, indeed, prefer the older child! Ricky was a bundle of constant activity and always was causing some kind of trouble for her, she reported. She felt she must constantly be on the watch to see that the older boy did not get hurt by Ricky, who was so mean.

The family had moved a number of times since Ricky was born because of the father's employment changes as a university teacher and researcher. Father was often away from home working on special projects or teaching in the evening. He was a small, passive man who let his wife run the home and children almost completely. The occasional exceptions were episodes of criticality during which he lectured the wife and boys on their shortcomings. Mother was a very attractive woman who related to people in a strong, assertive way. She tended to "mother" her husband, and to exalt him to others. Privately, however, she felt angry and thwarted by his lack of effectiveness in the family and unappreciated and ignored by him. Ricky resembled his father in appearance very much; the older son resembled the mother.

Ricky was referred to the psychologist's office by a neurologist. A school psychologist had suggested that some of Ricky's low achievement and hyperactivity patterns might have a physical basis since the parents were at a loss to know what to do with him. The neurologist could find no physical problems, however, and the family pediatrician described him as being in good health.

Projective techniques (see Chapter Four) for Ricky revealed that he was an insecure boy with intense feelings of inferiority and inadequacy. They showed his sense of self-esteem to be very poor because he could not find recognition and acceptance from either his peers or his parents. He felt lonely and isolated, and he filled his solitary hours with fantasies of heroic achievement. He said that he hated to look in the mirror because he was so ugly, feeling especially sensitive about his large front teeth. (In reality, he was a good-looking child who had overreacted to the uneven tooth development of children of his age.) He felt intensely angry toward both parents and viewed them as being potentially very harmful to him. The rivalry between Ricky and his brother was heightened by his feelings of being ignored and exploited in comparison with him. The tests also showed an overwhelming hunger for love and nurturance, which mother had denied him. Consequently, he tended to relate to everyone in a clinging, demanding way since he felt unable to act independently and take initiative without the support of other people. As a result of these test findings, it was recommended that Ricky and his parents receive psychotherapeutic help.

The goals of the therapy with Ricky were to enable him to better understand his outbursts of aggression and emotion and some of the reasons for his unhappiness, and to learn to talk out rather than act out his internal tension and anger. Also, the corrective emotional experience with an adult male figure as a special friend was directed toward helping him view himself in a new and less critical way: as a more worthwhile person. The underachievement at school was temporarily ignored except for encouraging him to explain how he felt about the situation there.

The goal of counseling with the parents was to help them understand some of their maladaptive ways of relating to Ricky. This included the father's aloofness in the family situation that Ricky had interpreted as rejection, the mother's transference of her disappointment with her husband to the boy who resembled him so much, and her open preference for the older brother. The parents were urged to correct their criticality ratio in interacting with Ricky. For example, it was observed that the older boy tended to receive rewards in the form of praise and attention at a rate of about four to every one punishment; Ricky, on the other hand, received almost the opposite treatment: he received the pathology-producing ratio of about one reward to every four criticisms. It was recommended that both parents try hard to be warmer, more affectionate, and more responsive to the small, good things that Ricky would do.

It was suggested that the parents individualize activity with the two boys as an antidote to the intense sibling rivalry. That is, father and mother were to spend at least one or two hours every week with the boys separately. This could symbolize to the child his worth in father's eyes, that he would take time from his busy schedule just to be with him. It also provided the boys with masculine identification experiences that were meaningful to them. Furthermore, the constant direct comparison between the two boys would be absent during these times for both parent and son.

Efforts were made to help mother become more aware of her rejection of Ricky and open preference for the older brother. In therapy sessions with mother alone, her anger toward her husband and parents was explored; and she began to understand how she had come to develop a pattern of withdrawal of love and affection when others did not meet her demands and expectations. Results of research indicating the need for nurturance from mother in encouraging young boys' achievement in school was interpreted to her.[20] Accordingly, her own role in Ricky's scholastic underachievement was discussed at length. In her weekly special times alone with Ricky she was encouraged to relate to him as warmly and responsively as she could. It was emphasized how very important it was for Ricky to choose and be highly involved in the activity himself, so that deficiencies resulting from her negative feelings toward him could be less obvious. A list of possible activities was drawn up with Ricky and both parents in order to facilitate the carrying out of this plan.

A work schedule was devised with both boys for tasks at home, and extra awards were given weekly for a perfect score. Failure to perform the tasks for more than three of the five weekdays included was to result in a previously agreed upon punishment which the children considered meaningful and fair.

In regard to the school situation, the psychologist discussed with the teacher Ricky's problems and needs for finding success experiences in the school setting. She agreed to work on establishing a four-to-one reward-punishment ratio for him, also. She further agreed to channel his needs for constant attention into more constructive lines by making him a classroom monitor to hand out papers and collect milk money. His seating arrangement was changed to include him with two studious but friendly boys who were asked privately by the teacher to experiment with befriending Ricky. The teacher was well-motivated to follow through on these suggestions because of Ricky's extremely disrupting influence in the classroom.

Within five months Ricky's grades had come up to a B average. Ricky, himself, said that he liked school better, and thought the teacher was beginning to be nicer. The parents reported the situation at home significantly improved. When the parents failed to maintain their high reward to punishment ratio or the individuated times were ignored for several weeks, progress was temporarily halted. Because of the parents' personal difficulties in following through with the therapeutic regimen, Ricky and his parents continued to visit the psychologist on an intermittent basis for a total of twenty-five interviews over a period of about a year. At that time a considerable reduction in Ricky's symptoms was

[20] Heilbrun, Alfred B., Jr.; Harrell, Samuel N.; and Gillard, Betty Jo. "Perceived Maternal Childrearing Patterns and the Effects of Social Nonreaction upon Achievement Motivation." *Child Development*, 38:267-281; March 1967.

noted, the result of more benign relationships becoming established with the people significant to him, and therapy was discontinued. He had begun to find certain areas of school work genuinely attractive, and he developed extracurricular interests which further augmented his academic interests. His grades rarely fell lower than C in any of his subject areas.

Although the solutions to Ricky's difficulties required the special attention of several different people in his environment, sometimes the situation is even more complex. For example, children who have physical problems can, and frequently do, have psychological problems at the same time, just as it is possible to have a broken arm and measles both at once. In the same way that the treatment for measles will not be sufficient treatment for the broken bone, psychological problems coexisting with physical problems must have separate treatment.

The following case illustrates how neurological difficulties can be compounded by pathogenic home conditions to produce a situation requiring special care.

CASE C

The convergence of neurological and psychological problems. Danny was a nine-year-old "charmer," an outgoing, skilled talker, and a manipulator of people. Although his intelligence was only somewhat above average, he made an excellent first impression of being very bright and witty. He was a small, slightly built boy who looked more like a child of seven. He had been evaluated by a neurologist because of his hyperactive behavior at school, which the teachers found very troublesome. The neurologist's findings were that Danny appeared to have severe visual-perceptual difficulties as well as the hyperactivity considered to be related to central nervous system dysfunction. The neurologist also felt that psychological problems were present in the child which reflected difficulties at home. Medication was tried for two years, but was not found to be helpful.

Two years after the referral had been made to the psychologist's office by the neurologist, Danny was at last brought in for a detailed study. During the interim, mother and father had been seeing a psychiatrist regarding their own emotional problems. Two months prior to Danny's first appointment, the father rather suddenly developed lung cancer and died. Following this, Danny's problems became acute.

Danny's presenting symptoms were: stealing from stores, friends, relatives; refusing to accept limits and constantly testing limits by doing things such as setting fires in wastebaskets and shorting out light sockets; making self-destructive threats, which included drinking Clorox and taking large amounts of aspirin; regressing continually in the quality of his school work; and constantly quarreling with and agitating his dying father. His deeply bitten fingernails provided mute evidence of the severity of his inner tensions.

Both parents had many problems of their own ever since childhood. Danny's paternal grandfather had been mentally ill and finally committed suicide. At the time of this death, Danny's father began drinking heavily and was not sober one night in the next seven years until his terminal illness. Nevertheless, he had been able to continue his job as head accountant of a large business firm, a position which he had earned after hard driving. It was a considerable increase in status over his own father's rather menial factory job. Both Danny and his older sister were quite aware of their father's obvious drinking problem. Danny and his father had bickered and quarreled constantly, and Danny told his mother he was glad his father had died. The father had openly rejected Danny and plainly preferred the sister.

The mother was an attractive woman who had not been to college as her husband had. They were married for twenty years, and in spite of their many marital problems, she found living alone after her husband's death very difficult. As a child she was very frightened of her own father, who also had had a serious drinking problem. Because of her father's alcoholism, the family had been quite poor and she felt intensely sensitive about this. She acknowledged that her own felt rejection as a child made her far too permissive, overly helpful, and unable to set limits on her own children. She was constantly afraid that they would not "really love her" if she were too firm and punishing. She and her husband had argued frequently in front of the children about her own tendency to be overly lenient and the father's strictness to the point of being brutal. Each would admit their excessive behavior, but justified his own actions because of the opposite extreme of the other.

The projective tests showed Danny to be an extremely immature, dependent child who felt rejected and deprived and very insecure. He saw everyone and the whole world as being ominously dangerous and destructive toward him. He was shown to be extremely self-centered, interested in other people only as a means to gain his own ends, and capable of being cunning, devious, ruthless, and even sadistic to achieve what he wanted. He operated psychologically on the assumption that "the best defense is a brisk offense." However, being a physically small child, he could not resort to physical power to manipulate and control other people, so he turned to the development of his verbal ability and wily personality to influence and "con" others. His tests indicated a strikingly advanced sociopathic personality for a child still so young, being well on the way toward becoming a sly, "confidence man" type of individual.

In therapy sessions with mother and Danny, efforts were made to correct the precipitating pathogens of: inconsistency and lack of firm limits; complete lack of responsibility assumption skills; lack of a healthy masculine identification; rejection by father due to his partiality, criticality, and death; and Danny's guilt over angry death wishes involving the father. Much of the therapy centered around a corrective emotional experience with an acceptant, nonhostile, nondestructive male therapist. From almost the first session Danny told his mother he enjoyed coming for the interviews because "a boy needs a man to talk to." To obtain maximum relationship value Danny's sessions were held in a psychotherapy playroom. While talking over problems and feelings he would often choose to assemble a plastic car model and ask the therapist to sit very closely beside him "to help." This afforded many opportunities for providing Danny with a high reward to punishment ratio for accomplishments performed. It also provided many opportunities for consistent gentle firmness in limit setting in regard to such matters as primarily talking about important issues, observing time limits, and cleaning up after his projects. Danny regarded each completed model as a prized possession, which he took home and guarded closely. "The models in my room are just like you coming to visit me!" he told the therapist.

As Danny and the therapist continued to work on relationship-oriented activities, Danny became more and more comfortable about talking over his fears, worries, conflicts, and angry feelings toward his sister and mother. A discussion of Danny's nightmares led to the use of his dreams in the therapy. He was intrigued to learn that dream symbols might mean something. He and the therapist talked about "befriending" his dreams, and they were described as "messages from the unconscious part of him that wanted to help him grow and be happy." He brought out dreams involving themes of anger toward nearly all of the significant people in his life at home and at school. Death wishes directed toward his father were very evident, as well as the burden of guilt which accompanied these feelings. Through discussion of these dream experiences as very real indicators of the way he was when he was alone in the dark hours of the night, he came to understand that these unacceptable feelings were a part of his personality. But, since these negative feelings did not alarm the therapist or result in Danny's rejection, he came to accept the idea that he was still a worthwhile person even with these kinds of feelings, and, as a matter of fact, that most people have such feelings, which are, however, neutralized by their capacity for love and concern for others. Consequently, he became less apprehensive and diffusively fearful of the world about him into which he had projected so many angry and destructive emotions. He became more tolerant of personality difficulties in other family members this way, too. One of his comments during a session was, "Gee, it's easy to have problems. I guess my dad had lots of 'em and that's why he treated me so mean."

Although his stealing continued for some time, he soon stopped stealing candy (which represented desire for infantile love and affection) and turned to more masculine objects, such as pocket knives, small wrenches, and flashlights. Efforts to curtail this behavior began with insistence that he return the stolen items to their owners with an apology for the inconvenience caused. Furthermore, his mother was advised to give him masculine-type chores around the home for pay so that he could purchase rather than steal his masculinity symbols. The fire setting and nailbiting subsided without being discussed in any way as therapy progressed and as he became less angry and anxious.

The focus of the work with mother was to help her establish consistent gentle firmness as a means of dealing with Danny's testing of any and all limits she imposed. Mother was quite dependent and needed considerable help in doing this. It was pointed out to her that giving in to his constant demands would only ultimately destroy him, and she must demonstrate her love and concern for him by no longer permitting him to be the dictator of the household. At first as she began to do this crises between herself and Danny were continuous. He told her outright, "Since my father is dead, I am boss of this house and you must do as I say!" During this period the mother called the psychologist almost daily on the telephone. She was consistently and systematically counseled to maintain her ground in setting limits but also to maintain a high reward to punishment ratio in relating to him generally by offering praise and affection for any minimal desirable accomplishment or act of self-control. After about three weeks of very stormy limit testing, the home situation quieted down. Mother began to feel more competent and optimistic that she would be able to win this major battle with Danny without needing to depend so heavily upon the therapist.

Mother made efforts at finding other strong male persons who could assist in Danny's masculine sex-role identification. Fortunately, two of her brothers lived fairly near and were interested in him. He was enrolled in Cub Scouts, and at the request of the psychologist, the school was able to place him with a male teacher.

Inasmuch as Danny had set fire to a wastebasket at school once earlier in the year and had been a troublesome pupil, the school personnel were aware of his emotional problems and were particularly motivated to cooperate with the therapist. The principal of the school at the time of the fire setting had called the psychologist to find out what to do about his misbehavior. The school was advised not to expel Danny for the incident as they were considering doing. Instead, he was shifted from his teacher, who was a nervous, high-strung woman, to a male teacher who was more capable of handling Danny's angry outbursts without becoming upset himself. The principles of consistency, gentle firmness, a high reward to punishment ratio, and Danny's desperate need for an acceptant father figure were discussed with this teacher. The severity of Danny's emotional difficulties was explained, and the teacher was advised to be as patient as possible and not expect immediate recovery. However, the teacher called back after only a few weeks to say that the techniques discussed had proved so successful that Danny had had no more defiant, destructive episodes. In fact, he had become something of a model child in the classroom. It seemed quite clear that the fire in the wastebasket was a reflection of Danny's despair at having a teacher who became emotionally upset and ineffectual with him in the same way as his mother.

Therapy with Danny, and the accompanying supportive work with his mother, continued for forty-two one-hour sessions over a period of ten months; at which time there was sufficient improvement in symptoms for mother and her family to feel confident of being able to cope with Danny by themselves.

"Rx" FOR SYMPTOMS

The cases just reviewed provide some specific examples of basic therapeutic techniques which have been found to help children with emotional problems. It will be noted that several general principles were common to the treatments of all three cases in spite of the considerable variation in the symptoms and pathogenic experiences of the children. These general principles may be viewed in much the same way that extra rest, proper nourishment, and fresh air and sunshine are considered basic factors in the healing of physical difficulties. Since these psychological principles are not generally as familiar as their physical health counterparts, some elaboration of the rationale for their adoption may be helpful.

CORRECTIVE EMOTIONAL EXPERIENCE

Victor Hugo's central character in Les Misérables provides a classic example of what we mean by a corrective emotional experience. In this story, Jean Valjean is depicted as a lad with a great many strikes against him who has come to consider himself part of the scourge of the earth. His life is transformed, however, by the influence of a kindly priest who takes an interest in him and helps him to feel like a worthwhile person. This is exactly what must happen when a child's self concept has become badly damaged: someone has to step in and provide that child with the interest, concern, and positive situational structure which will change his view of himself and his environment. In nearly all cases this needs to be a sustained, consistent effort over a considerable period of time.

Adults other than the child's own parents can be particularly effective in such a relationship.[21] As mentioned earlier, aunts, uncles, grandparents, a minister or Sunday-school teacher, family friend or neighbor, are all excellent candidates for being this one "special friend." One characteristic of a really good schoolteacher—the one teacher whom we remember as having really helped us is likely to be the ability to relate uniquely to each individual in the classroom. This kind of teacher takes the time and has the emotional energy to care about each child and his concerns, problems, interests, goals, hopes, fears, home life, and so forth; and he orientates his instruction to this knowledge.

Not only do particularly concerned adults serve to correct wrong or inadequate parenting, but they are able to increase greatly the child's sense of personal worth: it is as if children felt, "Mom and Dad care for me because they have to—but that other person must really *like* me!" Furthermore, adults of this type add a greater adult-oriented reference group for the child and help stabilize roles and values. A good child psychotherapist must be able to be a good children's friend.

REWARD TO PUNISHMENT (R-P) RATIO

Considerable emphasis was placed during the treatment plans in our illustrative cases on the reward to punishment ratio. The reason for this involves the two fundamental ways of shaping behavior. An attempt is made either to stamp in correct responses with rewards or praise, or to discourage undesirable behavior by punishment. Too much focus on punishment with children tends to produce undesirable effects, while not producing the desired results. In particular, punishment tends to cause angry feelings and often drives the behavior underground, where it continues at a passive-resistive, slyly hidden or fantasy level. It has been observed that a reward to punishment ratio that does not drop below four-to-one will help guide and direct a child's behavior with a minimum of these bad side effects. By rewards, we do not necessarily mean a quarter or an ice-cream cone, but anything that is ego-enhancing, that is, anything that makes the child feel good about himself and his

[21] Stevenson, Harold W.; Keen, Richard S.; and Knights, Robert M. "Parents and Strangers as Reinforcing Agents for Children's Performance." *Journal of Abnormal and Social Psychology,* 67:183–186; August 1963.

potential ability to master his environment, that helps him enjoy the rewards of capabilities, and that is a sign of the goodwill of significant adults. Thus, rewards include such behaviors as a pat on the shoulder, a warm smile, a statement like "That was fine" or "You really did a good job with that," or even a simple "Thanks." By punishments, we mean anything that is ego-reducing, which means that it diminishes the child's sense of feeling like a worthwhile person. A frown, stony silence, being sent off alone, deprivation of privileges, or a remark such as "What's wrong with you again?" would be typical examples.

We have observed that a reward to punishment (R-P) ratio of five rewards for every one punishment is about optimal in guiding and directing a child's behavior. However, when the R-P ratio falls down to only two rewards for every one punishment, neurotic symptoms begin to develop, especially those of inferiority and inadequacy and a generalized fear of failure. When the R-P ratio drops further to one-to-one or even below, the child begins to despair of ever winning the adult's approval, and hostile, angry, feelings arise. Predelinquent acts are often observed in children who chronically experience this R-P level.

This emphasis on establishing a specific mathematical ratio does not ignore the fact that there are qualitative differences in rewards and punishments. Certain punishments are obviously more devastating than others. However, for the parents and teachers who have the best interest of the child as their prime concern, and who are not basically hostile and destructive themselves, the R-P model can enable them to keep track more effectively of this extremely important dimension. For example, one mathematically oriented father of a severely emotionally disturbed boy, after careful deliberation, exclaimed in a choked voice, "Good God! My R-P ratio must be one-to-five hundred!"

Parents and teachers often ask a psychologist, "How should children be punished?" or even, "Should children not be punished at all?" Our answer to these questions would be:

1. Punishment *is* needed because the child needs limits, which must come from external sources until he can develop his internal controls.

2. These punishments and limits must be rendered consistently and with gentle firmness.

3. Punishments will only be effective if enough rewards are given

so that the child really wants to please the adult in the hope of securing future rewards.

4. Punishments are only effective when they immediately follow the incorrect behavior.

One additional problem that arises in conjunction with rewards and punishments is misbehavior in a manner that makes it obvious that a child is seeking out punishment. Even in these cases where it might appear that the child is "asking for trouble," he is still really seeking the reward of attention from an adult who has ignored or been indifferent to him and his problems. To a child, we often find that the best possible thing is to be rewarded. The worst thing is to be ignored, and in between, far closer to the reward end of the continuum, is the verbal reprimand type of punishment in which he is at least noticed. Thus, one of the strongest forms of punishment for a child is to be ignored, and the puzzled adult wonders why the child is being so petulant. One major problem for adults when working with children is "being present where you are":[22] maintaining an on-going sensitivity to the individual children in their midst, to their feelings, needs, frustrations, and goals.

CONSISTENCY AND GENTLE FIRMNESS

A central task in children's development is that of finding a "modus operandi"—a pattern of living and getting along in the world. If there is not some consistency within the significant adults in his environment, he will not be able to learn how to predict them and their response to him. As George Kelly pointed out, a person's personal construct system (personality) is based on his ability to make somewhat accurate predictions regarding life.[23] For adults desiring to help children through difficult situations, the primary objective regarding consistency is to determine the specific areas where consistency is markedly lacking in the child's environment. The next step is to proceed to alter the environment so that the child can come to improve his ability to predict the

[22] Steere, Douglas. On Being Present Where You Are. (Pendel Hill Pamphlet No. 151) Wallingford, Pa.: Pendel Hill, 1969.

[23] Kelly, George A. The Psychology of Personal Constructs. New York: W. W. Norton, 1955. I, Chap. 3.

confusing teacher or to please both parents at the same time or to cope with whatever the problem situation may be. In most instances this will involve working with the adults and communicating to them the conflicting expectations and incongruities which produce tension for the child. The success of this venture usually depends largely on the degree of motivation of the adults involved. Since the life styles of these grownups have come to include the inconsistent patterns, change for them may be extremely difficult and require sustained effort.

Ideally, serious attempts should be made by parents to achieve *intra-parent* consistency, wherein both mother and father strive to be consistent within themselves. The same holds true for the rest of us who work with children. If we set a limit for the child, we must enforce it. The goal to be maintained is *gentle firmness,* or what is sometimes referred to as "the iron hand in a velvet glove." In an age of flowering permissiveness, this may sound like something out of the Dark Ages. However, it appears to be the only way children can feel secure enough and have sufficient modeling experience to develop reasonable limits and controls of their own.

Inter-parent consistency is equally important for the child. Mother and father must attempt to work out their disagreements in expectations, goals, and child-rearing techniques if this is to be achieved. This should *not* be done in front of the children! Arguments and discussions of this type usually serve to provide children with ammunition which they will later use to play one parent off against the other in order to get their own way. If parents are unable to do this privately by themselves, they should seriously consider employing the help of a trained, neutral person such as a minister or counselor.

No parent can expect good school performance from a child who hears the teacher being lampooned and disparaged at home: his family loyalties generally are too well-entrenched to be seriously undermined by the demands of school. In "blue-collar" families, formal education sometimes is not highly valued. A different pattern, but one which produces the same results, can be observed in well-educated families where the parents consider themselves brighter and more knowledgeable than the teacher—and say so, in front of their child. Teachers usually must work hard to open and maintain good communication channels with the home in order to reach agreement over discrepancies in values and work techniques.

One additional point of considerable significance regarding the setting of limits involves the age at which limit setting is begun. It is extremely difficult to change a youngster who has been reared for five years in an ultra-permissive setting into a well-adjusted pupil who can respond to the many limits which group instruction in school usually requires. Parents and other concerned adults would do well to avoid child-rearing techniques which raise expectations that cannot be maintained as the child matures. The earlier the child learns to accept reasonable limits, the easier it becomes for him to adapt to the requirements of interpersonal and group interaction.

MASTERY AND RESPONSIBILITY ASSUMPTION

In discussing the pathogenic counterpart of this principle, we pointed to the need which children feel to be useful, contributing members of society. Sigmund Freud's goals for emotional maturity were *"lieben und arbeiten"*—to love and to work.[24] One of the ways to help children feel a success in being responsible is to let them begin early working *with* a parent in various home chores. Typically, a little girl of five or six will want to help mother wash dishes or even help cook, and she should be given such opportunities. Mother can pull a chair to the sink and let the child help, and she should praise the child for the accomplishment, even though later, when the youngster is not present, she might have to redo some of the task. Fathers find, oftentimes, that a young child will enjoy "helping" him with home repair jobs by doing such things as holding tools or carrying items. He can systematically praise and reward the child for "helping work" and "being a good worker."

One reason that parents probably do not do this more frequently is that including the child makes the project take longer than it would if they just did the task themselves. However, the investment in extra time is crucial in helping the child develop an increased sense of ego-adequacy and a feeling of potential competence as a productive worker when he grows up. It is extremely important that the parent reward highly even minimal accomplishments as the child begins a new learning experience. The parent must remember that this is a child learning lessons in responsibility assumption and ego mastery. He should not be

24 Jones, Ernest. *Years of Maturity: 1901–1919.* Vol. II, *The Life and Work of Sigmund Freud.* New York: Basic Books, 1955.

judged as an adult worker would be nor expected to produce the quality, quantity, or speed of an adult. At the time of its emergence, each new bud of ego development is very fragile and needs to be nourished and protected by considerate adults.

As children grow they should be given regular chores within their scope of ability for which they have full responsibility and for which they receive praise and reward for accomplishment. For example, a shiny penny or a story read to him might be a nightly incentive for a three-year-old to pick up his clothes and put them away at bedtime. A few years later when he has begun to read, a work chart can be devised on which chores are listed with the days of the week so that accomplishments can be recorded. Rewards, punishments, and the jobs themselves should be discussed with the children so that all elements are considered fair by all parties concerned. This technique can eliminate the constant nagging and reminding which parents, teachers, and children all find so unpleasant. In making out a work schedule, children will often tend to have exaggerated ideas about what they can do. It should be kept in mind that the schedule is only a technique for shaping behavior by consistently rewarding the child for his successes and punishing failure. Hence, chores and goals included on the chart must fall well within the child's actual range of accomplishment so that failure experiences are limited. If the child fails to get his tasks done very often, the jobs and goals have been set too high for him. In such an event the schedule should be reappraised and made more realistic for the youngster. Incidentally, this technique can help parents and teachers become more aware of their own inconsistent tendencies in assigning work, setting goals, and providing rewards: many an adult has given up using a work check list, not because the children were uncooperative but because they themselves failed to be consistent in checking it and following through with the rewards and punishments.

POSITIVE SOCIALIZATION EXPERIENCE

Socialization begins with the child's relationship to his parents. Efforts must be directed toward resolving difficulties in this area whenever help is undertaken. This is very basic and usually requires the assistance of a well-trained specialist when the problems are severe between parent and parent, or between parent and child. However, adults not so experienced may serve to correct some of the home deficiencies, as pointed out earlier. A little girl who has good times with an aunt whom she admires will suffer a little less even though her own mother is very rejecting. Friendly letters can mean a lot to a lonely child. With other children in the family, a sympathetic outsider may be able to organize, on some regular basis, happy, noncompetitive activities such as hikes in the woods, picnics, and visits to museums or plays. The teacher in school is in an unusually good position to employ social interaction strategies designed to include isolated or "problem" children. The more seriously disturbed the child is, the more conscientious and persistent the efforts must be to provide him with happy experiences with other people. It usually requires some careful planning and ingenuity to keep activities from backfiring and causing the youngster increased unhappiness. For an individual with severe problems, it may be necessary to begin with just one other child or adult in order to help him learn to reach out without being overwhelmed. As confidence and positive social skills are developed, the circle can be widened. Consistent efforts need to be made to enable the child with difficulties to view the world as a more benign and friendly place. He must especially be encouraged to develop feelings of empathy and sympathy for others, and he should be praised and rewarded for any small acts of helpfulness and unselfishness.

TIME

One of the biggest difficulties which the psychotherapist faces in dealing with problems in children is impatience on the part of the parents, and sometimes, the teacher. Emotional difficulties and maladaptive attitudes and actions have usually taken years to develop, and these habitual modes of response cannot be changed overnight. No one expects recovery from a serious physical illness to occur in one or two days. The usual expectancy about the length of cure for emotional difficulties is not so generous, however. Too often, people react to a child's troublesome symptoms as if he should willfully curtail his maladaptive behavior on the spot, or else be regarded as a hopeless case. It is a sad commentary on the state of knowledge about mental health that parents tend to look almost hopefully to the physician when their child shows evidence of having problems. It is as if the outlook for the treatment of a serious or even irreversible defect such as a central nervous system dysfunction was somehow brighter than the outlook for dealing with situational factors and psychological problems in which the parents themselves are involved. We hope the preceding actual examples of children who were in trouble have made it abundantly clear that the opposite is true. Please note that the cases discussed were selected because of the variability which they represented, not because their treatment was exceptional. The time and effort that it takes for substantial changes to occur on a permanent basis, for helping the child feel like a worthwhile, useful person, can only be regarded as one of the best possible investments.

THERAPEUTIC SPECIFICS

Everyone who has anything at all to do with children under stress should keep in mind the principles of establishing a corrective emotional experience, maintaining a high reward to punishment ratio, being consistent and gently firm in setting limits, assisting the development of ego mastery and responsibility assumption skills, promoting positive socialization experiences, and maintaining a reasonable time expectancy. However, a multitude of factors exist in the life of each child which are unique to him alone. It is due to these specifics that one youngster becomes a bed-wetter and another steals or becomes an underachiever in school. There is a great danger in focusing too much on the presenting symptoms alone, however. The general principles outlined above should be given primary emphasis in attempts to help children out of their troubled situations. If this is conscientiously done, dwelling on the symptoms is not necessary at all; the symptoms will simply drop away as the child's underlying needs are consistently and more adequately met.

Nevertheless, parents and teachers do persist in their concern over specific symptoms. They are not always able to extrapolate from a more general overview of basic approaches, and they ask for concrete advice regarding the particular symptoms in the child for whom they are concerned. *Because of the unique aspects of any one problem situation, across-the-board answers are usually inadequate and may even be wrong. Furthermore, the literature on nearly all of the specific symptoms is considerable and constantly changing as new and more effective techniques for dealing with the symptoms are developed. It is not possible to provide a comprehensive review of this material in the general discussion which we have undertaken.* However, if these limitations are kept in mind, the following recommendations regarding some of the specific symptoms listed earlier may be helpful.

Attention-getting Behavior (Showing Off). *Don't* ignore the child. He needs more of your time and concern; that is what he is trying to tell you!

Do upgrade the quality and quantity of your response to him. Be less critical, distant, indifferent, and busy. Work to provide him with a better position in the family and school group, and give him much more recognition for positive accomplishments. Consistently punish misbehavior according to the gentle firmness principle, but be certain that a high R-P ratio is maintained.

Bed-wetting and Soiling (No physical cause). *Don't* punish, embarrass, or threaten the child for his accidents. He is probably already a tense, high-strung youngster who has underlying angry and resentful feelings.

Do see to it that he has a thorough medical checkup to make certain there are no physical reasons for his symptom. If none are found, try to find pathogens at home that need to be corrected, especially involving the child and his mother. If the child is otherwise happy and well-adjusted, try a conditioned response device for bed-wetting (enuresis) available commercially. Read William Homan's remarks on this matter in his book *Child Sense*[25] for more understanding of this problem.

Bowel accidents which are recurrent in an older child usually are indicative of much underlying anger which is being suppressed. The environment should be examined carefully to determine what is causing the anger, insecurity, and resentments—and these pathogens corrected.

Daydreaming, Fantasy, Social Withdrawal. *Don't* scold or isolate the child for such behavior.

Do look for pathogens causing him unhappiness, such as family tensions and criticality excesses. Make real life much more rewarding for him. Praise him highly for small accomplishments, and gently help him to develop social skills by having happy experiences with limited numbers of other people, one at a time if necessary at first. If withdrawal

[25] Homan, William E. *Child Sense: A Pediatrician's Guide for Today's Families.* New York: Basic Books, 1969. Chap. 4.

is so thoroughgoing that the child is reluctant to be pulled back into reality with increasing frequency, urgent help from a psychotherapist is needed.

Defiance (Smart-alec Behavior). *Don't* laugh, show anger, or otherwise reward his attempt at exercising power through poor manners. Don't provide him with a model for telling people off. Don't passively permit this to become a habit.

Do respond as neutrally as possible as long as the child is only "blowing off steam" in a harmless, nondestructive way and proceeds to do what he is asked to do anyway. For the more chronic and blatantly defiant type of behavior, firmly take the child aside and let him know immediately that such behavior and speech are not acceptable. Isolate him from others until he is able to control himself. Work hard to upgrade the R-P ratio for this child generally, however. Give him more responsibility and status in the family and school group. Encourage him to discuss what he feels are unfair, unnecessary demands placed upon him. Help him to develop social interest and a feeling of adequacy in helping others by encouraging him to help teach a child having special problems, assisting in helping another child who becomes injured or sick, discussing how other people react to unfortunate circumstances, and so forth. Help him deal directly and more acceptably with angry, resentful feelings.

Depression and Apathy. *Don't* overlook this symptom. When it is chronic and intense in a child, it is serious.

Do try to understand the child's life space. Be his friend. Encourage him to talk about feelings of loneliness, resentment, anger, hurt, and hate, if possible; and accept his statements sympathetically. Psychological evaluation by a clinician should be considered if the symptom is pronounced and persistent.

Eating Problems. *Fussy Eating:* *Don't* continually worry about what the child eats unless a physician has indicated that he is actually malnourished. Don't permit between-meal snacks and candy. Don't reward the child for this symptom by paying attention to his fussiness.

Do give him regular, well-balanced meals. Do increase the amount of attention he receives for desirable behavior in other areas a great deal.

Ignore what he eats and doesn't eat. Try to help him view eating as a privilege rather than a responsibility to the adult to clean up the plate.

Obesity (Nonglandular): *Don't* attempt diets without a physician's help. Don't tease, ridicule, or ignore this child because of his problem.

Do work with a physician on dietary regulation for the youngster and any other family members with a similar problem. Look for family-related pathogens which could be causing him basic unhappiness and insecurity, and work hard toward correcting them. Examine, especially, the relationship between the child and mother since food is usually a symbol of maternal love and affection, for which the child may have a great craving. Other obese family members should strive to overcome their own problems in this area in order to reduce the modeling effect of eating to reduce tension. Upgrade the frequency of rewards for positive accomplishment in other areas, and encourage vigorous physical activity which can help use up food.

Anorexia (Not Eating): *Don't* overlook the importance of a thorough physical examination and close, continued medical attention. However, psychological factors must not be ignored. Don't badger the child about his not eating.

Do regard this as a fairly serious symptom if weight loss is becoming severe. Try to ease tension and reduce demands upon this child. Include him in friendly, nonstrenuous outdoor activities such as taking walks regularly and talking about things of interest to him. Investigate pathogens such as overcontrol and family tensions needing correction. Referral for psychological evaluation is strongly indicated when medical treatment is not effective and the symptom becomes extreme.

Excessive Emotionality, Hypersensitivity. *Don't* scold the child for crying, but don't be overly solicitous, either.

Do try to reduce the inconsistencies, pressures, and excessive demands on this youngster. Keep things simple. Help him have success experiences in accomplishing chores and school tasks by assigning jobs well within his ability level. Pathogens responsible for maintaining his high anxiety level must be corrected. Be sure he has plenty of regular sleep and rest periods. Try to be as neutral as possible about his crying in order to minimize its reward value in terms of gaining attention, but give him plenty of attention for positive accomplishments. Encourage the development of musical interests or art skills in which he may be able to channel some of his emotionality more productively. If he frequently begins crying in a situation when laughter would be more appropriate, and laughs when the more typical response would be unhappiness or sadness, he is in need of professional psychological scrutiny.

Fearfulness. *Don't* make fun of the child's fears or force him into situations in which he will become terrified. Avoid being overprotective and pampering.

Do encourage this youngster to feel more confident and adequate by teaching him to make things, acquire skills, and perform useful chores for which he can be highly rewarded. Guide him into new situations gently, but encourage independence. Extinction of specific phobias may require the help of a psychotherapist.

Fire Setting. *Don't* overreact and become greatly upset.

Do take prompt action to curtail and punish this behavior within the realm of gentle firmness. Be sure the child understands the possible consequences of his act. Look for pathogens which may be responsible for causing him extremely angry and destructive feelings, and work toward their alleviation. Provide him with more acceptable outlets for his aggressive feelings through vigorous, large-muscle activity. If the child is a boy, make an effort to improve his relationship with his father and other adequate, male figures in his life. If other psychological symptoms are noted or the behavior is recurrent, clinical psychological treatment should be considered.

Hair-pulling, Eyebrow Plucking (The child's own hair or brows). *Don't* slap, scold, or embarrass the child.

Do try to ignore the symptom. Investigate possible pathogens in the home situation producing conflict, anger, and guilt feelings in him. Look especially for angry feelings toward father in the hair-pulling boy; look for an intense, but conflict laden relationship with mother in the brow plucker. Work to correct such pathogens, and strengthen the quality and quantity of the relationship between the child and the same-sexed parent. If severity persists, the help of a psychotherapist may be necessary.

Health Worries, Hypochondriasis. *Don't* fail to have the child undergo a complete and thorough physical examination. Don't exhibit excessive concern over physical complaints in family members. Avoid the tendency to dismiss symptoms altogether just because they may not have a physical cause, however.

Do explain the dangers of becoming a hypochondriac. Parents or other significant adults with overconcern for health and body functions should receive counseling so that the modeling effect on the child is reduced. Firm limits should be set on school attendance. Requirements regarding staying in bed all day without television, books, or other entertainment when school is missed for sickness should be strictly enforced unless it is a matter of a long convalescence from a serious illness or broken bone. Respond to illness in a kindly and attentive, but primarily matter-of-fact way. Give him much more of your time and attention when he is feeling well, and reward him more for positive accomplishment.

Hyperactivity, Hyperkinesis. *Don't* punish the hyperactive child by making him sit still for a specified length of time or depriving him of recess or activity periods. Don't confuse this child with inconsistent demands, or overstimulate him with a frenetic environment. Don't yell and make threats that you are not fully willing and able to carry out. Don't expect the child to perform work requiring an unusually long attention span.

Do simplify the environment for him. Set a model for calmness and consistency. Give him many useful but physically demanding chores at home and at school such as carrying things up and down stairs, emptying wastebaskets, raking leaves, gathering kindling wood, exercising the dog, helping the janitor, picking up litter in the school yard. Punishment for him might be having to run around the school building or walk up and down the stairs a few times. Do have the child evaluated by a pediatrician or a pediatric neurologist when hyperactivity is persistent, because medication may be useful in helping the child slow down and lengthen his attention span when there is a physical basis for the hyper-activity. Make concerted efforts toward helping this child learn to talk out rather than act out his tension and anxiety.

Hostile and Aggressive Behavior, Cruelty, Excessive Fighting. *Don't* give the child a model by being a hostile, abusive adult.

Do set firm limits on this child in a very consistent fashion, but greatly increase the rewards he gets for socially acceptable behavior. Maintain a high R-P ratio. Search for pathogens of inconsistency, partiality, rejection, and the possibility of overcoercive parents—especially the same-sexed parent. Try to engage him in competitive games and active sports in which his tension can be released less destructively. Encourage him to talk out his anger, and accept what he says without moralizing. Read Dorothy Baruch's book *New Ways in Discipline*.[26] Persistent and excessive behavior would suggest that psychological evaluation is in order.

Lying. *Don't* label the child a liar. Don't set a model for deceitfulness and cunning. Don't ask impossible questions of him, such as "What's the matter with you all the time?" and "Why do you always do the wrong thing?"

Do reward the child for telling the truth. For example, punishments for misbehaviors honestly reported to the parent or teacher might be reduced; whereas the punishments for behaviors lied about would be increased. Try to improve communication with this child. Read Haim Ginott's book *Between Parent and Child*[27] for specific suggestions for accomplishing this.

Nervousness, Tenseness, Nailbiting, Tics (muscle spasms). *Don't* put a lot of pressure on this child. Don't punish him by withdrawing love and affection. Don't subject him to noisy threats or a confusing environment. Don't call attention to the manifestations of his nervousness.

Do simplify things. Greatly increase the amount of warmth, basic nurturance, and affection that the child receives. Keep things quieter, more structured, and more consistent. Ignore nervous mannerisms as much as possible since he is undoubtedly already sensitive about them. Give him tasks well within his ability level and reward him highly for their accomplishment. Maintain high consistency and work to reduce environmental tensions, especially those in other people who are significant to this child.

Passive Resistance, Sullenness (Just not working; sit-down-strike behavior). *Don't* be arbitrary, illogical, overcontrolling, and inconsistent.

---

[26] Baruch, Dorothy W. *New Ways in Discipline*. New York: McGraw-Hill, 1949.
[27] Ginott, Haim G. *Between Parent and Child*. New York: Macmillan, 1965.

Don't set excessively high goals that the child feels little hope of being able to attain.

Do set fewer limits on this youngster, but be very consistent in enforcing the ones that are set. Be sure he completely understands and is really able to do the tasks assigned him. Help him to talk about other things at home and at school that make him angry, and respond sympathetically. Work out goals and assignments *with* him, and make some compromises to help him feel less defensive. Reward small positive accomplishments highly and frequently. Help him achieve a sense of greater freedom and independence by allowing him more real choices of his own, structuring less of his time for him, and trying to develop a warmer and less formal relationship with him. Use a daily work chart to help provide consistency and immediate knowledge of results for work assigned.

Perfectionism (Excessively high goals resulting in compulsions, rigidity, or failure). *Don't* direct unusually high goals and demands toward him yourself. He already has incorporated more than are good for him. Don't make him feel that he must work to earn your friendship and affection. Don't concentrate on manneristic compulsions such as chronic hand washing, and thus call attention to them.

Do be consistently warm and outgoing toward this child, especially when he feels he may have failed at doing something as well as he had hoped. Help him broaden his horizons, and spend time with this child just talking and exploring a wide variety of topics which he tends to ignore in pursuit of his usual goals. Help him have many good times with other people in friendly, noncompetitive situations. Work to develop his social interest by exposing him to details in the lives of those less fortunate whom he might help, such as by bringing homework to and visiting with a child with a broken bone, becoming friends with an especially lonely child, discussing in some depth the problems of a mentally disadvantaged youngster. Engage him in ordinary, earthy, routine work, such as disposing of trash, washing out wastebaskets, feeding and cleaning up after pets, in which there is no goal other than to do the job each day. Praise him highly for getting along well with and doing things for other people, especially his peers. Discuss his goals with him in a friendly, sympathetic way in terms of their effect on what he does and how he spends his time. Help him learn to know that you value him as a person regardless of what his accomplishments are. Significant adults in his environment who persist in stressing formal relationships and high goals could profit from counseling if they are not otherwise able to alter their patterns of relating to him. Keep work charts at home and at school so that immediate, realistic feedback is constantly available regarding his accomplishments, but do not encourage rivalry.

Psycho-sexual Problems (Effeminate boys, excessively tomboyish girls). *Don't* develop an extremely warm "special" relationship with a child who is not the same sex as your own. Avoid all forms of sexual seductiveness with children, including coyness and flirting. Don't reject opposite-sex children, but don't try to be both parents at once.

Do attempt to help the child develop his proper psycho-sexual identity by making certain he has a close, warm relationship with adults of his own sex. Ideally, the most important person to him should be his same-sexed parent. He should particularly like and feel he understands this parent best, but have respect and affection for the opposite-sex parent. In order to ward off tendencies for a child to become promiscuous in later years, he or she should receive plenty of love and attention from the opposite-sex parent; but care must be taken that this is not over-done. When a parent is absent for large amounts of time or otherwise unable to assist in this very basic task in the child's development, it is extremely important that substitute adults be enlisted to help. Boys often profit greatly from increased attention from male relatives other than father and a conscientious effort on the part of an adequate male teacher to be his friend. Woman teachers, relatives, and mother in particular should not disparage men whom the young boy admires. Rather, they need to promote friendships between the boy and men who are worthy of the child's emulation. Read Ostrovsky's book *Children Without Men*[28] for an elaboration of the problem and more specific recommendations for parents and teachers. Little girls whose mothers are rejecting or absent desperately need a consistent, warm, and nurturant female to sustain an interest in their development. Parents who are so close to their opposite-sex child that they feel reluctant to let go, should seriously consider psychotherapeutic counseling for themselves before the damage to the child's psycho-sexual development becomes extreme.

[28] Ostrovsky, Everett S. *Children Without Men*. New York: Collier Books, 1962.

School Phobia (Actual fear of attending school). *Don't* scold, threaten, or otherwise increase the child's discomfort over the idea of being at school. Don't emphasize his failures or past fears about this matter. Don't permit him to stay out of school while the solution to his problem is being sought.

Do investigate pathogens contributing to anxiety on the child's part. Is he unable to cope with some aggressive children at school or hopelessly mismatched with his teacher? Is he excessively dependent on an overprotective adult at home? Is he anticipating failure in the class work? Is he worried about mother's health or safety due to her physical condition or recent violent arguments at home? Check out these possibilities and work with the school psychologist if the problem is persistent. If even this does not help and there are other prominent symptoms in the picture, more intensive clinical help would be in order.

Self-abasement, Accident Proneness. *Don't* chide, scold, or overrespond to such symptoms. Do not reward maladaptive tendencies by giving them extra attention.

Do look for pathogens causing anger and guilt feelings in the child. Especially check out excesses of criticality, an aloof and rejecting quality in parenting, a tendency to overlook and ignore this child by significant others in his life. Work to correct such pathogens, and encourage him to talk about things that make him feel guilty. Help him learn to express the anger he must also be feeling in regard to these matters. Greatly increase the amount of attention and rewards he gets for acceptable accomplishments and behaviors. Treat injuries gently, but matter-of-factly. Work hard on helping him feel more worthwhile and cared-for as a child.

Sexual Disturbances (Exhibitionism, peeping, public masturbation, homosexual acts). *Don't* overreact. An occasional misdeed of this nature is common and usually the result of a young child responding to some information or misinformation that he has received. Don't confuse the occasional masturbation of normal development with pathogenic symptoms.

Do correct any misinformation and explain the limits of socially acceptable behavior without embarrassing or shaming the child. However, consider continued behavior of this kind to be a fairly serious symptom of emotional disturbance or an indication that the child has become a follower of a deviant group of usually older children. In such cases, a more detailed evaluation of the underlying significance of his behavior should be undertaken by an appropriate mental health professional. Masturbation accompanying the vacant staring of social withdrawal should be ignored, but concerted attention should be directed toward treating the withdrawal symptom.

Sibling Rivalry. *Don't* allow your schedule to become so full that siblings must compete excessively for your time and attention. Do not point out faults of a child in the presence of the other children. Avoid making invidious comparisons between siblings and the tendency to make one child a scapegoat or "bad guy" in the family situation. Do not give siblings parallel, competitive-type chores.

Do attempt to increase the R-P ratio for all children in the family to the same, high level. Praise and reward each child frequently in the absence of the other children. Let each child overhear you make good comments about him to outsiders. Individualize time spent with each sibling: mother and father should each take time about once a week to do something with every child separately that is planned out by just the two of them. Find chores for the children that can complement what other siblings in the family do. For example, a younger child can gather trash from the wastebaskets and an older one can carry it out and dispose of it. An older child can put plates and silverware where a younger child can reach them and set the table. Praise and reward siblings highly for cooperative achievements and give them many opportunities to do this. Punish both children *equally* when misbehaviors have been significant, regardless of who started it. Permit a certain amount of noisy argument between siblings without interference as long as no one gets hurt and it is not excessive. Teach them to attack problems, not each other, in their disagreements.

Sleep Disturbances (Bad dreams, difficulty getting or staying asleep). *Don't* overstimulate the child in the evening with television violence, family arguments, terror stories, or a power struggle over his going to bed.

Do be sure his sleep periods are regularly maintained, that he knows when the lights must normally be out in his room, and what are the acceptable exceptions to this rule. Enforce this consistently and firmly. Encourage outdoor, large-muscle activity during the day. Encourage him to discuss dreams, especially bad dreams, with a sympathetic adult who can reassure him that everybody has frightening dreams when they are troubled or angry or unhappy about something in the daytime. It should be explained to him that the dreams come from within himself and are a part of him that is trying to understand the complicated world in which he lives. Help him view his bad dreams as "friends" in the same way that happy dreams are, since in the bad dreams his unconscious mind is making pleas for help to the significant adults in his life so that he need not become so afraid. Learn something about the meaning of dream symbols. For example, children who dream of being chased or trapped by a spider often have problems with a mother who tends to be overly protective and overly helpful to the child. Children who have nightmares of being chased by monsters, robots, huge animals, or big machines, or snakes often have a fear of father, whom they perceive as omnipotent, frightening, and overpowering in their lives. Read Carl Jung's book *Man and His Symbols*[29] and Emil Gutheil's *Dream Analysis*.[30] Help the child view his unconscious mind as a benign and friendly part of him that wants to help him be happy in life.

Stealing, Predelinquent Behavior. *Don't* label the child a thief or delinquent. Don't pamper him and let him expect that anything he wants he always gets.

Do greatly increase the amount of attention, affection, and interest from others that he receives for positive accomplishment, especially from the same-sexed parent. Concentrate on providing him with a high R-P ratio. Punish misbehavior firmly and consistently. Make sure he personally returns or pays for with money he has earned any stolen or damaged items. Pay him money for work he performs in addition to regular chores so that he is able to buy rather than steal items he desires. Improve his status in group situations, and work to provide him with friends who are not predelinquent themselves. Give him identification experiences with a warm, same-sexed adult whose life style varies sig-

[29] Jung, Carl G.; Von Franz, M. L.; Henderson, Joseph L.; Jacobi, Jolande; and Jaffe, Aniela (eds.). *Man and His Symbols.* Garden City, N.Y.: Doubleday, 1964.
[30] Gutheil, Emil A. *Dream Analysis.* New York: Washington Square Press, 1967.

nificantly from the deviant group with whom he may come to identify so that he has a viable alternative to choose.

Stuttering. *Don't* tell him not to stutter. Don't call attention to this problem or give him advice such as "slow down" when he tries to speak. Don't discuss his problem in his presence or encourage others to do so.

Do be very patient. Listen to *what* he says rather than how he is saying it. Give him much more approval and acceptance, especially from mother. Encourage him to talk, and engage him in conversations. Reduce demands on him. Have a more relaxed, easy-going environment. Try hard to reduce bickering, quarreling, and other tensions in the home. Get help from a speech therapist and professional counseling for family members when such recommendations as the above cannot be carried out effectively and the child is becoming anxious about his speech difficulties.

Temper Tantrums. *Don't* give the child a model for having a temper. Don't overindulge him or let him feel that getting angry makes people give in to him. Don't rise to the bait of head-banging or other such behaviors by rewarding it with special attention. Children seldom really hurt themselves in this way and soon tire of such antics if they fail to upset the adults present.

Do ignore the temper tantrums as much as possible. If behavior is extreme and disruptive to others, put the child off in a room by himself where he can lie down until he regains his composure. After the outburst has subsided, try to discuss with him the factors that have made him so angry. Point out how ineffective his temper episode has been in achieving what he desired, and help him think of more adaptive ways of channeling his feelings. Work at home and at school on setting firmer, more consistent limits for him. If the temper outbursts are very extreme and involve complete lack of emotional control as well as potentially destructive or hurtful behavior to other people, this would imply that the angriness is associated with major personality deterioration, and a prompt referral to a psychologist or other mental health worker would be in order.

Thumbsucking. *Don't* call attention to this behavior and make an issue of it. Don't slap, scold, or otherwise embarrass the child about it.

Do provide the child with a more predictable, stable, and happy environment. Upgrade the relationship with mother, especially, and work on maintaining a high R-P ratio. Work to increase his sense of mastery by teaching him skills, giving him regular chores, and letting him take responsibility as much as he can. Help him feel more adequate and capable in confronting his environment. Encourage independence but be sure tasks assigned are well within his ability level. Work to make growing up more desirable and less punishing for him. If the symptom persists after the age of nine or ten and there is a pile up of other symptoms, professional psychological evaluation would be recommended.

Underachievement. *Don't* badger, embarrass, or otherwise increase the child's tension about doing school work. Don't criticize the teacher or school in front of him.

Do find out as reliably as possible what the child's actual academic potential could be. An individualized testing by the school psychologist on a device such as the Wechsler Intelligence Scale for Children would be adequate. Check out and work to correct pathogens such as: physical problems, home attitudes toward school, perfectionism in parents and child, maternal rejection, intense sibling rivalry, inconsistency and insufficient structure at home and at school, other emotional problems. Increase communication between home and school. *Greatly* increase the R-P ratio the child experiences. Be very consistent, and provide plenty of structure. Increase his status in the group at school and his position in the family. Help him discuss areas in his life that are making him angry and resentful. Read Howard Halprin's article "Can Psychotherapy Help the Underachiever?"[31] for more specific suggestions.

PITFALLS TO TREATMENT

Not all efforts to help children are successful. Well-meaning adults may try one thing after another only to find a child's symptoms more persistent and troublesome than ever. It may be useful at this point to

---

[31] Halprin, Howard M. "Can Psychotherapy Help the Underachiever?" *Underachievement,* ed. Milton Kornrich. Springfield, Ill.: Charles C Thomas, 1965. Pp. 579–593.

review what are some of the more common things that can go wrong in treatment attempts.

LACK OF OBJECTIVITY

Probably the most confounding factor in guiding change in a young person's life is our inability to see the degree of our own involvement in the problem. It is for this reason that even children of psychologists and psychiatrists may fall far short of the goals of optimal personality development. Most adults feel that they are doing the best they can in caring for their children. They are unable to approach problems in a neutral way, however, due to their own rationalizations and response tendencies involving these children with whom they have come to identify over a long period of time. No one can be objective with members of his own family or with cases in which he is closely involved emotionally. It is for this reason that good friends, teachers, ministers, and especially a professional mental health worker can be so helpful. Enabling one to recognize faults and deficiencies in the adult-child relationship is only one aspect of how an outsider can be instructive. More importantly, persons who are more objective in the situation are better able to maintain the perspective needed for suggesting truly effective treatment procedures.

LACK OF KNOWLEDGE

As it was pointed out earlier in this discussion, many answers are still tentative, and techniques for dealing with specific problems change as our knowledge increases. Most educated adults would no longer beat an older child for a urinary accident at night. This was a common response to this problem some years ago, however, and parents who simply do not know any better persist in this technique. Obtaining reliable knowledge is not always easy. Well-conducted research and clinical experience continue to be primary sources for new ideas and techniques. To the average person, however, these efforts often appear to be communicated in a jargon intended only for other professionals. The conservative tenor of respectable scholarship may further complicate the matter for the uninitiated: by the time the limitations and doubtful aspects have been reviewed, the reader may feel ready to dismiss the entire work as not applicable to his own situation. In the information limbo that is left, the individuals who expound their ideas in the loudest voices and with the most flair come to be heeded. It is hoped that the present venture will serve a useful purpose in providing, in distilled form, some basic and practical knowledge for understanding, relating with, and helping children who are experiencing some degree of psychological conflict.

LACK OF MOTIVATION

Not all adults are able to maintain the best interests of children as their primary objective. Even though they know what should be done, they can't bring themselves to forgo their own pleasures and other commitments. Rather than viewing the matter of emotional difficulties sympathetically, a hard-nosed, "Well, I made it; why can't he?" attitude prevails. The rationalizations are almost endless: demands of work are more important, therapy costs too much money, the psychologist doesn't know what he is talking about, the neighbors will gossip, there is nothing wrong that can't be taken care of at home, and so on. What is often being reflected, however, in such cases is the emotional immaturity of the adult who has never developed enough social interest and concern for those around him to be willing to be inconvenienced, even temporarily, for another person's good.

One aspect of our materialistic culture related to the problem of motivation has to do with the matter of fee setting for psychotherapy: free advice is usually regarded as worthless advice. Parents who are not moved to make changes in themselves by their child's suffering will often be cooperative with a therapist just to get their money's worth. When they have a financial stake in altered behavior, they tend to be more highly motivated and to follow through with a therapeutic regimen that can speed the corrective process on its way. Hence, most psychotherapists and mental health agencies have found necessary a sliding fee scale that is adjustable to family income resources but still provides the incentive to minimize extended treatment and keep down expenses.

INABILITY TO FOLLOW THROUGH

A great many sensitive adults attempt to do more than they are able to do. They see the vast amount of distress around them and vainly try to be everywhere at once, raising the hopes of the troubled persons that help is on the way. In a short time their energies are depleted, however, and they come to realize that they just cannot continue. The raised hopes are dashed back into oblivion, and increased bitterness takes their place. What children with problems do not need are "do-gooders" like these! Repeated experiences of being "burned" in this way only serve to increase the difficulty involved when sustained treatment is available. The child who has been shunted back and forth from one well-meaning person to another with only superficial attention to his distress may even develop a bitter pride in stumping the experts. When an adult has a genuine concern for a child who is suffering emotionally, he must be aware of the self-discipline required on his own part for maintaining this concern and expressing it in a consistent fashion until the suffering is actually alleviated. It may take a considerable period of time before the child is clearly "out of the woods."

INADEQUATE FACILITIES AND SHORTAGE OF TRAINED PERSONNEL

People often do not know where to go for help when emotional problems in their children get out of hand. Working with the school psychologist or school counselor in conjunction with the family physician is a good place to begin. On the basis of their assessment of the situation, either the matter need go no further, or more intensive attention may be recommended. In the latter case, referral to a clinical psychologist who works with children, a family service agency, or a child guidance clinic would likely be the next step. If there are physical complications, or psychiatric hospitalization seems necessary, a psychiatrist who has had experience and training with children is needed. The areas of specialization that have developed in the mental health field are numerous and titles can be confusing. Not all psychiatrists and psychologists work with children. A counselor should not be expected to do the work of a psychotherapist. Professional competence to deal with certain problems varies with the theoretical bias of one's professional training. Readily available literature, such as Public Affairs Pamphlets,[32] can help provide a clarification of such matters.

Unfortunately, adequate facilities and trained personnel tend to be available only in larger cities and population centers. Because of this

[32] Ogg, Elizabeth. Psychologists in Action. (Public Affairs Pamphlet No. 229) New York: Public Affairs Pamphlets, 1955; and Psychotherapy—A Helping Process. (Public Affairs Pamphlet No. 329) New York: Public Affairs Pamphlets, 1962.

shortage of manpower, natural laws of supply and demand do not prevail and there are many undertrained and incompetent individuals dispensing advice and collecting fees in mental health matters. For this reason, it is well to go further than the Yellow Pages of the telephone book in seeking reliable help. Ask people who are in a position to know if the person or agency being considered is qualified and reputable. Be wary of individuals who advertise their services or who promise quick, "miracle" cures or results. Ask about the training of the individuals. For example, a psychiatrist should have, in addition to a completed medical degree, a two-year residency in an approved psychiatric training center as well as certification that he has passed the state board examination in psychiatry. Psychiatrists tend to fall into two groups: those who deal with problems organically and treat primarily with medication or shock treatment, and those who have a more psychoanalytic bias. For children, it is generally conceded that the focus of treatment must be placed on understanding the psychological and social network of the family and its tensions, and the psychiatrist should be skilled in this type of function.

A clinical psychologist in private practice should have an undergraduate degree in psychology or one of the related social sciences, plus an additional four or more years in clinical psychology toward obtaining Master's and Ph.D. degrees in this specialty. In addition, he must have had two years of supervised experience before functioning independently, and he should be certified by the state psychological association. The clinical psychologist is generally oriented toward depth personality evaluation and psychotherapy in which no medication, electroshock, or tranquilizer is prescribed.

Other persons who have not completed this amount of training frequently work under the supervision of a psychiatrist or clinical psychologist or mental health agency. The psychiatric social worker has an undergraduate degree in psychology or sociology, which is followed by an intensive two-year course including thorough training in psychotherapeutic techniques. Psychotherapy is a process of looking inward to find the source of personality disturbance, the aim being one of basic change in attitudes toward life. Counseling, on the other hand, looks outward at some of the problems which individuals encounter in school, in parent-child relationships, in coping with physical disabilities, and the like. The counselor generally is not trained to change basic personality. Counseling functions are frequently performed by school counselors, school psychologists, student advisors, and religious leaders with pastoral counseling background. The local community welfare council or council of social agencies is an excellent source of information about counseling services and family group therapy. Some colleges and universities have counseling centers staffed with well-qualified doctoral counseling psychologists which are open to the general public.

When entire groups of children show signs of emotional disturbance, special training in group techniques is required. The work of A. S. Makarenko in the Soviet Union, for example, has demonstrated that highly antisocial groups of children can be restored to useful, well-socialized members of society. His method is based on an enduring and intensive personal relationship which can serve as a consistent model and reinforcer for constructive behavior, group-oriented discipline techniques, and group commitment to shared superordinate goals.[33] Research efforts in recent years in the United States have come to substantiate the efficacy of this approach.[34] Incorporation of these techniques in a manner that would be consistent with the values of American society may prove to be extremely useful in the future.

It is apparent from the foregoing discussion that in only certain geographical and economic areas does the American population have even moderately adequate mental health services at the present time. People who are isolated or victims of severe educational and economic deprivation are being badly neglected. Since the need is so great, teachers, parents, and other concerned adults must do all they can to understand and learn how to deal effectively with troubled children.

SUMMARY

The techniques and approaches suggested in this chapter for dealing with children's difficulties can go a long way toward limiting problems

[33] Bronfenbrenner, op. cit. (n. 19).
[34] Some prominent examples include:
Bandura, Albert. *Principles of Behavioral Modification*. New York: Holt, Rinehart and Winston, 1968.
Sherif, Muzafer; Harvey, O. J.; White, Jack B.; Hood, William R.; and Sherif, Carolyn W. *Intergroup Conflict and Cooperation: The Robbers Cave Experiment*. Norman: University of Oklahoma Book Exchange, 1961.
Sherif, Muzafer. *In Common Predicament: Social Psychology of Intergroup Conflict and Cooperation*. Boston: Houghton Mifflin, 1966.

when conscientiously applied. Even though perfect resolutions of particularly troublesome situations are not forthcoming, at least further compounding of the difficulties can be avoided in many cases. Bear in mind, especially, the basic therapeutic principles of establishing a corrective emotional experience, maintaining a high reward to punishment ratio, being consistent and gently firm in setting limits, assisting the development of ego mastery and responsibility skills, promoting positive socialization experiences, and maintaining a reasonable time expectancy. Set the stage for good mental health. Many children would be able to make it on their own after having received enough of a helping hand at the right time.

SUGGESTED READINGS

Ackerman, Nathan W. *The Psychodynamics of Family Life: Diagnosis and Treatment of Family Relationships.* New York: Basic Books, 1958. This is a classic on family interaction and treatment procedures which teachers and professional counselors would find highly useful.

Erikson, Erik H. *Childhood and Society.* 2d ed. New York: W. W. Norton, 1963. One of the most influential books in recent years in the field of child development theory, this work is a "must" for people working with children.

Guerney, Bernard G., Jr. (ed.). *Psychotherapeutic Agents: New Roles for Nonprofessionals, Parents, and Teachers.* New York: Holt, Rinehart and Winston, 1969. Here is a compilation of ideas and specific techniques with which nonprofessionals can be effective in working with disturbed children.

Kessler, Jane W. *Psychopathology of Childhood.* Englewood Cliffs, N. J.: Prentice-Hall, 1966. Deviations from normal child development are systematically presented in this volume with thorough discussion of the more common symptoms and disorders of childhood personality.

Wicks, Frances G. *The Inner World of Childhood: A Study in Analytic Psychology.* Rev. ed. New York: Appleton-Century-Crofts, 1966. A highly readable and sensitive view of the child's world valuable for both parents and teachers.

SIX · THE DEVELOPING SELF:

THE PARENTAL ROLE

Helen Felsenthal

The preceding chapter is concerned with the repair of a child's damaged self concept. The authors have lucidly explained the work of the parent and teacher in helping a child regain psychological adjustment. They emphasize, however, the importance of preventive measures. In many instances the behavioral problems could have been avoided by earlier implementation of parental conduct conducive to the development of a positive self concept. When such behaviors are introduced early in a child's life, they are not considered corrective measures but, instead, become a way of life which helps the child to develop as an assured individual capable of achieving his potential.

I have two young children, a six-year-old daughter and a son of eight years, both of whom appear to possess a positive self concept. Their acquisition of a favorable self concept was not accidental, however. From birth, and indeed before birth, my husband and I made a conscientious effort to develop this self-esteem. Unfortunately, many parents do not understand the necessity and importance of encouraging self-esteem, and some have never given thought to it.

Recent interest in the education of the disadvantaged child has launched exploratory studies of the influence of early environment on the cognitive development of children. Many of these studies were an outgrowth of the federally-financed Head Start program. This research has not been particularly productive, however, of specific suggestions about what parents can do during the child's preschool years to improve his learning ability or intelligence, and most investigators would admit that answers to parental inquiries have to remain fairly broad and general.[1]

[1] Freeberg, Norman E., and Payne, Donald T. "Parental Influence on Cognitive Development in Early Childhood: A Review." *Child Development,* 38:65–87; March 1967.

Therefore, when we discuss the elusive psychological construct of "self concept" and examine its relationship to both cognitive and emotional development, we are drawing mainly upon our collective experiences and observations rather than any established body of research. In helping the parent and teacher understand these relationships, we must glean our information from various realms of knowledge—from child development, psychology, sociology, history, and even from personal insight. Much of our present understanding of early cognitive development has been derived from a psychologist discussed in Chapters Two and Three, Jean Piaget, who used his own children as subjects.

How does a parent know his child has a positive self concept? And more importantly, what parental behaviors lead to this development? Observation will partially answer the first question. Children with high self-esteem are self-assured and confident. They are not frightened or intimidated. When you speak to them, they look you in the eye and do not hang their heads or answer in a whisper. One can tell that they have never heard the dictum, "Children should be seen and not heard." They relate well to others, adults as well as peers. They have a strong sense of right and wrong, and they know how to distinguish between the two. They are open, and if they do something "wrong," there is seldom a need to explain their erroneous behavior to them. Most children with high self-esteem are happy, vibrant, and energetic. Sullenness and withdrawal are seldom observed. Unhappiness is usually expressed verbally and repression has not become a defense mechanism. They are well-liked and accepted by others, especially their peers, and this acceptance constantly reinforces their self-esteem and helps develop their leadership qualities. Finally, and perhaps most importantly to educators, the children display achievement, academic and otherwise, consistent with their apparent ability. They believe they are capable of learning and have confidence in their own abilities. While not all high achievers possess a favorable self concept, studies have demonstrated a positive correlation between these behaviors.

The second of the two questions asked above—What parental behaviors lead to the development of self-esteem in children?—is the main concern of this chapter. Although the emphasis will be on the parental role, teachers in the preschool and primary grades often act as a surrogate parent to the child. Hence, the teacher must be knowledgeable in the development of the self concept, complementing and/or guiding the parent in his relationship with the child. In some cases—as the Kirkharts have indicated in Chapter Five—when the parent is unable to identify and implement the behaviors affecting the developing self concept, the teacher must assume his role. The teacher becomes the "significant other" in a child's life and therefore holds the responsibility to compensate and help fill a void in the child's world. Moreover, even though the seeds of a child's self image are sown long before he enters school, the self concept is not a constant; rather it is emergent, and it is thus amenable, especially in the young child, to environmental influences. Thus the study of the child's developing self concept encompasses his family life as well as his role in a school-centered society.

In focusing primarily on the role of parents in the development of the child's self concept, the origins of self concept will be examined first. This initial development occurs mainly in the prenatal and infancy stages of life and continues throughout the preschool and early school years. The discussion will concentrate on those parental behaviors which influence the developing self concept. Some guidelines for parents in their attempt to enhance the child's self-esteem will be offered. Knowledge of family dynamics will also aid preschool and elementary teachers as they make a conscientious effort to facilitate the emotional as well as the intellectual development of the child.

THE DAWN OF SELF CONCEPT

"As searchers after identity contemporary youths are pioneers, and as teachers of the systematic way of the search we social scientists are beginners. We know enough for a beginning but our body of knowledge is riddled with gaps and guesses, and we are not always in agreement with each other."[2]

Each child at birth assumes his role as a member of the family unit. Most children enter a family in which both biological parents reside in the home. Often an older sibling is also present. Although the size and structure of the family affect the emerging self concept of the child, as we shall see later, it is the mother who assumes the most important role in the child's early psychological development. The mother-child

[2] Nixon, Robert E. *The Art of Growing.* New York: Random House, 1969. P. 29.

dyad is the earliest and perhaps the most fundamental human relationship.

PRENATAL CONCERN

Mother's conscious or unconscious concern for the child begins before birth in her relationship with the developing fetus. Physicians and psychologists, despite some recently acquired knowledge about fetal development, know little about the dynamics of the psychological development of the fetus and, in particular, about the prenatal mother-child psychological correlates. The physiological growth of the unborn child has been examined as a function of the physical condition of the mother, but little is known concerning the relationships between a child's life in the womb and his later personality development.

Some studies have suggested that stress experienced by the pregnant mother can alter the movements of the fetus from normal to hyperactive. Further, fetal hyperactivity in the last months of pregnancy can manifest itself after the baby is born in feeding difficulties, failure to gain weight, sleep problems, general irritability, distractibility, and other conditions that make adjustment to postnatal life difficult.[3] Animal experimentation has revealed the relationship between conditions of emotionality in pregnant females and the similar emotionality in their offspring. In these experiments, some pregnant laboratory animals were placed in a stress-filled environment while others were placed in a normal environment. The behavior of the offspring from each group of animals was generally similar to the behavior displayed by their mothers prior to birth. Moreover, emotional disturbance in the mother makes birth complications more likely and increases the probability of damage to the baby's central nervous system. When the central nervous system is damaged behavioral abnormalities are frequently manifest.[4] Longitudinal studies concerning the prenatal psychological conditions of the mother which may have a lasting influence on the child are, however, limited in both number and scope.

Thus far, our attempts to establish a relationship between the prenatal

[3] Hurlock, Elizabeth B. *Developmental Psychology.* 3d ed. New York: McGraw-Hill, 1968. P. 90.

[4] Ferguson, Lucy R. *Personality Development.* Belmont, Calif.: Brooks/Cole Publishing Co., 1970. P. 30.

thoughts or emotions of the mother and postnatal physiological or psychological characteristics of the baby have been largely based on conjecture and/or superstition. The little that is known indicates nonetheless that concern for the child's psychological development should begin during the prenatal period. However, most expectant mothers consider the prenatal psychological development of their children beyond their control and consequently focus their attention on their babies' physical well-being.

The mother should know that a physically healthy child has a greater chance for an adequate psychological development, since the concept of a child's physical self plays an important part in the entirety of the self concept. From the moment of birth the individual meets stress, and a healthy body contributes to the ability to meet life's many demands. The mother's awareness during pregnancy of the importance of adequate rest, nourishment, periodical examinations, and of refraining from drugs or conditions which might unknowingly affect the fetus, is the beginning of a deliberate concern for the child's welfare.

Early and what may turn out to be continuous rejection of the child can be manifested in unwillingness to accept the pregnancy and any subsequent alteration in life style which is needed to enhance the child's chances for normal development. Extreme and absolute rejection comes, of course, in the form of abortion. Although the number of abortions, either legal or illegal, is not accurately known, it is generally the case that most normal pregnancies result in the birth of a child regardless of the desires and wishes of the mother. In most states decisions favoring legal abortion are usually based on physiological reasons, e.g., the high risk of infant malformation because of the mother's contraction of German measles during the first three months of pregnancy.

Several questions need to be considered when studying the psychological development of the expected child. Do mothers who profess rejection of pregnancy later adjust to the birth without adverse consequences to the child? How often and how long does rejection continue through the child's early years? How crucial is the unfavorable relationship between mother and child in the first months of life to the later personality development of the child, and, in particular, to the development of his self concept? While most arguments against legalized abortion are based on religious and/or ethical beliefs, pre- and postnatal maternal rejection and its potential effects on the child have not been

adequately taken into consideration. The attitude of the courts toward abortion has been changing rapidly. Current abortion laws are under scrutiny with many states studying the revision of these laws.[5] More recent concern has centered around the psychological consequences to both the mother and the unwanted child. Although systematic research in this area is limited, one longitudinal study has shown that a significant percentage of unwanted children later develop psychiatric instability.[6]

THE FIRST MONTHS

During the first months of life, the baby is almost totally dependent on the mother or mother substitute. The mother, in turn, finds her life dominated by the continuing needs of her baby. The mother's initial job is fulfilling the child's biological needs. Usually with the help of a physician, she determines the amount and kind of nutrition needed, keeps the baby clothed and clean, and is alert to any symptoms of bodily disturbances. The new mother becomes attuned to the eating, sleeping, and elimination patterns of the new child. She may attempt to control these patterns with a particular feeding schedule or by putting the child to bed when she wants him to sleep. Sometimes the mother's decisions on these matters are influenced by social pressures based on theories of child rearing. For example, she may adhere to a traditional schedule which allows for feeding every three or four hours, or she might adopt a philosophy which stresses greater freedom for the child in the form of a "demand feeding schedule." Often decisions are difficult for the new mother since this country has experienced several wide swings in child-rearing practices during the past fifty years.

Because the newborn is completely at the mercy of others for survival, the satisfaction of these biological needs greatly influences the

[5] For a review of existing abortion laws see the following:
Ayd, Frank J., Jr., "Liberal Abortion Laws," *America*, 120:130–132, February 1, 1969.
Smith, David T. (ed.). *Abortion and the Law*. Cleveland: Press of Case-Western Reserve University, 1967.
U. S. Department of Labor. *Report of the Task Force on Family Law and Policy to the Citizen's Advisory Council on the Status of Women*. Washington, D.C.: U. S. Government Printing Office, 1968.
[6] Edge, David (ed.). *The Formative Years*. New York: Schocken Books, 1970. P. 30.

child's security. Kagan characterizes this relationship between the infant and the mother as "a ballet in which each partner responds to the steps of the other."[7] The mother's actions mold the infant's behavior, but the relationship between mother and child is also affected by the infant. The mother is more likely to attend a crying infant than a quiet one. The infant who smiles or coos will elicit a similar response from his mother. From the early days of life, some of the infant's behaviors will be selectively strengthened and certain others will be selectively weakened. The foundation for later interaction between the mother and child begins in these early weeks, as the mother learns to recognize and adapt to her infant's individual reaction patterns and requirements.[8] It is this quality of "individualized adaptation" to the child's needs that distinguishes good mothering from the inadequate mothering which is frequently experienced by institutionalized infants who receive rather impersonal care.[9]

The infant's sense of well-being is affected by the mother's emotional state as well as her attention to his physical needs. The fulfillment of the child's psychological needs is also necessary for his adjustment to the new environment. Some of the child's non-biological needs include trust, security, recognition, and love. The child's need for love may develop out of the mother's role in satisfying many of his biological needs, such as feeding him when he is hungry or thirsty, changing him when he is cold and wet, and putting him to bed when he is tired. According to Erikson,[10] the balance of "trust" against "mistrust" which characterizes the experience and behavior of each infant in the oral period depends on the extent to which the mother proves a reliable source of gratification and security. Trust is the basic issue to be resolved in the early mother-infant relationship. But the amount of trust derived from early experiences does not seem to depend on absolute quantities of food or demonstrations of love, but rather on the quality of the maternal relationship. Mothers create a sense of trust in their children

[7] Kagan, Jerome. "The Child: His Struggle for Identity." *Saturday Review of Literature*, 87:80–82; December 7, 1968. Quoted from p. 80.

[8] Ferguson, op. cit. (n. 4), p. 31.

[9] Yarrow, Leon J. "The Relationship between Nutritive Sucking Experiences in Infancy and Non-nutritive Sucking in Childhood." *Journal of Genetic Psychology*, 84:149–162; March 1954.

[10] Erikson, Erik H. *Childhood and Society*. 2d ed. New York: W. W. Norton, 1963.

by combining sensitive care of the baby's individual needs with a firm sense of personal trustworthiness.

There is still much to be learned about the exact nature of the infant's needs and about the relative importance of the mother's behavior in satisfying them. Studies such as those by Harlow and Zimmerman[11] using newborn monkeys have made important contributions in this area. These studies indicate that there is a strong need, apparently innate, for tactile stimulation and that one of the most important functions of the mother is to provide this form of contact and comfort. There must be other basic needs of this kind which influence the developing human being, but, unfortunately, systematic research has been extremely limited. Although considerable attention has been given to the general effects of weaning, toilet training, and similar bodily functions, very few attempts have been made to study the early response patterns between a mother and her child.[12]

> . . . information on the specific ways in which the infant's temperament and idiosyncratic reaction patterns modulate the effects of maternal care and reciprocally modify maternal feelings and attitudes is derived more from common sense and sensitive clinical observations than from research evidence. Current lively interest in this area is likely to produce a good deal more research in the near future.[13]

Without advance preparation, the new mother will find the additional demands on her time and energy almost overbearing. The physical and emotional fatigue which frequently accompanies birth can amplify a mother's lack of preparedness for her new task. These factors can cause a mother to impart a sense of frustration and resentment to the child. In a country which emphasizes higher education and job training programs, it seems strange that so little importance has been attached to preparation for motherhood. Perhaps because mothering in lower animals seems instinctive, it is fallaciously assumed that humans can respond in a similar way. For example, my own education had progressed through the

11 Harlow, Harry F., and Zimmerman, Robert R. "Affectional Responses in the Infant Monkey." *Science*, 130:421–432; August 1959.
12 Caldwell, Bettye M. "The Effects of Infant Care." *Review of Child Development Research*, I, eds. Martin L. Hoffman and Lois W. Hoffman. New York: Russell Sage Foundation, 1964. Pp. 9–87.
13 Ferguson, op. cit. (n. 4), p. 34.

Master's degree before my first child was born, yet nothing in my formal training had prepared me for woman's "prime task." What little help I received came solely from such sources as Dr. Gesell and Dr. Spock, and I blundered my way through the first critical months of my child's life. The psychology and education courses I had taken earlier did certainly increase my basic knowledge of general human development, but none of this prepared me specifically for my role as a mother. Doctors, teachers, carpenters, and plumbers all have apprenticeships of one sort or another, but the new mother is left almost completely to her own resources. If mothers are to have similar opportunities for training, a sponsoring agency needs to be found. Should "mother-training" be offered through the school, the government, the community, the church, or organized professions?

When the mother-child relationship is satisfactory, the child becomes a compatible and integrated member of his new environment. He develops a self-attitude consistent with those expressed by the significant others in his world. As discussed in Chapter One, this self concept is largely derived from the reflected attitudes of those around him. It is a learned constellation of perceptions, cognitions, and values, and an important part of this learning comes from observing the reactions one gets from other persons.[14] External appraisal serves as a gauge for self-evaluation. The young child observes how others regard him and accepts this valuation of himself.[15] The child's self image, thus formed, serves in turn to guide and maintain his further adjustment to the external world. Since the parents are the persons who are present earliest and most consistently, they have the unique opportunity to reinforce selectively the child's learning about self.

PARENTAL BEHAVIORS WHICH INFLUENCE SELF-ESTEEM

Speculation concerning the major factors which affect the developing self concept has existed since the development of modern psychology in the latter half of the nineteenth century. Freud placed emphasis on

[14] Wylie, Ruth C. The Self Concept. Lincoln: University of Nebraska Press, 1961. P. 121.

[15] Mead, George H. "Self." George Herbert Mead on Social Psychology, ed. Anselm Strauss. Chicago: University of Chicago Press, 1964. Pp. 199–246.

the general relationship between early environmental deficiencies and later maladjustments, the implication being that the absence of such deficiencies is uniformly associated with good adjustment. However, recent research indicates that no patterns of parental behavior or attitudes are common to all parents of children with high self-esteem. After studying the antecedents of self-esteem, Coopersmith[16] concluded that *general* conditions associated with producing high self-esteem have been established but not all of these conditions are essential to development of self-esteem in any given individual, nor is any single condition sufficient to produce a favorable self concept.

Many educators and psychologists have focused on the importance of the self concept, but studies concerning the direct relationship between parental behaviors and the emerging self-esteem of the child are few. In an extensive review of the research in this area, Wylie[17] concluded that there are no true antecedent-consequent (stimulus-response) designs of study. Most studies emphasize the correlational responses of parents and children. In this type of study direct cause-effect inferences cannot be derived. Such a paucity of studies is understandable, for moral considerations restrict placing children under adverse circumstances for purposes of research. However, the need for the personal parent-child relationship has been well established. Children separated from their mothers exhibit overt symptoms of anxiety. Not only may this anxiety be intense but sometimes it lasts a long time. The work of Bowlby[18] and his colleagues has shown consistent patterns of behavior both during and after the separation period.

One obvious behavior of the child separated from his mother's care is fretfulness and crying. "Many people have found it difficult to believe that even when a child is with kindly people in a good environment he is still unhappy for much of the time and still wants to get back to his family; but I think the evidence is unmistakable."[19] A second observable

16 Coopersmith, Stanley. *The Antecedents of Self-Esteem.* San Francisco: W. H. Freeman and Co., 1967.

17 Wylie, op. cit. (n. 14), p. 135.

18 Bowlby, John. *Child Care and Growth of Love.* Baltimore: Penguin Books, 1966.

Heinicke, Christoph M., and Westheimer, Ilse J. *Brief Separations.* New York: International University Press, 1965.

19 Edge, op. cit. (n. 6), p. 20.

behavior is the child's fear of another separation. The younger the child, the more evident are these behaviors.[20]

There appear to be several basic needs which must be fulfilled if a child is to consider himself a worthy person. These needs are met in the reciprocal love relationship between the parent and child. The prime parental behaviors which make up the relationship of love and which appear to have the greatest effect on self-esteem are: (1) consistent acceptance with respect and concern and (2) freedom and independence within carefully defined limits. The person with high self-regard usually has experienced a combination of these qualities. It is helpful, therefore, to describe the actions which constitute these important qualities and the conditions which might result from their deprivation.

TEACHER AND PARENT WORK TOGETHER

Most children in our society are born into a family whose parents are willing and anxious for each child to develop his capabilities as fully as possible. Parents generally love and have a genuine concern for their child. Instances of child brutality or extreme neglect are usually indications of severe emotional disturbance on the part of a parent and occur relatively infrequently in the general population. The prime question, then, is not exclusively the amount of love for the child but how a parent expresses this love. If all love was expressed in a manner conducive to good personal adjustment, we could expect that the majority of children would develop self-esteem adequate to enhance development of their potential. If this were true, the teacher's role in the developing self concept would encompass narrower dimensions and would be restricted to his role within the classroom exclusively. Parental education on the psychological needs of the child would not be necessary.

However, a willingness by parents and teachers to help in the child's full development and their declaration of genuine acceptance are not enough. A knowledge of behaviors which enhance the child's self-esteem is also necessary. This is where the teacher's understanding can influence parental behaviors. Limited parental intellectual ability is usually not the problem, rather it is a lack of knowledge of the dynamics of human development. In Virginia Axline's moving book *Dibs: In Search*

[20] Ibid., pp. 20, 21.

of *Self*,[21] for example, the parents possessed exceptional mental abilities with concurrent professional success. But they were ignorant of the basic needs of their child as an emerging individual. Consequently, the child was functionally retarded and completely lacking a sense of individual worth.

The teacher can work with the parent to help him understand the importance of the self concept and how it affects all areas of the child's life. The teacher can view the child more objectively and knows what to expect for a particular age or grade level. Frequently the parent has a limited frame of reference from which to work. His expectations are generally comparative rather than cumulative. An older child in the same family or perhaps a neighborhood child of the same age provides the limited basis of comparison. The teacher also has knowledge of various aspects of the child's life and can integrate information concerning social adjustment, physical and intellectual growth, and psychological development. A deficiency in any one of these areas might influence the development of the child's self concept.

The parent can make himself more aware of the child's self concept by answering, perhaps with the teacher's assistance, the important questions relating to self-esteem:

1. Does the child appear to have self-confidence? Verbal clues from the child will assist the parent in formulating an answer. Comments such as "I'm stupid," or "I can do that easily" indicate how the child feels about himself.

2. Is the child fearful of new experiences? The child who is hesitant to try the unknown indicates mistrust of his own abilities. A child who is afraid to make a mistake will not want to try the unknown since there is a chance for failure.

3. How does the child handle failure? Failure is inevitable in life and often an important part of the learning process. If the child seeks constant perfection, he excludes experiences which can lead to initial failure but also to eventual success.

4. Does the child continually boast or make up tales to enhance his status? The boastful child is often trying to compensate for weaknesses. Unfortunately, the untruths usually have an effect contrary to the desired one and cause a lack of trust by others.

[21] Axline, Virginia M. *Dibs: In Search of Self*. Boston: Houghton Mifflin, 1964.

5. Does the child have an unusually strong need for positive reinforcement? Constant need for encouragement and positive feedback is a help signal indicating a lack of confidence.

6. How does the child feel about his physical appearance? The child needs to be proud of his appearance since this is his most noticeable characteristic.

7. Is the child possessive of material objects? If the child does not relate well to other people, he can become overly concerned with inanimate objects and find security in material possessions. He will be extremely hesitant to share these possessions with others.

8. Does the child seek opportunities for independence? The desire to make decisions indicates a confidence in ability and a willingness to take responsibility.

9. Is the child permitted and willing to express his own ideas and opinions? A child indicates confidence in his own worth when he is willing to vocalize his thoughts.

10. How does the child handle responsibility? A willingness to accept increasing responsibility indicates continuing growth.

As the parent answers this type of question, he becomes more aware of the child as an individual and realizes the importance of affective factors to the child's growth. The enlightened parent knows that he is a significant model for the child, who looks to the parent for guidance in his own psychological development.

THE PARENT AS A MODEL

The baby's need for a dependent relationship allows the parent to become the center of the child's world. But the identification between parent and child becomes stronger even as the child becomes less dependent on the parent to satisfy his needs, for while seeking his own independence, the child needs a model or an example to follow.

Early learning is often imitative; thus the first words a child learns closely resembles the words he hears most often. Imitative learning is not restricted to overt action, however. Feelings and attitudes also can be learned through identification. Self-awareness, too, is learned mainly through identification and imitation. The newborn has no self-awareness since his actions are determined by bodily needs and not by any reference to a self. The ability to think of oneself as an object and to have feelings about oneself evolves throughout childhood.[22] An example of this process is the child's identification with a person of his own sex. Wylie[23] found that sex identification factors were evident in cases where children with high self-esteem (compared with children of low self-esteem) viewed their own self concept as being more congruent with the self concept of the parent of the same sex.

The child first learns about himself by observing those close to him. The word "me" has great meaning for the child; the pronouns most frequently used by a toddler are "me" and "mine." The child is making a conscientious effort to understand himself in relation to others. However, the young child has a particularly difficult time learning to use personal pronouns correctly. His initial use of "I," "me," "mine," and "your" is confused and inaccurate. He may refer to himself in the third person, for example, "Johnny wants that." Increasing accuracy in the use of pronouns indicates the child's maturing conception of his existence and individuality.[24]

The parent can help in this maturation process by verbally aiding the child in his attempts to use language to define the self. Because a very young child cannot communicate well verbally, parents may erroneously believe they do not need to react verbally to the child. The child's listening ability is developed long before his verbal communication skills. Children do not need to understand every word or phrase for complete comprehension. Nonverbal behavior, volume, and/or intonation patterns are frequently sufficient clues to the child to permit understanding. Intelligence or understanding is not measured validly until much later in the child's life, but some psychologists feel that infants have the capacity to interpret meanings and feelings from the parents' verbal expressions without understanding the words themselves. Few preschool children use language, a major component in intellectual evaluation, as their chief source of communication. Feelings such as anxiety involving the self and other people are developed long before

[22] Lindesmith, Alfred, and Strauss, Anselm. *Social Psychology*. New York: Holt, Rinehart and Winston, 1968. Pp. 314–316.

[23] Wylie, op. cit. (n. 14), p. 135.

[24] Lindesmith and Strauss, op. cit. (n. 22), pp. 317–318.

language can define with any accuracy or precision exactly what it is that is anxiety-provoking.[25] Even as the child becomes more fluent and able to understand his own and others' feelings, he is usually discouraged from expressing these feelings. Strong emotions such as anger or hostility are repressed in our society. Childhood is supposed to be a happy and carefree time, and the parent tries hard to make the child happy even if this means denying him opportunities to experience emotions basic to life.

The interaction between fathers and mothers of children with high self-esteem is marked by greater compatibility and ease than is the case with parents of children with low self-esteem. High-esteem children appear to have mothers who are themselves rated higher in self-steem and who are more stable emotionally than mothers of children with medium or low esteem. The high self-esteem mothers are more likely to accept their role as mother and to carry it out in a realistic and effective manner.[26] But mothers do not need to devote full time to child rearing to fulfill their role adequately. The *quality* of the relationship between the mother and child is more important than the *quantity*. Children whose mothers work outside the home do not necessarily feel that they are rejected or unimportant.[27] High-esteem mothers do not profess child rearing as their only interest but are often involved in activities or interests unrelated to home life.

Parents do not need to be affluent to provide a suitable environment for psychological growth. Socio-economic status is not a prime determinant of high self-esteem. The psychological bases of esteem are more dependent on close, personal relationships in the immediate environment than upon material benefits or prestige rankings in the community.[28]

Parental influence on the child's cognitive development is also marked. Benjamin Bloom[29] plotted the pattern of development of individual characteristics and concluded that half of all growth in human intelli-

[25] Sullivan, Harry S. *Conceptions of Modern Psychiatry*. New York: W. W. Norton, 1953. Pp. 19–23.
[26] Coopersmith, op. cit. (n. 16), p. 116.
[27] Ibid., pp. 91–95.
[28] Ibid., p. 86.
[29] Bloom, Benjamin. *Stability and Change in Human Characteristics*. New York: John Wiley and Sons, 1964.

gence takes place between birth and age four, another 30 percent occurs between the ages of four and eight, and the remaining 20 percent between eight and seventeen. Research evidence increasingly reveals the effect of early environmental influences on intellectual development. Some of the major environmental characteristics which can affect the development of general intelligence or school achievement, either positively or negatively, are now being specified. However, one of the limitations of research in this area is the need to rely upon retrospective reports by the mother regarding parental practices in early childhood. The investigator must assume a continuity of home environment over the period of years from early childhood to the later grades, as well as some measure of accuracy on the part of the mothers.

Evidence from such studies indicates that children of superior intellect come from homes where parental interest in their intellectual development is evident. This interest is manifested by pressures to succeed and assistance in doing so, particularly in the development of the child's verbal skills.[30] Parents help language development by encouraging verbalization, providing reading materials for their children, reading to the young child, and arranging for various experiences and materials which supply a wide range of opportunity for language usage.

The recent emphasis on education of the culturally deprived child has concentrated on specialized training methods to improve intellectual performance. Longitudinal studies which pinpoint the results of specific methods could benefit any parent. Researchers are also investigating parents' perception of their role in the rearing process and the influence of this rearing on cognitive growth. However, the paucity of information regarding parents' attitudes to their own potential influence upon intellectual development has constituted a major obstacle to the increase of knowledge in this area.[31]

ACCEPTANCE AND RESPECT FOR INDIVIDUALITY

Each child is unique in himself. No two children look exactly alike, think, or act alike despite similarities in experiences. Furthermore, one cannot predict precisely how any one child will act in a given situation. Each birth offers an entirely new creation. The essential factor in ac-

[30] Freeberg and Payne, op. cit. (n. 1), p. 71.
[31] Ibid., p. 82.

ceptance, then, becomes the awareness of and respect for individuality. Respect implies equality, but the definition of equality needs clarification. Many parents interpret equality as complete surrender to the demands of the child. Still other parents refuse to accept the child's right to equality on any terms. They feel their position as parent entitles them to unquestioned authority and unchallenged decision-making.

Adults expect a certain amount of respect from one another regardless of the relative status or importance of the interacting individuals.

> Very little interaction occurs, even between total strangers, without some element of code, norm, or rule entering into the interaction. This is true even where conflict exists between the interactants or [even] where the interaction actually takes place around a conflict—[such] as in a boxing match or in warfare.[32]

In adult society, under most circumstances one does not rudely disagree with an idea expressed by another. Generally, disagreements will focus on differences in interpretations. Personal attacks accompanied by charges of incompetence or inferiority are avoided as much as possible. If two adults disagree, argument may be firm, but it is nevertheless conducted with careful consideration to the feelings of the other person. Could there be any reason why the "rules" of polite disagreement should not apply in adult-child interaction, in particular the parent-child relationship? Children seldom experience the respectful treatment from adults which adults afford each other. The adult expression of anger, "Do not treat me like a child," exemplifies this.

Children soon learn that they have a restricted "voice" in their family; limitations are placed on their prerogative of disagreement. When differences of opinion do become voiced, they are often rejected in a manner that would be considered disrespectful were the rules of adult interaction in effect. But it must be remembered that often a young child's interpretations or explanations of behavior can enlighten the parent because the child is able to view a problem from his own unique point of view. Much guessing and speculation could be eliminated if the child were included in the discussion. In addition, the child would gain the feeling that his opinion (and he himself) is worthy. He would not be relegated to a submissive position because of his age or dependence.

A child's feeling of weakness and worthlessness is likely to derive from

[32] Lindesmith and Strauss, op. cit. (n. 22), p. 296.

the authority structure of the family. In the authoritarian family, irrational authority is a rule. Rules are followed and orders obeyed, not because they are inherently sound or correct but because they are transmitted from a superior (parent) to an inferior (child). The child's independence and spontaneity tend to be smothered, resulting in weakness, helplessness, and an absence of dignity. This weakness and worthlessness lead to debilitating effects on the self concept.

A lack of respect for the opinions voiced by youths can continue while the child is dependent on the parent but a time comes when the child is ready to leave the home. Most adolescents learn to make the transition into maturity without alienation from the family, but there are some who seek their autonomy by complete rejection of their families. The alienated youth who explicitly rejects his family, sometimes to the extent of leaving the home and joining a cultural subgroup, has become the topic of current popular literature. This movement has resulted in formation of whole communities of alienated youth, e.g., the Haight-Asbury district in San Francisco. Frequently, these young people come from affluent homes where the parents profess ignorance of the reasons for the child's rejection of family values and aspirations. Typically, the parents state that the child was given every advantage and opportunity. The errant adolescent is often considered bright and has usually been encouraged to develop his potential through participation in traditional middle-class institutions (e.g., advanced education in prestigious universities, opportunities for travel or public service, etc.).

The current youth revolt has had a short history, and much of the literature which attempts to explain these groups is speculative at best. Some additional questions need to be asked. Could the alienation have begun long before the teen-age years and manifested itself only after the individual was physically able to leave the nest? What kind of self concept do these youths have? Do their independence and professed free thinking indicate a high positive self concept, or is the reverse true? They have, in fact, acknowledged their perceived inability to alter the "establishment," and so they have chosen instead to sabotage the offending society.

Alienation thus can result from a real or felt disability before the demands of our society. Those who are unable to meet a demand have two alternatives: they can accept the legitimacy of the demand and with it their own inadequacy, or they can repudiate the demand so as to retain their self-esteem.[33]

Have the parents of these youths confused acceptance with overindulgence? In America today not only does the child want to live up to parental expectations but the parent also wants to live up to the child's expectations. The child of previous generations was torn between what he wanted and what his parents wanted. The contemporary parent is divided between what he thinks is good for his child and what he believes would gratify him in the parent-child relationship. Behavioral inconsistency stemming from this dilemma tends to confuse the child.[34] There is a distinction between overindulgence and wholehearted expression of love and acceptance. Adler[35] warned against the destructive effects of overindulgence; he believed that pampered children develop an unrealistically inflated value of their worth. This self-centeredness leads to unwillingness or a lack of readiness to engage in mature reciprocal social relationships.

SIBLING RELATIONSHIPS

The parent can be influential in helping the child prepare for independence and social responsibility by encouraging a spirit of trust and camaraderie in reciprocal relationships within the home. Ideally, this relationship, first experienced in the home, will then be extended by the child to the larger society.

In the home the child enjoys security and can function without fear of rejection; here he can explore and identify his feelings of hostility, anger, jealousy, and sexuality.

Emotions are vital to existence; suppressing them does not erase them. Therefore the parent needs to learn to distinguish between the act and the feeling. It is often difficult for the parent to condemn an act yet convey the acceptance of the feeling involved with the act. Feelings can both precede and run concurrent with actions, i.e., a child may first become angry with a sibling and then strike him. Usually parents attempt to stop the overt action which results from these emotions. Frequently,

[33] Keniston, Kenneth. The Uncommitted. New York: Dell Publishing Co., 1965. P. 386.
[34] Henry, Jules. Culture against Man. New York: Random House, 1963.
[35] Adler, Alfred. The Science of Living. Garden City, N. Y.: Doubleday, 1969.

in rejecting the actions the parent also rejects the child's right to full expression of his feelings, or, at best, strongly encourages their control. Perhaps an example will help clarify this point. Two brothers are arguing over a toy belonging to the younger boy. He refuses to share the toy, saying that he has the right to determine its use. The older boy becomes angry and begins to hit his brother. The mother does not permit the fight to continue, but she does not need to demean the older brother for becoming angry with the younger one, although she may condemn the physical attack. Instead, she can sympathize and say that she understands why the older boy is unhappy and angry but that deliberate attacks on others are not permitted.

If a parent cannot distinguish between acts and feelings, the child will also be unable to do so. Thus some of the important emotional elements of self-identity are discouraged and repressed. Anger, for example, is a common emotion in both adults and children. During maturation the child encounters many incidents which lead to frustration and anger. The young child has not yet learned to suppress this anger, and outbursts of frustration can be daily occurrences. However, as the child develops socially he learns that anger is "bad." Anger is not experienced as a natural expression of differences but rather as something unacceptable and to be avoided. Jules Henry suggests a reason for this in our culture:

> A lack of tolerance for anger is probably related to the fact that since modern American parents often attempt to create a home atmosphere of permissiveness and yielding, the appearance of anger finds the child relatively unprepared. It may also be that the parent himself is uncertain about his anger; anger is almost immoral in the contemporary American family, and mothers show great anxiety over their impulses to scream at their children.[36]

Children react differently to similar circumstances. Thus, an act which might provoke anger in one child might lead to curiosity and exploration in another child. Further, parents should be aware that any one child might react differently at different times to similar circumstances. The knowledgeable parent is not surprised at differences between siblings; rather, he is fully aware of them and he accepts such

[36] Henry, op. cit. (n. 34), pp. 138–139.

differences. The unknowledgeable parent, on the other hand, expresses unhappiness verbally when one child does not react in the same way as another child or even like the parent himself.

The specific effects of sibling rivalry are unknown, but there are indications that they might have implications for the study of the self concept. Research suggests that the only child tends to have a more favorable concept of self than children with brothers and sisters. A possible reason for this is the comparatively larger amount of time and interest given the only child, which results in increased opportunities for verbal interaction with adults. Sibling relationships may have an adverse influence on the developing self concept, especially in those families where parents are unaware of the detrimental effects of their comparative evaluations.

Although strong attachments between siblings may lead to imitative behavior, the parents should respect the right of each child to make alternative identifications with nonsiblings. If competition is keen in a family, or if one child is constantly compared to another, the younger or more inferior child may even be forced to choose other behavioral alternatives, possibly negative in nature, in order to maintain his own dignity and individuality. The parental expectations must be realistic in terms of the child as an individual.

ESTABLISHMENT OF REALISTIC EXPECTATIONS

There is a sense of security in being able to predict behavior, and some parents feel that they have lost control when behavior deviates from their expectations. Often this deviation comes in the form of failure to meet parental goals. It is part of "the American Dream" for a parent to desire his child to achieve higher than the preceding generation. In actuality, this often means that the child must strive for goals which somehow eluded the parents (e.g., how many "Little-League fathers" are frustrated athletes?). Achievement should be encouraged but the encouragement should take the form of guidance with respect for the desires of the children rather than coercion to fulfill the desires of the parents.

When a child is unable to meet parental expectations he may, in fact, take a course of action in direct opposition to the parents' goals. This selected behavior may be detrimental to the child; it often manifests itself in "the decision to fail,"[37] although some children are driven to achievements beyond their abilities or interests. The child who does not dare oppose an overpowering parent can instead defy the parental substitute, the teacher, by not learning. By employing such negative behavior, the child can effectively punish the parents to whom he is otherwise subservient. A calculated failure to learn has become the "commonest whip that the middle-class child can hold over a parent whose pride is deeply hurt by the child's academic failure."[38]

One of the ways parents can provide for success and minimize loss of self-esteem is by helping the child avoid situations which will inevitably and unnecessarily lead to failure. The parent can, for example, provide toys which will challenge but not frustrate the child. Some parents attempt to give their children a "head start" in education by trying to teach them to read before they show readiness for this skill. Often this is done to enhance the parents' esteem rather than for the ultimate benefit of the child. Research indicates that early readers do not necessarily continue to progress at an accelerated rate.

The child's own criteria should be used as a means of individual evaluation rather than comparison with another child. Unfortunately, some adults tend to assume the role of the evaluator, or in more precise terms, "the corrector." Holt[39] criticizes educational methodology which rewards "right" answers and punishes "wrong" responses. Parents and teachers feel that an important part of their instructional role is pointing out or correcting all mistakes as soon as they are made. Thus the child's self-checking and self-correcting skill does not develop and he gains little self-confidence.

A prime task of parents is the development of independence in their offspring. The growth of independence should be gradual but consistent and begin early in life. Prenatal life is one of complete dependence, and postnatal life is at first entirely controlled by the mother. But from birth onward the parental goal should be the eventual autonomy of the child. The development of independence by the infant is first seen in his willingness to let the mother out of sight without undue anxiety be-

[37] Bettelheim, Bruno. "The Decision to Fail." *Conflict in the Classroom*, eds. Nicholas T. Long, William C. Morse, and Ruth G. Newman. Belmont, Calif.: Wadsworth Publishing Co., 1965. Pp. 435–446.

[38] Ibid., p. 438.

[39] Holt, John. *How Children Learn*. New York: Pitman Publishing Corp., 1967.

cause she has become an inner certainty as well as an outer predict-ability. Such "consistency, continuity, and sameness of experience" provides a sense of identity which relates inner feelings with outer ex-periences involving familiar and predictable things and people.[40]

How much of a problem dependency is in adulthood depends in large part on whether the mother is sincere in her efforts to push her children to independence and on whether she is supported by her husband in this effort. Least likely to succeed are mothers like those of alienated youths, women whose own conflicts lead them to pull their sons toward them at the same time that they push them away.[41]

FREEDOM WITH CONTROLS

The young child realizes that his power within the family is limited. Major decisions such as where the family will live and how they will spend money are made by the parents, usually without consulting the child. Daily decisions such as the time and content of meals are also made by the older members of the family. Many children do not gain experience in the decision-making process, even though there is much more opportunity to do this than is generally recognized by the parent.

Maintaining the authoritarian role, the parent is reluctant to give up his authority and allow the child to learn to make decisions. Some parents feel that release of authority will lead to loss of control. They are accustomed to imposing external controls on the child and do not give him an opportunity to develop internal controls. A preschool or primary child, for example, can choose the clothes he will wear for the day. Consequently, he should be encouraged to do so. In this way he learns to combine and harmonize colors and styles and to take pride in his appearance. The mother may need to guide the child at first, but, surprisingly, these skills can be learned quickly. The young child can also choose what and how he wants to play. The teen-ager can purchase his own clothes and perhaps contribute to their cost by holding a job which helps him become self-supporting.

The opportunity for children to make decisions and live with the consequences of these decisions is important in building self-esteem.

[40] Erikson, op. cit. (n. 10), p. 219.
[41] Keniston, op. cit. (n. 33), pp. 304–305.

Helpful parents will permit greater power as the child manifests greater ability and maturity of judgment. Denial of expression by parents produces a subverting effect on the child by reinforcing his underlying doubts of unworthiness and incompetence. Conversely, the permissive atmosphere which permits free expression of ideas and does not resort to harsh or frequent evaluative comparisons enables the individual to know and accept himself. Conflicts can be averted if parents accept the views and values of the child, although they need not necessarily agree with him.[42]

Parents can confuse equality of rights with equality in expectations. The parent must be aware of the age and maturity of the child and must not impose adult standards on child behaviors. For example, a two-year-old would not be expected to make decisions about bedtime. A fourteen-year-old should be able to make this decision. Individuals differ on their food preferences. Adults generally do not eat the foods they do not like. Why are children forced to eat everything put before them? How many homes experience regular arguments at the dinner table with the absolute power of the parent eventually directing the amount and content of food intake?

When a child is permitted to control, in part, his own destiny, he acquires a sense of appreciation for his own views and the ability to resist group pressures to conform without consideration of his own needs and opinions. This development of social poise, leadership, and independence may result at times in extremely assertive and exploratory actions, actions which can be interpreted by parents and teachers as rude or discourteous. Coopersmith[43] found that the child with high self-esteem is likely to be a "considerable source of travail and disturbance to his parents, teachers and other persons in authority, and the child with low self-esteem is more inclined to be overtly submissive and accepting."

SUMMARY

How one feels and thinks about himself has an effect on every act performed. The various chapters of this book have illustrated how the

[42] Rogers, Carl R. *Client-Centered Therapy*. Boston: Houghton Mifflin, 1951. Pp. 502–503.
[43] Coopersmith, op. cit. (n. 16), p. 253.

home, school, and other institutions are critically involved in helping the child develop the concept that he is a worthy person who can contribute to the world around him.

Teachers, counselors, psychologists, and other professional personnel who work with children are all concerned with the child's self concept, but the parent is the key person in its development. The first years in the lives of most children are in the home. Even when the child enters school, or participates in other activities, he still returns to the home, which remains the center of his life until he begins to make his own home. Consequently, the role of the parent in a child's psychological development assumes prime importance. Parents seldom have to be instructed to keep their children physically healthy. They are aware of the need to provide food and shelter and to protect the child from harm until he is old enough to protect himself. But physical development is only one component in the child's growth. Psychological growth is also vital, yet parents do not automatically or instinctively provide the conditions for their children which will lead to a positive self concept. Parental planning which includes knowledge of the dynamics of child development is necessary. This knowledge involves a realization of the importance of the first months of life and the continual awareness of the parental behaviors which influence the child's development, in particular, his developing self concept.

Someone once told me that the important things in life always take hard work and commitment to purpose. Parenthood is certainly an important part of most people's lives. Indeed, the only significant accomplishment in the lives of some individuals is the birth and rearing of a child. Certainly this rearing of children is "hard work." Much of this work concerns itself with the knowledgeable and systematic planning of conditions and behaviors which will lead the child to develop his potential fully.

SUGGESTED READINGS

Bowlby, John. *Child Care and Growth of Love.* Baltimore: Penguin Books, 1966. A leading researcher reviews the effects of early environment on the child's ability to love and be loved.

THE DEVELOPING SELF: THE PARENTAL ROLE / 203

Coopersmith, Stanley. *The Antecedents of Self-Esteem*. San Francisco: W. H. Freeman and Co., 1967. An investigation of the conditions and behaviors which affect the developing self concept.

Ferguson, Lucy R. *Personality Development*. Belmont, Calif.: Brooks/ Cole Publishing Co., 1970. A coherent account, illuminated by theory and based on empirical evidence, of the development of the child's interpersonal relations from birth to adolescence.

Ginott, Haim G. *Between Parent and Child*. New York: Macmillan, 1965. A handbook of practical suggestions for dealing with daily problems in child-rearing.

Redl, Fritz. *When We Deal With Children*. New York: The Free Press, 1966. A psychiatrist presents information based on his many years of experience on problems in parent-child relations.

Young, Leontine. *Life Among the Giants*. New York: McGraw-Hill, 1965. The author explains what it is like to be a child and teaches her adult readers how to be children again by helping them understand the world from a child's point of view.

SEVEN · THE SELF IN EARLY YEARS:

DISCUSSION

Editor's Note: This chapter derives largely from a discussion meeting held on May 9 and 10, 1970, at Meadow View Farm, Hudson, Ohio. All authors, as well as discussants (see p. vi), had read the preliminary drafts of the chapters in this book to prepare for this gathering where various relevant topics were elaborated, clarified, and summarized. Many specific comments and suggestions were made on each chapter and these have since been incorporated into the final versions presented in this book. Nevertheless, some of the remarks and interactions seemed general and interesting enough for recapitulation. What follows, therefore, is the selected and partially edited proceedings of this meeting. Although the draft for the chapter has been cleared with the six authors, some instances of misstatement and misinterpretation may still remain. Needless to say, the responsibility is solely the editor's.

(In the discussion, the participants are simply identified by alphabet, *A* for the person who spoke first, *B* the second, and *O* the last. No correspondence is to be found between these symbols and the participants' actual initials.)

A. Let me lead off the session by quoting from the 1967 Plowden Report, which, in my opinion, should be required reading for every teacher and teacher-aspirant. "A school," says this British report, "is not merely a teaching shop, it must transmit values and attitudes. It is a community in which children learn to live first and foremost as children and not as future adults. In family life children learn to live with people of all ages. The school sets out deliberately to devise the right environment for children, to allow time to be themselves and to develop in the way and at the pace appropriate to them. It tries to equalize opportunities and to compensate for handicaps. It lays special stress on individual discovery, on firsthand experience and on opportunities for creative work. It insists that knowledge does not fall into neatly separate compartments and that work and play are not opposite but complementary."[1]

B. That is a beautiful statement on what the ideal school should be. As I understand it, there was another British report in 1931 (the Hadow Report) which was already paying much attention to what Piaget had to say and which had led to various curricular innovations in English schools.[2] Some of these, for example, the "project," "center of interest," and "theme" methods, are discussed also in the 1967 report, as well as in a book by Marshall.[3] In any case, the earlier report argued strongly for an interpretation of curriculum in terms of experience and activity, rather than in terms of something out there, facts and information.

C. I find it interesting that you are both referring to documents not originating in the United States. It is unfortunate, but our teachers tend to be woefully ignorant of what is taking place elsewhere in the world. Even such neighborly educational systems as the British, French, or German ones are not really familiar to American teachers, except perhaps in historical terms through Froebel, Pestalozzi, Montessori, Herbart, and the like. Actually, their current educational thoughts and practices merit our close study. When it comes to, say, Soviet pedagogy, who can say he knows anything at all?

B. Yes, few of us can even identify Anton Semyonovich Makarenko! I believe that the reported emphasis in Russian education on functional integration of the family and society and on rewarding individual performance in terms of its contribution to group achievement is worth our while to ponder.[4]

[1] Central Advisory Council for Education (England), chaired by Lady Bridget Plowden. *Children and Their Primary Schools,* Vols. I and II. London: Her Majesty's Stationery Office, 1967. (Available from British Information Services, 845 Third Avenue, New York, N. Y.) Quoted from Vol. I, p. 187.

[2] Consultative Committee on the Primary School, chaired by Sir Henry Hadow. *Report of the Consultative Committee on the Primary School.* London: His Majesty's Stationery Office, 1931. (Reprinted in 1959.)

Also see: Consultative Committee on Infant and Nursery Schools, chaired by Sir Henry Hadow. *Report of the Consultative Committee on Infant and Nursery Schools.* London: His Majesty's Stationery Office, 1933.

[3] Marshall, Sybil. *Adventure in Creative Education.* New York: Pergamon Press, 1968.

[4] Bronfenbrenner, Urie. *Two Worlds of Childhood: U. S. and U. S. S. R.* New York: Russell Sage Foundation, 1970.

(Continued on next page.)

D. To a certain extent, we can say the same thing about various thoughts and practices within the United States. We are often unaware of what is going on right in the next system, next school, or even next classroom!

E. Not only are we ignorant but perhaps also afraid? People are hesitant to examine the unknown.

F. The other side of the coin is the all too familiar tendency to adopt fads and fashions in education. When something gets to be familiar, it becomes an idol for a decade or so. Acceleration came and went. Creativity was in and then out. Teaching machines, behavioral objectives, ability grouping, modular scheduling, and so on and on. I think Sorokin was right in his trenchant analysis of amnesia and the discoverer's complex in the social sciences.[5] Most of us do not pay any attention to what has transpired before our time and behave as if the neglect of our historical heritage and its significance gave us more freedom instead of shackling us.

B. I know what you mean. While basic ideas seem to remain the same, interests wax and wane with the vogue of the time. If current activities, for example, on learning disabilities indeed add anything novel and insightful to similar attempts in the 1930's and around 1900, we can rejoice in our progress. I am afraid, however, that most of our new Columbuses repeat the old mistakes of earlier voyagers by not even studying their navigational charts and records.

D. So long as the map does not show it, there could not possibly be a mountain. Ignorance is bliss, indeed!

F. Some of us are terribly afraid of unfamiliar people, things, and events. We do not know what to do with them and typically keep our distance from them. This does not help improve human relations, but at least in our children such a defensive attitude may be kept at a minimum by efforts to familiarize the unfamiliar. For example, some children's books nowadays treat the subject of exceptional children in

Makarenko, A. S. *The Collective Family: A Book for Russian Parents.* Garden City, N. Y.: Doubleday, 1967.

Redl, Helen B. (ed.). *Soviet Educators on Soviet Education.* New York: The Free Press, 1964.

[5] Sorokin, Pitrim. *Fads and Foibles in Modern Sociology and Related Sciences.* Chicago: Henry Regnery, 1956.

a sensible manner.[6] Likewise, there are books on ethnic experiences and relations.[7]

E. And books for teachers on these matters.[8]

G. Some television writers are also working to make the unfamiliar more familiar. Their themes are often the "deviant" aspects of our society and these programs make the unfamiliar understandable and thus less "deviant": children without parents, children of unemployed fathers, ghetto life, auto accidents and resulting injuries and deaths, deaf and mute children, the mentally retarded, and so on.

D. There always will and should be the novel and unfamiliar in a

---

[6] Some examples are:

Caudill, Rebecca. *A Certain Small Shepherd*. New York: Holt, Rinehart and Winston, 1965.

Little, Jean. *Mine for Keeps*. Boston: Little, Brown, 1962.

Wrightson, A. Patricia. *A Racecourse for Andy*. New York: Harcourt, Brace and World, 1968.

[7] Jones, Weyman. *Edge of Two Worlds*. New York: Dial Press, 1968.

Snyder, Zilpha K. *The Egypt Game*. New York: Atheneum, 1967.

Steptoe, John. *Stevie*. New York: Harper and Row, 1969; and *Uptown*. New York: Harper and Row, 1970.

Taylor, Theodore. *The Cay*. Garden City, N. Y.: Doubleday, 1969.

Weiner, Sandra. *It's Wings That Make Birds Fly*. New York: Pantheon Books, 1968.

[8] American Library Association, Children's Services Division. *Notable Children's Books*. Available from the Association, 50 E. Huron Street, Chicago, Ill. Issued annually, individually dated.

Epstein, Charlotte. *Intergroup Relations for the Classroom Teacher*. Boston: Houghton Mifflin, 1968.

Koblitz, Minnie W. (ed.). *The Negro in Schoolroom Literature: Resource Materials for the Teacher of Kindergarten through the Sixth Grade*. New York: Center for Urban Education (33 West 42nd Street), 1966.

National Education Association. *An Index to Multi-Ethnic Teaching Materials and Teacher Resources*. 1968. Available from the Association, 1201 Sixteenth Street, N. W., Washington, D. C.

Rollins, Charlemae (ed.). *We Build Together: A Reader's Guide to Negro Life and Literature for Elementary and High School Use*. 3d ed. Champaign, Ill.: National Council of Teachers of English (508 South Sixth Street), 1967.

Sugarman, Daniel A., and Hochstein, Rolaine A. *Seven Stories for Growth*. New York: Pitman Publishing Corp., 1965.

Trubowitz, Sidney. *A Handbook for Teaching in the Ghetto School*. New York: Anti-Defamation League of B'nai B'rith (315 Lexington Avenue), 1968.

child's life, but there is no reason why his response should remain fear, suspicion, hostility, and rejection.

H. I am inclined to argue that there are good reasons for these reaction patterns to persist. They serve definite protective functions, don't they? To use a parallel example here, it is useless to argue with schizophrenics or paranoiacs, pointing out that there is no rational reason why they should behave in such and such ways. So long as their ways of life solve their perceived problems, these will bring rewards and thus be perpetuated.

D. I see what you are saying and I must reluctantly agree with you that these defensive, as well as offensive, responses are often successfully employed to attain certain goals. What I am concerned about is the implicit or explicit encouragement our culture is giving its members to resort to these means. We ought to be helping reshape the looking glass itself.

I. Going back to the resource materials on various facets of human relations, the fact of their availability does not mean that they are used, does it?

G. That is right. Children may not be choosing the books that teachers and librarians are hoping they will. For example, pupils in my class are encouraged to select their own books in an individualized reading program. As a result of this freedom, a large segment of the group has gotten into a kick on séances, spiritualism, ESP, Bishop Pike, and the like, and it has been a bit tricky to handle. I have had one parent complain about it and another supply the children with more books on the subject! It has not been a big problem, but it is the kind of thing that happens in children's independent reading selections. No matter how much is written to combat prejudice, there is no guarantee that these will be the books that children will read; however, it is wonderful to have the books available and to have talented writers incorporating open-mindedness and sensitivity in their themes and plots.

I. I guess that same kind of thing can be said of many "good and nice" things parents, teachers, and schools buy for children: language laboratory facilities, slides, films, and projectors, closed-circuit television, programmed learning materials, and so on. Some fancy products of so-called educational innovation have been standing in a closet covered with dust after a considerable investment of time, money, and energy.

C.   One problem is that too many of us do not know how to use them well, and so the children are not taught to appreciate them.

G.   Yes, that seems to be true. For example, few of us teachers consider it our responsibility "to turn the passive reception into active intake and integration on the part of the young" (p. 22). But we should! Stressing critical listening and critical thinking with TV being a central target would be a good case in point.

J.   But, don't children learn these things anyway? Aren't they more skillful than we are in critical watching, and so forth? After all, children spend more time watching TV than attending school!

K.   I don't think so. One can certainly argue that since a child's own interest is the best master of his action, no external agents ought to intervene. It is easy to sympathize with this position, but the contention seems to confuse the energy for growth with the direction of growth. By all means, let a child's natural curiosity and spontaneity move him! But, let's not assume that having this delightful enthusiasm will enable him to duplicate single-handedly all the major human feats within a few short years and without suffering negative results. After all, there is such a thing as a disciplined pursuit of excellence — a child's liking to bang on the piano may be a good starting point, but it is absurd to expect him to acquire the virtuosity of a Franz Liszt or Ignace Jan Paderewski with no guide, no model, and no companion. A star must be there to which he can hitch his wagon, you know.

L.   How to preserve, enhance, and channel the bubbling spring of children's minds — that seems the challenge for parents and teachers. In any case, one crucial ingredient is the active involvement of children in raw, or primary, life experiences as a basis for learning. This is exactly what is likely to be missing in vicarious TV-type participation. You see, the whole exercise is secondary, or abstract, in nature and by-passes the primary process of immersing oneself in the stream of life itself. Without the secondary process of reflection we remain impulsive visceral man but, without the primary experience, we become feelingless cerebral man. Either way, man is not man anymore.[9]

I.   Watching and critiquing the seemingly effortless performance of

[9] Bronowski, J. *The Identity of Man*. Rev. ed. Garden City, N. Y.: The Natural History Press, 1971.
Lewis, C. S. *The Abolition of Man*. New York: Macmillan, 1965.

masters, be it in the arts, scholarship, or sports, without having even once experienced firsthand the agony and the ecstasy involved — that is at best a poor substitute for learning through immersion. Appreciation of and respect for one's brothers do not come from such a practice. That is why it is essential for us not to perpetuate in children the modern trend for nothing but an imitation of life, with no emotion nor involvement. Preselected and predigested versions of someone else's experiences may be safe, convenient, and inexpensive, but also tend to be superficial, joyless, and dull.

M. A "borrowed" sort of life just is not very satisfactory for anybody, is it?

C. In this connection, some of the recent educational games may be a good thing for teachers to consider. Although these are called games, or simulation, children become quite involved and, with a little guidance, they can learn a lot about social relations and the like.[10]

G. Do you remember that teacher somewhere in Iowa who "simulated" ethnic discrimination by giving differential treatments on the basis of the color of children's eyes? The blue eyes vs. brown eyes? I guess teachers who have duplicated the experiment have found that children can get very serious about even as innocuous a difference as eye color, and some wise handling of the situation is essential if they are to understand the dynamics of it all and not get hurt emotionally. In my school, the experience was so upsetting to children it had to be stopped.

L. And the same applies to many things they watch on TV.

N. Also, let us not forget that the ubiquitous mass media are often used, not for their rightful purposes of communication, but rather for shielding us from the essential encounter with ourselves in solitude. To be alone and at ease with the self, I believe, is both a necessary condition for, and a certain result of, mature life.

H. Yes, that is an important point. Mrs. Lindbergh said it beautifully (see p. 20), and Erich Fromm also observed how difficult it is to be alone with oneself. According to him, this ability to stand on one's own feet constitutes the prerequisite for mature love. "Paradoxically, the

[10] Boocock, Sarane S., and Schild, E. O. (eds.). *Simulation: Games in Learning.* Beverly Hills, Calif.: Sage Publications, 1968.

Carlson, Elliot. *A New Approach to Problem Solving: Learning Through Games.* Washington, D. C.: Public Affairs Press, 1969.

ability to be alone is the condition for the ability to love."[11] Otherwise, the relationship is that of dependence, not one of love. Unless one can stand alone, he cannot be of any assistance to others.

K.   That perhaps applies equally to the teacher as an individual, the teacher and students as a group, and teachers as a group. Just as a teacher needs a place and a time to be alone with himself, so must any group have an opportunity to be alone to look at itself.

J.   Unfortunately, a typical teacher in the lower grades does not have any place to be alone since his classroom is his office. I often wonder why this particular spatial arrangement has been uniformly adopted in our elementary schools. Besides, teachers are seldom able to take advantage of each other's presence while on duty.

D.   Some teachers are undoubtedly overdependent upon their pupils and this complicates the already delicate parent-teacher relationship. A. S. Neill of Summerhill talks about the unconscious adoption of pupils by the teacher and warns: "They [teachers] strive, without realizing what they are doing, to steal the child from the parents. It is really necessary that a teacher be analyzed."[12] He meant psychoanalysis here, I guess.

N.   Similar recommendations were made by such people as Anna Freud and Jersild.[13] The main thing is that the teacher comes to know himself by whatever means is available to him. I do not think orthodox psychoanalysis is to be interpreted as the royal road to self understanding; if used sagaciously, various forms of therapy, sensitivity training, encounter groups, Zen, et cetera, can also help teachers come to know themselves better.

D.   I think that some systematic preparation of teachers for parenthood further helps in this regard. Most young teachers will be parents themselves, and they can certainly use better formal education in the art of becoming human parents. Besides, if they appreciate what it takes

[11] Fromm, Erich. *The Art of Loving.* New York: Harper and Row, 1956. P. 112.

[12] Neill, A. S. *Summerhill.* New York: Hart Publishing Co., 1960. P. 330.

[13] Freud, Anna. *Psychoanalysis for Teachers and Parents.* Boston: Beacon Press, 1960.

Jersild, Arthur T. *When Teachers Face Themselves.* New York: Bureau of Publications, Teachers College, Columbia University, 1955.

Jersild, Arthur T.; Lazar, E. Allina; and Brodkin, A. *The Meaning of Psychotherapy in the Teacher's Life and Work.* New York: Bureau of Publications, Teachers College, Columbia University, 1962.

to be a parent, teachers can be more understanding in their work with their pupils' mothers and fathers. Hopefully, teachers and parents can be allies, instead of being competitors for children.

F. I think it pertinent here to recall what Bloom found in his research.[14] He concluded that there is a marked decrease over time in the effect of better environment on behavioral changes (intelligence, achievement, aggression, et cetera) in children. The critical period is during the very first few years of life and, there, parental teaching is the only ally educators have.

O. Yes, indeed! Some experts have argued that our schooling begins when, for all practical purposes, it is too late to do anything fundamental. This is especially true with underprivileged children.[15]

F. Besides, maternal expectations and styles of teaching are very different between working-class and middle-class homes. Often working-class mothers expect little of their children and cannot offer much help in the mastery of cognitive tasks.[16] Both these orientations are bound to feed negative self concept in children.

B. In discussing this kind of thing, however, we must be careful not to overlook large variations within the same social class. It must also be remembered that some middle-class homes are far more deprived emotionally and culturally than many lower-class homes.

F. That is right. But let me add one more relevant finding. Hess and Shipman observed that working-class mothers tend to look at school as just another bothersome institution for their children to cope with. The school is about the same as the police, welfare agency, tax collector, or prison in this sense. It is definitely not a place of learning.

N. A related matter is that it is sometimes advisable to move a child, especially a boy, from a female teacher to a male teacher. In the United States boys from homes in which male figures are absent (for occupa-

[14] Bloom, Benjamin S. *Stability and Change in Human Characteristics.* New York: John Wiley and Sons, 1964.

[15] Bettelheim, Bruno. "How Much Can Man Change?" *Profile of the School Dropout,* ed. Daniel Schreiber. New York: Random House, 1968. Pp. 215–224.

[16] Brophy, Jere E. "Mothers as Teachers of Their Own Preschool Children: The Influence of Socio-economic Status and Task Structure on Teaching Specificity." *Child Development,* 41:79–94; March 1970.

Hess, Robert D., and Shipman, Virginia C. "Early Experience and the Socialization of Cognitive Modes in Children." *Child Development,* 36:869–886; December 1965.

tional or familial reasons) tend to have identification problems, and these can be aggravated in the female-dominated lower grades.

A. We hear often about the adverse effects of an all-female teaching staff, but how solid is the evidence? I get the impression that general clinical observations and case studies on the possible effects of father absence have been more or less logically extended into the argument of the need for male teachers in school. Although it seems true that appropriate sex-role identification is hindered by the lack of the same-sex models,[17] I know of no direct investigation of the allegedly remedial effects of the presence of male adults in the classroom.

E. That is a good point, even though the general pattern of data seems to support the inference. In spite of some ready rationales, little actual research has been done concerning the differential patterns of teacher-pupil interactions as a function of teacher and/or pupil sex, and much less about the curative results of such interaction patterns.

L. Probably more important than the presence or absence of male "bodies" would be the fact that the school is essentially a woman's world, governed by such characteristically female values as cleanliness, obedience, decorum, and passivity.[18] Masculine values of movement, independence, aggressiveness, et cetera, are not particularly encouraged in the classroom. So the situation may not be materially improved by adding many male teachers so long as our schooling lacks active, explor-atory, and imaginative qualities.

C. And we go back to the Plowden Report, Dewey, Montessori, and all the wise teachers who have been trying to tell us the same thing, that is, learning must be an adventure into the mysteries of life itself.

N. Male or female, there can, in addition, be cases of simple teacher-pupil incompatibilities. Some parallel to the clinician-client relationship should perhaps be established in the school so that such possibilities of

[17] Deutsch, Martin; Katz, Irwin; and Jensen, Arthur R. (eds.). *Social Class, Race, and Psychological Development.* New York: Holt, Rinehart and Winston, 1968.

Ostrovsky, Everett S. *Children Without Men.* New York: Collier Books, 1962.

Pettigrew, Thomas F. *A Profile of the Negro American.* Princeton, N. J.: D. Van Nostrand, 1964.

Yarrow, Leon J. "Separation from Parents During Early Childhood." In Martin L. Hoffman and Lois W. Hoffman (eds.), *Review of Child Development Research,* Volume I. New York: Russell Sage Foundation, 1964. Pp. 89–136.

[18] Sexton, Patricia A. "Schools Are Emasculating Our Boys." *Saturday Review,* Educational Supplement, June 19, 1965, p. 57.

incompatibility are honestly faced and handled by the principal and teachers. Some routine procedures may be established for reassignments without any accompanying trauma or stigma. These will serve to protect both teachers and children. Just as some therapists work better with certain clients than with others, it should be expected that different teachers show differential patterns of effectiveness with different pupils.

K. Of course, we should not be looking for a storybook classroom where no conflicts arise, no unpleasantness is felt, and no crises are met. That would again be an imitation of life. To remove sources of unnecessary and unreasonable pressure is one thing, but it is another to build an overly aseptic environment, trying to protect children from all stressful experiences.

H. Remember those studies reporting on highly effective individuals?[19] They were characterized not by the absence in their early years of traumatic events but rather by the way they faced and handled these potentially growth-inducing experiences.

B. It seems likewise important for us to realize that some negative components in the self concept may be essential. An overemphasis upon self-consistency can be misleading, since inconsistency in our concept of self may open up more choices and directions for growth.

G. Yes. A self-accepting person is willing to sacrifice the guarantee of security in a closed, consistent self concept for further growth. Sort of a vitality over security, self before self concept, you know. I believe that growth is more personally valuable than the preservation of a rigid self concept. We must be willing to try out different pictures of self, so to speak, to find out how well they fit the self. Perhaps some such movements as the hippies are indications of this desire on the part of our young people. In any case, preservation of our present concept of self should not be our ultimate goal; that is what is wrong with neurotics and psychotics, isn't it?

A. Right. But before anyone can dare try to revise his self concept, he must have basic trust in this self. Otherwise, the center will not hold and the whole being may collapse. Self-esteem means something like having faith in the self and letting the self concept settle where it belongs, not the other way around.

[19] MacKinnon, Donald W. "The Highly Effective Individual." *Teachers College Record,* 61:367–378; April 1960.

H. That was also stressed by Fromm: "Only the person who has faith in himself is able to be faithful to others."[20]

N. In my clinical work it has been impressive to note that whenever a child comes through strong in spite of seemingly overwhelming odds against him, I can look for and always find someone in or out of his home who has served as a source of sustaining influence. Some adult who has "tuned into" the child.

M. And the teacher can be that adult. A teacher who cares.

H. Yes. Again Fromm has pointed this out so well. He says that one of the most important conditions for the development of a child into a happy, loving, and rational being is "that the significant person in a child's life have faith in these potentialities. The presence of this faith makes the difference between education and manipulation."[21] And he also says this: "While we teach knowledge, we are losing that teaching which is the most important one for human development: the teaching which can only be given by the simple presence of a mature, loving person."[22]

O. The simple presence of a mature, loving person who conveys something of the values, attitudes, and aspirations of human beings as human beings.

I. Teachers in general tend to underestimate their influence in this sense. They feel that whatever they can do within the huge, technological superstructure amounts to little or nothing, but I believe they are mistaken. They *do* affect eternity at the most fundamental level.

J. Incidentally, Stephens raised the same point as Fromm about the rock-bottom requisite for viable education: the presence of an interested adult merely to tend to the organic process of learning.[23]

E. That brings us to the matter of, say, affective education as against the familiar cognitive education. Not that the two are mutually exclusive but, rather, that cognitive efforts will not get anywhere unless placed on a secure foundation of affective education. I think that we often try vainly to build the cognitive without the affective.

K. Absolutely. We must free children and also prepare teachers to

[20] Fromm, op. cit. (n. 11), p. 123.

[21] Ibid., p. 124.

[22] Ibid., p. 117.

[23] Stephens, J. M. *The Process of Schooling.* New York: Holt, Rinehart and Winston, 1967.

deal intelligently with values and emotions. After all, feeling is a way of knowing and an important way at that.

I. Can we reverse it? Knowing is a way of feeling?

K. No, not necessarily. There is knowing and there is knowing. Some knowing is done with feeling, while other knowing is nothing but a mechanical increment of information. To understand one's self involves feeling and valuing, an experience going beyond a descriptive analysis.

E. Unfortunately, the latter kind of knowing is about the only thing ever evaluated in school. Most of our instruments of psycho-educational measurement are geared to a narrow range in the cognitive domain.

I. And we are inclined to interpret teaching as merely instruction. Even when demonstration is included, teaching is taken to represent nothing but intentional efforts. I feel it is important for us to realize that there are unintentional kinds of teaching going on every day, just as there are many unintentional sorts of learning.[24]

D. Teachers need to remember that the role of information transmitter is probably the least vital of all the roles he, as a unique human being, can perform. This is the function advances in educational technology are most likely to take over. It reminds me of what Sanford said about the mistaken notion of learning as an accretion of information. According to him, "Most of the psychology of learning deals only with how content is registered and remembered, failing to recognize that education really has more to do with unlearning, with motivation, and with relationships with teachers than with recall of facts. One of the most important functions of education is to erase wrong attitudes acquired in earlier periods, something that cannot be done simply by superimposing more knowledge on the wrong foundations that happen already to have been set up."[25]

M. That is very interesting. I have never thought of unlearning when I discuss teaching. How to facilitate the process of unlearning in our pupils through our teaching? That says something about the curriculum also, doesn't it?

B. I think we are indeed trapped in the information-accretion model of learning when we think of any fixed curriculum. We should recast our curricular questions into a more functional form and quit asking about

[24] Yamamoto, Kaoru. "Many Faces of Teaching." *Teaching: Essays and Readings,* ed. Kaoru Yamamoto. Boston: Houghton Mifflin, 1969. Pp. 3–16.

[25] Sanford, Nevitt. *Where Colleges Fail.* San Francisco: Jossey-Bass, 1968. P. 169.

different ways to organize compartmentalized subject areas into a static schedule of one type or another. As I recall, Tumin phrased more meaningful questions thus: "What do we want our children to come to *value*? What do we want them to be able to *feel and see and hear and smell and touch*? From what do we want them to learn to *get pleasure*? What do we want them to *understand about themselves* and *the world of nature and man*? How do we want them to *behave toward other human beings*? To what do we want them to be inclined to *commit themselves*? What technical *abilities* do we wish to *cultivate* in them?"[26]

C.   That is really good! That puts the whole thing in perspective: more process-oriented thinking about curriculum.

F.   I especially like his emphasis on valuing, feeling, committing, and the like. Most of these processes are nonverbal and even preconscious, but there is admittedly a tremendous need for us to cultivate awareness and receptiveness at these levels.[27]

O.   Not to raise a specter here, but I wonder whether some teachers and teacher-educators have been using these same pleas to rationalize the lack of intellectual astuteness in their undertakings.

G.   That is an important point. A plea for better affective education should not overlook the fact that while education is meant to develop the totality of man, not just this aspect or that aspect, schools are to contribute to such development largely through an intellectual discipline. Other social institutions also help in their respective ways, but the school ought to fulfill its unique function that cannot be accomplished elsewhere. Processes of thinking must remain the central concern of schooling and teachers themselves ought to be good at rigorous but heuristic thinking.

F.   We should also remember that today's children are growing up in a highly technological culture. While some teachers shun the fruits of technology and many educational critics argue as if we could simply wish away the technologically-oriented values, the fact remains that this historical epoch too will run its full course before any remarkable changes come in sight. What I mean is that we should be in a position

[26] Tumin, Melvin. "Teaching in America." *Childhood Education*, 44:347–353; February 1968.

[27] Huxley, Aldous. "Education on the Nonverbal Level." *Contemporary Educational Psychology*, ed. Richard M. Jones. New York: Harper and Row, 1967. Pp. 44–60.

to help students attain the feelings of adequacy through the mastery of technical skills and knowledge and, in turn, use this competence in developing their humane concern and innovative potential. Cognitive and affective education must be an integrated whole. It is difficult for a child to sustain and enhance his sense of adequacy when he cannot in fact cope with challenges in his daily life.

J. I think I am not mistaken in saying that our teacher-aspirants are themselves revolting against the familiar Mickey-Mouse courses no matter how they are disguised. The fact that they are going to work with young children is no excuse for oversimplifying these college students' educational experiences. That is actually an insult to their own intellectual prowess. Students are slowly but surely pressing for both competence and compassion in their teachers, not just one or the other.

M. An insult in the same sense that adults' mimicking infantile language in the name of better communication is an insult to children. Talking down to students is more subtle than, but as invidious as, laughing at them.

O. Besides, it takes the highest degree of intellectual astuteness and emotional maturity for teachers at any level to look at themselves. Open, intuitive, and original persons who master the art of teaching are a far cry from shallow, obtuse, and defensive individuals who bear false witness to scholarship and teaching.[28]

A. Although there is always the danger of our going to the other extreme of pedantry, many people mistake the art of plain talk, let us say, for the abolition of technical jargon. Some college students also mistrust all big words, insisting that there is no need for them, but what tends to be overlooked in such an argument is that precise and succinct communication of more complex concepts demands increasingly elaborate symbol systems. A particular word may be more useful in this sense than another because it stands for a more inclusive, though abstract, concept. We can, for example, express most mathematical relations in plain English, but the operation will certainly be less efficient and more confusing than the comparative one in a numerical symbol system.

F. In a similar manner, we can argue for the need for teachers to

---

[28] Borton, Terry. *Reach, Touch, and Teach.* New York: McGraw-Hill, 1970.
Leonard, George B. *Education and Ecstasy.* New York: Dell Publishing, 1968.
Postman, Neil, and Weingartner, Charles. *Teaching as a Subversive Activity.* New York: Delacorte Press, 1969.

familiarize themselves with American dialects other than their own, not to speak of foreign languages. Even though most expressions are roughly translatable across different dialects (the lower-class Southern white, middle-class Northern black, et cetera), it will not do for teachers to insist that a single code which happens to coincide with their own be used by everyone. A language is powerful because it symbolizes people's style of life, their accumulated ideas, emotions, hopes, and dreams. It is obviously ridiculous for us, for example, to insist that an Eskimo child not use his fine conceptual discrimination of "snow" in the ten or twenty or thirty different words available in his language for that very purpose.

K. Perhaps this is stretching the point a little bit, but can't the same thing be said about any conceptual schemes or theories we have? They are coding systems for making some sense out of what we come into contact with and they can be a powerful aid to our understanding of ourselves and others. For example, why do we struggle with Piaget's or Vygotsky's system? Because it shows us a way to communicate with a child. This particular language allows us to "read" his development, adjust our expectations, and arrange an optimal educational environment for him. A theory is no vain frill. As someone said, a good theory is the most practical thing there is.

G. As it is true with a language, so it is true with a theory. Neither stays put, because both are continuously open to revisions and changes. Dialects are crossbred with each other and apparent differences are ironed out to suit the users of this or that dialect at a particular time and place. Theories are not sacred rules. As a matter of fact, if they are immutable, they are probably dead. In this context, teachers may look into the recent trend toward unification among seemingly discrepant theories.[29]

H. And the practical importance mentioned goes not only for refined theories but also for any piece of information derived from solid research. For example, the findings on nursery children's conflicts help an alert teacher to maximize the learning potential of the school environment. The incident of quarrels tends to be higher if play space is more

[29] Koestler, Arthur. *The Ghost in the Machine.* New York: Macmillan, 1967.
Mehrabian, Albert. *An Analysis of Personality Theories.* Englewood Cliffs, N. J.: Prentice-Hall, 1968.
Von Bertalanffy, Ludwig. *General Systems Theory.* New York: George Braziller, 1968.

restricted, if movable equipment and toys are absent from the play-ground, or if sand play is the major activity.[30] Or the findings about the relationships between dependence conflict and competence: disadvan-taged lower-class children, who do not develop trust in adults and hence cannot utilize physical and emotional support from the grownups in their environment, fail to develop confidence in themselves and are unable to function independently and self-sufficiently.[31] These data should be regarded as essential elements which go into any careful edu-cational planning.

M.   Codes for curricular planning. Communication in the broadest sense, right?

D.   Fuchs says of Harlem kids that they have accurately perceived teachers' dislike for them by some such observation as teachers' uncon-sciously backing off from children whenever they approached teachers.[32] Simple but quite revealing.

H.   This is the point Hall argues in his two books on the silent cul-tural or subcultural languages.[33]

C.   Ruesch and Birdwhistell have also been studying this important aspect of human communication.[34]

K.   In that sense, there is not such a thing as classroom routine, is there? How the teacher manages these activities tells much about his values, attitudes, and intentions.

O.   In just such a way various administrative arrangements, including grouping, grading, and regulations on dress and conduct, communicate

[30] Swift, Joan W. "Effects of Early Group Experience: The Nursery School and Day Nursery." *Review of Child Development Research,* Vol. I, eds. Martin L. Hoffman and Lois W. Hoffman. New York: Russell Sage Foundation, 1964. Pp. 249–288.

[31] Beller, E. Kuno. "The Evaluation of Effects of Early Educational Intervention on Intellectual and Social Development of Lower-Class, Disadvantaged Chil-dren." *Critical Issues in Research Related to Disadvantaged Children,* ed. Edith Grotberg. Princeton, N. J.: Educational Testing Service, 1969. Pp. 201–247.

[32] Fuchs, Estelle. *Pickets at the Gates.* New York: The Free Press, 1966.

[33] Hall, Edward T. *The Silent Language.* Garden City, N. Y.: Doubleday, 1959; and *The Hidden Dimension.* Garden City, N. Y.: Doubleday, 1966.

[34] Birdwhistell, Ray L. *Introduction to Kinesics.* Louisville, Ky.: University of Louisville Press, 1952; and *Kinesics and Context.* Philadelphia: University of Pennsylvania Press, 1970.

Ruesch, Jurgen, and Kees, Weldon. *Nonverbal Communication.* Berkeley, Calif.: University of California Press, 1964.

loud and clear the basic philosophy of the school and the community. These organizational or procedural plans are codes through which we reveal what we have in mind.[35]

E. And children do get the message! It somehow reminds me of the study which showed that while teachers were saying that school marks meant little to elementary pupils, children themselves were quite concerned about their academic performance and the meaning of marking systems![36]

B. In the everyday encounter with, say, 30 children, a teacher is required to "read" at least 30 different codes, because each child has his unique life style. The challenge is for the teacher to be one genuine person and, at the very same time, 30 authentic teachers, geared to each of his pupils.

N. George Kelly said something like, a good teacher is the one who can take 30 children and latch onto all 30 different personal construct systems without losing himself.[37] Every person interprets his experiences within the frame of his personal construct system and he makes a choice in terms of the alternatives *he* sees open to him. For the moment, the "personal construct" can be equated with the self concept. A pupil uses his map, not the teacher's. It is therefore up to the teacher to "read" the 30 maps.

J. But if, in the process, the teacher loses sight of his own self, he cannot be of much help to anyone. It takes faith in himself (self-esteem) not to superimpose his map on the child's.

E. Yes, the teacher must somehow let each child feel his presence.

B. As a mature, loving adult. Not as an artificial collection of role performances. New teachers often try to cope with ambiguous situations by applying a preconceived set of rules, acting some allegedly cure-all

[35] Eddy, Elizabeth M. *Walk the White Line.* Garden City, N. Y.: Doubleday, 1967.

Fuchs, Estelle. *Teachers Talk.* Garden City, N. Y.: Doubleday, 1969.

Moore, G. Alexander. *Realities of the Urban Classroom.* Garden City, N. Y.: Doubleday, 1967.

Waller, Willard. *The Sociology of Teaching.* New York: John Wiley and Sons, 1965.

[36] Boehm, Anne E., and White, Mary A. "Pupils' Perceptions of School Marks." *Elementary School Journal,* 67:237–240; February 1967.

[37] Kelly, George A. *The Psychology of Personal Constructs.* New York: W. W. Norton, 1955.

roles, and forcing (!) themselves to be spontaneous. Teacher education programs should be careful about giving students nothing but crutches of this sort, instead of letting them learn to be themselves. Teachers need to be well prepared but, in their contacts with children, they must be natural, they must be authentic.[38]

G.   Right. And to convey one's genuine presence in the classroom is to mobilize all there is to human communication, all the different senses, all the different codes, and all the different experiences.

H.   But without adding to the already staggering amount of "waiting" time in the classroom which Jackson spoke of? Children are always required to wait their turn, delay their actions, and often settle for denied desires.[39]

I.   That is quite a job. But if a teacher trusts himself and is trusted, he is willing to learn and able to change to meet the demands of a changing situation. That is a part of his professional integrity.

O.   He must be forever trying to synthesize a facilitative environment for children from conflicting pieces. He has to be a person highly tolerant of ambiguity.

L.   I am afraid that most of us fall short of this ideal, but our struggle can itself be a good educational model. Professionals ought to bring pressure for self-improvement upon each other.

C.   Now what about all those specific action suggestions in Chapter Five? Would they work with children of varying ethnic and socio-economic backgrounds? They use different behavioral codes, don't they?

N.   I think we can argue that, basically, children are children, and emotions are emotions. Therefore, whatever works with one group of children tends to work with another.

C.   But their behavioral modes (symptoms) may be different.

M.   And so are the meanings of these symptoms, aren't they?

N.   Actually, any set of specific recommendations is itself a deciphering code. It may work or it may not. At least, however, such a code adds to the list of potential alternatives in action to help children. Do's and

[38] Burkhart, Robert C., and Neil, Hugh M. *Identity and Teacher Learning.* Scranton, Pa.: International Textbook Co., 1968.

   Shumsky, Abraham. *In Search of Teaching Style.* New York: Appleton-Century-Crofts, 1968.

[39] Jackson, Philip W. *Life in Classrooms.* New York: Holt, Rinehart and Winston, 1968.

Don'ts should not be accepted as sacred, magic rules. They are hypotheses to be tested in each unique situation.

L. One thing is clear in any case. When children are experiencing difficulties and some intervention is indicated, the younger they are, the better the prognosis. Also, it is true that treatment of a child in isolation is not so effective as working with the whole family. The point is that the child began acting in a certain manner in response to the total matrix of his environment. He cannot be expected to change his behavior when the dynamics of the family life remain unchanged.

J. That is well described in two case studies by Baruch and Axline (see p. 23).

L. The same comments apply when school-home conflicts are involved.

M. Also to things like masturbation?

E. Yes, there will be no reaction unless there is an action. Exploration with one's body is as natural as exploration of external objects. It is generally the way those around a child handle his action that determines his subsequent behavior.[40] Sex-related "problems" are good examples.

I. By the way, there are some good materials on these matters for teachers and parents, available from SIECUS, as well as from the N.E.A.[41]

N. Here in these areas of concern as elsewhere, it seems important for teachers to tune in to the affective message of a behavioral pattern, rather than to the cognitive message. For example, a friend of mine decided to set aside ten or fifteen minutes every morning to "feel about" children's dreams. Instead of going into a clinically intricate discussion of the contents of these dreams and their symbolism, the teacher

[40] Bettelheim, Bruno. *Paul and Mary.* Garden City, N. Y.: Doubleday, 1961.

Dreikurs, Rudolf. *Psychology in the Classroom.* 2d ed. New York: Harper and Row, 1968.

Neill, A. S. *Freedom—Not License!* New York: Hart Publishing Co., 1966.

Redl, Fritz. *When We Deal with Children.* New York: The Free Press, 1966.

[41] Lehman, Edna. *Talking to Children about Sex.* New York: Harper and Row, 1970.

Manley, Helen. *Family Life and Sex Education in the Elementary School.* Washington, D. C.: Department of Elementary-Kindergarten-Nursery Education, National Education Association (1201 Sixteenth Street, N. W.), 1968.

SIECUS (Sex Information and Education Council of the United States, 1855 Broadway, New York, N. Y.) publishes various leaflets, booklets, and reprints. See also SIECUS (ed.). *Sexuality and Man.* New York: Charles Scribner's Sons, 1970.

allowed her pupils to visualize each other's dreams and empathize with the emotions felt by the dreamer. Discussions of these feelings and attitudes followed. Children tremendously enjoyed this experience and found it very profitable. That is one way to facilitate children's self knowledge and also interpersonal communications in a broad sense.

D. I read about something like that also. A first-grade teacher in California tried this "dream time" idea and children not only told of their dreams but also drew these in pictures. She made it very clear that these dreams should not be interpreted or psychologized by the teacher. Children are allowed to share the experience with each other, to feel the emotions, and to extend the imaginative productions further. For children, this served to facilitate their preconscious functions,[42] while it allowed the teacher to gain better understanding of his pupils. The teacher confided: "Even though I am sure that I don't understand what the children's dreams 'mean,' I do feel that I am gaining an awareness of dimensions of their personalities that I would never have been exposed to had we never had dream time."[43]

K. And I bet that this teacher was also learning a lot about herself through that kind of sharing! As all sensitive parents and teachers know, children teach us a lot, mostly about ourselves. Teaching and learning are always two-way in this sense, I guess.

A. I began the session by quoting one useful source. Let me close this discussion by quoting another clarion call, this one from Kubie, who noticed that the world is full of the products of our educational system, men of erudition with little wisdom or maturity. "Self-knowledge is the Forgotten Man of our entire educational system and indeed of human culture in general. Without self-knowledge it is possible to be erudite, but never wise. My challenge to all of us is to have the humility to face this failure, and the determination to do something effective about it. . . ."[44]

[42] Kubie, Lawrence S. "Research in Protecting Preconscious Functions in Education." *Contemporary Educational Psychology,* ed. Richard M. Jones. New York: Harper and Row, 1967. Pp. 72–88.

[43] Werlin, Elena G. "An Experiment in Elementary Education." *Contemporary Educational Psychology,* ed. Richard M. Jones. New York: Harper and Row, 1967. Pp. 233–253. Quoted from p. 238.

[44] Kubie, Lawrence S. "The Forgotten Man of Education." *Contemporary Educational Psychology,* ed. Richard M. Jones. New York: Harper and Row, 1967. Pp. 61–71. Quoted from p. 71.

INDEX